POV Press
Books by Bethanne Kim

Survival Skills for All Ages:

> *#1: 26 Basic Life Skills*

> *#2: 52⁺ Everyday Recipes for Emergencies*

> *#3: 26 Mental and Urban Life Skills*

Scouting in the Deep End:

> *#1: Cubmastering: Getting Started as Cubmaster*

> *#2: Scout Leader: An Introduction to Boy Scouts*

> *#3: Citizenship in the World: Teaching the Merit Badge*

Not the Zombies:

> *#1: OMG!*

> *#2: BRB!*

> *#3: YOLO!*

The Constitution: It's the OS for the US

The Organized Wedding: Planning Everything from Your Engagement to Your Marriage

Forthcoming:

Survival Skills for All Ages:

> *26 Outdoor Life Skills*

> *Special Needs Prepping*

Scouting in the Deep End:

> *#4: Mentoring Youth in Scouts*

THE CONSTITUTION: IT'S THE OS FOR THE US

BETHANNE KIM

Photo by Bethanne Kim

1. Political Science–Civics & Citizenship
2. Political Science–Constitutions

Kindle ISBN: 978-1-942533-10-8
Paperback ISBN: 978-1-942533-09-2

Distributed by POV Press
PO Box 399
Catharpin, VA 20143

Printed in the United States of America

DEDICATION

To all those who have given their lives, their limbs, their health, and their freedom so the rest of us might have ours, and to their families who have also given so much for this Union, this book is respectfully DEDICATED.

TABLE OF CONTENTS

CONTENTS

CONTENTS

ACKNOWLEDGEMENTS

This book might not have happened if my mother-in-law hadn't forced me to look in a box of old books that included the inspiration for it, so thank you. And it definitely wouldn't have happened without the support of my husband, so thank you to him, my parents (Bob and Julie), and my sons for their unwavering support.

Thanks also to my reviewers and editors Bob Jones, Bob Jones (two different ones), Denise Oberlies, Francis Park, Barry-Buzz Heckard, and Carlene Strathmann, the artist who created the original cover art for the e-book as well as reviewing the text.

INTRODUCTION

This book started out as an update of William Giffin's late 1880s book *Civics for Young Americans.* In it, he writes about when "your father" votes for President. At first, I thought this was very sexist. Then I realized that women were denied the right to vote until the 19th Amendment was ratified in 1919! He wasn't being sexist—women simply didn't have the right to vote until over forty years after his book was published.

The 19th Amendment is far from the only change since Mr. Giffin wrote his book. Adopted in 1789, our Constitution itself was barely 100 years old at the time and had only 15 amendments, not the current 27. The Civil War and slavery ended less than twenty five years before Giffin's book was published. Giffin lived through the war, and possibly even served in it, and many adult blacks were themselves freed slaves. The USA was still young enough and weak enough as a nation that much of the original book was about Great Britain's government because the author expected everyone to be familiar with the government of one of the Super Powers of the time. To be clear, that meant the British Empire in 1888, not the United States of America. This shows how quickly a nation can stop being a Super Power.

In 1776, the British Empire was so large and powerful that the sun literally never set on it, much like the sun never sets on Disney theme parks today–Disneyland Paris, Walt Disney World in Florida, Disneyland in California, and Hong Kong Disneyland. Britain's major land holdings included the actual island of Britain (England, Scotland, and Wales); large chunks of North America, now part of the US and Canada; portions of Africa; and India.

Australia was also claimed by Britain but was not settled until 1788. After our Revolution, the British needed a new penal (prison) colony since they could no longer send their prisoners to America. They still had Canada but feared that sending prisoners so close to the new USA might stir up problems. Since Australia was far away, the British chose it as their new penal colony.[1]

Compared to the mighty globe-spanning British Empire, we were truly small, poor, and weak at the time of the Revolution. We needed help from a more powerful nation to successfully break away. France, a long-time enemy of Britain, helped us because the King of France wanted to hurt Britain and her King. Without French help and French gold, our Revolution would almost certainly have failed.[2] The irony is that the success of our Revolution against the British King inspired the successful French Revolution against the French King.

What does it say about the character and strength of the American people that we have inspired others to revolt against dictators and despots? Can you think of any other examples? Or do you disagree and think we did not truly inspire anyone else? If you disagree, then what do you think did inspire them?

Before the American Revolution, there were no countries with Democratic or Republican governments, although people had heard of them–and how they ended–from ancient Greek and Roman history. The Roman Republic, like earlier Greek city-states it was modeled after, was only large city-state itself, and it existed about 2,000 years before our Revolution.[3] A city-state is when a city and its surrounding areas, suburbs and farms, function together like a small country, and is similar to a modern "metropolitan area." The larger, later, Roman

Empire was an Empire, with an Emperor, not a Republic. The United States is the first attempt *ever* to create such a large republic. It was a wild gamble on a theory never before tried in the history of the human race.

When Gifford wrote in the late 1880s, there were no countries with Communist or Socialist governments–anywhere. It was a mere forty years since Karl Marx wrote *The Communist Manifesto,* although the idea of communal governments was discussed before, and only fifteen years since he penned the line "from each according to his ability to each in according to his needs" in *Critique of the Gotha Program.* Marx wrote this in 1875to describe the ideal Communist society.

Since even our enemies admit that the modern United States is rich, powerful and influential, it is easy to forget just how young our nation really is, and how fragile, poor, and weak it started out. Whether we are one of the richest might be argued today, but not whether we are still rich compared to many countries.

Electing national officials is normal throughout the world today, not an exception, but it wasn't like that before our Revolution. Even in states where corruption is wide-spread and elections do not remotely reflect "the will of the people" because the "elected" government is really a dictatorship, many regimes (the group controlling a government) apparently feel the need to pretend they have democracy. This widespread acceptance makes it is easy to forget how radical our form of government was when it was founded, and how fragile it remains.

The United States is unique in using "state" to mean the level of government below the national government. Most other countries use names like "province." Other than the 50 US states, "state" means roughly the same thing as "country" or "nation." That is why the State Department's job is foreign policy, dealing with other countries, and not domestic policy, dealing with the 50 states and their issues. This is because when the country was named, the Founders expected each of the former colonies to function like a country (state). (The newer US Constitution simply kept the name established under the

Articles of Confederation.) Both the function and the purpose of the larger national government were a bit unclear under the Articles of Confederation, but our very name clearly shows what a large role the Founders wanted and expected the states to play in governing our country. The states weren't an afterthought.

We retained many good traditions and institutions from the British, but we also kept one particularly bad one. Slavery was not particularly British, and definitely not particularly American, but it was part of both countries in the 1770s. Slavery and its related issues have caused more arguments and political problems in the United States than any other single issue except states' rights versus federal power, and some of those states rights/federal power problems were linked to slavery as well.

A federal system is one where power is divided between a national government and the states under it, which each have their own government. The national government for the US is referred to as the federal government.

This book discusses some of the economics of slavery and the history surrounding it, but the morality of it is not up for discussion. Slavery is an abomination that must be ended any time and place it appears, but that does not mean we shouldn't try to understand why and how it continued for as long as it did. Those who do not learn from history are doomed to repeat it. Understanding how it was retained when so many wanted it to end is important too. This is an example of a fairly small number of people effectively forcing the entire nation to do (or not do) what they want. (Many people tolerated slavery; few were actively involved in and highly supportive of it.)

This book contains the entire unedited text of the United States Constitution and all its Amendments, as of the 1992 passage of the 27th Amendment).[4] Underlined text in the Constitution is text that was later changed by an Amendment.

Historical context, what was happening and was common knowledge when each part was written, is the focus of this book because context matters. "Hand me those arms" means different things if the person speaking is a wounded vet who lost both arms to an IED (Improvised Explosive Device–a bomb), a doll maker making a doll, a SWAT team preparing to storm a building, or a furniture maker building a chair. When you ignore what is happening around an event or statement, it is easy to completely misinterpret it.

It is not my intention to advance any particular political point of view, but simply to educate the reader so that you may go and learn more yourself on anything you find interesting. (The Kindle version of this book is chock full of informational links.) You, the reader, do not need to have someone else tell you what to believe. Our Founders went to a great deal of effort to convince average citizens that the Constitution was best possible governing document for our new country. They believed average people could not understand the basic principles of it. Of course, it was written by lawyers and presented a new form of government, so the meaning and/or implementation of parts of it are and always have been very much up for debate, but the basic principles are clear.

Every book has an agenda, or something the author wishes to accomplish. That may be as simple as entertaining you. Here is my agenda: I want you, the reader, to think critically about our Constitution and our government and decide what *you* believe, not just repeat what you think others–including me–want you to believe or what you hear on the news. It doesn't matter to me if you agree with what I believe. It matters that you form your own opinion and do not just repeat what other people say without researching it to make sure it's true.

The Founders argued over how things were to be interpreted and it is fine to follow in their footsteps. Just be sure you are arguing your own opinions. Don't just repeat what someone else has told you to believe. Base your opinion on facts or actual experiences–not what someone told you they read on somebody else's blog. And always try to be civil (reasonably polite) when you talk about politics, even though it can be very hard to do.

There is a lot of historical information in this book. Hopefully you will be inspired to learn more about some of these areas. Ideally, the stories and explanations will help you to better understand how our government works and form your own opinions.

RESOURCES

1. Convicts and the British Colonies in Australia
australia.gov.au/about-australia/australian-story/convicts-and-the-british-colonies

2. France Allied with American Colonies
www.americaslibrary.gov/jb/revolut/jb_revolut_francoam_2.html

3. The Roman Republic and Ancient Greek City-States
www.ushistory.org/civ/6a.asp

4. Transcript of the US Constitution
www.archives.gov/exhibits/charters/constitution_transcript.html

CHAPTER 1
SOME FACTS FROM HISTORY

You have been taught some of our country's history from its discovery to the present time. Since the arrival of the Niña, the Pinta and the Santa Maria, one thing has not changed: People come here to make their lives better. Some come searching for a fortune in gold, or in land, or in something else. Many of the earliest colonists longed, more than anything, for freedom of religion. They fled the tyranny of state religions and despotic monarchs in Europe. Many immigrants still flee despots and religious persecution.

When the Seven Years' War began in 1756, the colonists were ready to help and fight for the English King, even though many had been badly treated in Europe. All through the nine long years of the Seven Years' War (called the French and Indian War in America) they fought bravely and well. At the close of the war, the colonies felt that they had borne the brunt of the conflict while England reaped all the glory. The war's very name was based on the European part of the conflict, which lasted seven years, and ignored the fact that it lasted nine years in America.

Because part of the war was fought to benefit the colonies and keep them safe, Britain felt that the Colonies should pay the war's costs. Until this time, the colonies had been very lightly taxed because there was very little to tax. The British citizens had both more taxes and a much higher tax rate than the colonists. The British government decided this was unfair and dramatically increased taxes on the now-moderately-prosperous colonies. In short, the Americans now had money they could use to pay taxes, so the British started taxing them. You can guess how happy this abrupt change made the Americans.

Americans were willing to accept paying somewhat more in taxes, but Britain increased the taxes dramatically within a short time (although still to lower levels than in Britain itself). The even bigger problem for America was the lack of American representatives in Parliament to protect American interests. This is where the slogan "No Taxation Without Representation!" came from. Under the British system, representatives do not have to live in the area they represent and they did not intend to change that to please the Colonists. They did not see a problem with someone who had never even visited America representing American interests.

Can you see a way the British system for allocating representatives might have influenced our Constitution? (Hint: you can't live in Oregon and represent Arkansas in Congress.) Do you think their way was good, bad, or neutral? Do you think things might have gone differently if the British had changed their system so that Americans and their interests were represented in Parliament? How much do you think the Colonial Representatives could have done to advance and protect American interests in a Parliament with hundreds of other Representatives?

The Navigation Acts,[1] the Stamp Act,[2] the Boston Massacre,[3] and the Tax on Tea were enough to make the colonies unhappy with the British government,[4] but King George III was guilty of many more injustices. Something can be unjust but still legal, and everything King George did was legal because we were still British colonies. For example, the king would not allow a man to cut down a tree on his own land without first asking permission.

Do you think our government does anything similar today? Do you think any of our current laws are unjust? Can people do anything

SOME FACTS FROM HISTORY

they want on their own property (like cutting trees, not like injuring others) or are there rules and laws to limit their actions?

The King would appoint a judge and then refuse to pay him unless he decided all the cases in favor of the king. He appointed many unnecessary officers and forced the colonies to pay them large salaries. (All of this was perfectly normal, accepted monarch behavior.) King George kept a large number of soldiers and many expensive officers in the colonies, even in times of peace. The colonists were unhappy about paying for the soldiers, particularly since they also had to house them in their own homes.

Despite it all, the colonies remained loyal to England. In fact, they petitioned for redress, for the King or Parliament to make things right, with the Olive Branch Petition.[5] Traditionally, "extending an olive branch" means making a peace offering. Their petition was answered by more arrogance. Already engaged in armed conflict (war) with Britain, there was only one path left to the colonies: Declare themselves free and independent of Great Britain and her King. This was done on the fourth day of July, seventeen hundred and seventy-six. It was not until seven years later that Britain acknowledged our independence, and it was not until after the War of 1812 that she really accepted our independence.

The initial willingness of all the colonies to accept British rule is important because not all of either the colonies or the colonists started out as British. Germans[6] and Dutch[7] were the dominant ethnic group in some areas, for instance. All the different groups who came here contributed something in exchange for the liberty and freedom they desired, as they still do today. But we could not function without a common government, a common language, and common values, and the government and language that have been accepted by all new citizens since our very first days were British.

Do you think Britain could have sent soldiers here quickly enough to make a difference when they were needed, especially on the frontier, if there weren't enough stationed here?[8] Remember that it took months for a letter to cross the ocean—one way. Do you think it was wrong of the King to keep soldiers stationed here? Was it wrong of him to expect the colonists to pay for keeping the soldiers here?

These British soldiers were sometimes guilty of crimes for which they went unpunished. How do you think that influenced colonial feelings? Did it influence our Constitution (hint: Bill of Rights)? What do you think about not punishing the soldiers' when they committed crimes?

Do you think the colonists found it acceptable? If it wasn't, do you think the colonists accepted it anyway? If something is accepted, it is something that is regarded as normal or at least not fought against. If it is acceptable, that means it is satisfactory or agreeable to one or more people. People can regard something they find very unsatisfactory as acceptable because they don't have a choice or because a better solution cannot be found. People can be forced to accept something they really think is unacceptable, as contrary and paradoxical as that sounds, but it usually leads to trouble eventually. Can you think of any examples? Did they lead to trouble?

When this happens in our modern government, how can we change what is unacceptable to either end the practice or change it to something that is acceptable?

Do you think that we have more officers than we need compared to the number of workers/soldiers/ sailors under those officers in our modern government? Do you think, historically, many countries have ended up with too many high level people and too few workers, or that is has happened in many places?

Most new immigrants did not want to harm their homeland and simply asked to be allowed to move to the New World where they could to live and worship as they chose. No matter where they came from or when, immigrants have always had difficulties to deal with. For the earliest settlers, these included the Starving Time in Virginia,[9] the Lost Colonies,[10] the ship voyages here, the even worse experience on slave ships,[11] and conflicts with Native Americans, who were *not* all peaceful.

Others, both white Europeans and black Africans, came here as indentured servants.[12] Later, many Africans came involuntarily as slaves.[13] Indentured servants came here under a contract to work for another person for a set period of time, usually seven years, to repay the cost of their voyage. Sometimes the conditions they lived and worked under were very much like slavery, except that it was for a set time, not for life. Most indentured servants were either poor people who could not afford to come here any other way or convicts avoiding a worse fate in Europe. In fact, if you read the news, you will see that even today there are people who agree to work in sweat shops and other places for years in return for being brought to the United States. The fact that this practice and the slave-like work conditions are illegal has not stopped it because there are always people desperate to escape their country and come here, no matter the price.

The first major wave of immigrants after our Revolution was the Irish.[14] They came because of the Irish potato famine and were met with racism. They also had to deal with prejudice and religious intolerance because they were Catholic, not Protestant like most of those who came before them.[15] They had to take jobs no one else wanted and live in areas no one else liked very well when they first arrived. Decades later, the Chinese started immigrating because of the Chinese Famine and Taiping Rebellion, and because they were needed to work on the transcontinental railroad.[16] Famines and rebellions have led many other groups to move here as well. As well as different cultures, many have brought new religions. Each has had unique assimilation, and racism, issues.

Chinese laborers did most of the extremely dangerous work blasting the transcontinental railroad through the hard rock of the Sierra Madres Mountains while the flatter eastern part of the railroad used mainly Irish workers. The famous picture of the Golden Spike Ceremony celebrating completion of the railroad shows the Irish workers and not a single Chinese worker. Anti-Asian racism was rampant at the time, but the formerly despised Irish had been assimilated into our melting pot.

Historically, any time a truly large number of people from one ethnic group immigrate here, it causes concern, and often racism, until it is clear that they are indeed learning our language and culture and becoming part of our country, or assimilating. Once that happens, acceptance generally follows. And so the cycle continues with new groups arriving and eventually being assimilated, only to make way for yet another new group to arrive, be discriminated against, and be assimilated.

Why do you think this might be? Why do you think a large group following a new religion can create so much tension? What do you think causes faster acceptance/assimilation of some immigrant groups, by both Americans and the immigrants themselves? What do you think might slow it down? Why do you think people choose to come here but not assimilate? What examples have you seen either way in your own life?

SOME FACTS FROM HISTORY

RESOURCES

1. Navigation Acts
www.britannica.com/event/Navigation-Acts

2. The Stamp Act
www.avalon.law.yale.edu/18th_century/stamp_act_1765.asp

3. The Boston Massacre
www.bostonmassacre.net/

4. The Boston Tea Party
www.boston-tea-party.org/tea-act.html

5. Olive Branch Petition
www.revolutionary-war-and-beyond.com/olive-branch-petition.html

6. Germans in America
www.loc.gov/rr/european/imde/germchro.html

7. Dutch Colonization
www.nps.gov/nr/travel/kingston/colonization.htm

8. Colonial Shipping and Town Development in Tidewater
www.virginiaplaces.org/transportation/colonialshipping.html

9. The Jamestown Starving Time
www.history.org/history/teaching/enewsletter/volume8/dec09/teachstrategy.cfm

10. Discovering the Lost Colony of Roanoke
www.kids.librarypoint.org/lost_colony

11. Conditions of Slave Ships
www.4thebest4e.tripod.com/id15.html

12. Indentured Servants Experiences 1600-1700
www.teachervision.com/slavery-us/resource/3848.html

13. Common Misconceptions about Colonial Slavery
www.teachinghistory.org/history-content/ask-a-historian/25577

14. Irish and German Immigrants
www.ushistory.org/us/25f.asp

CHAPTER 1

15. Chinese Immigrants
www.loc.gov/teachers/classroommaterials/presentationsandactivities/
presentations/immigration/chinese.html

16. Golden Spike Ceremony
www.up150.com/timeline/golden-spike-ceremony

CHAPTER 2
ABOUT THE FOUNDING FATHERS

The Founding Fathers were amazing men (women were not allowed to participate) who did amazing things, but they were far from perfect. Most of what you hear and read about them understandably emphasizes the great things they did but it can also make it seem like they rarely, if ever, made mistakes. Other books and articles focus on their faults, which is hardly fair either. Like the rest of us, they were simply human.

Great men and women start out as kids who get in trouble with their parents and don't like all their school subjects, just like everyone else. They may make a lot of friends, or a lot of enemies. A few of the Founders were successful very quickly in their job or business, but others failed equally quickly. A few failed many times. What made them great was that they learned from these things and *kept trying* until they got to where they were meant to be. They were also great because of what they accomplished by working *together*. No colony anywhere in the world had ever before successfully revolted and won independence from their colonial parent country. Please take a moment to think about that—*no one had **ever** done it before, anywhere.*

There are some men that everyone includes on a list of Founding Fathers, such as George Washington, but there were dozens if you include all the possibilities. Potential Founding Fathers include those who attended the Constitutional Convention, wrote the Declaration of Independence or the Articles of Confederation, and more. There is no complete definitive list in the way that there is a complete list of signers of the Constitution or the Declaration of Independence. There was a lot of variety among these Founding Fathers.

Looking at photos of the Founders, it is easy to think that they were all very similar—rich, old, well-educated, white guys whose families had been here for a long time. Few things were common to all of them, except that they were all well-educated for the time. This did *not* mean a fancy degree from a famous university or even any degree at all. Well-educated people can be self-taught, even today. Some Founders, such as West-Indian (Caribbean) born Alexander Hamilton, were immigrants themselves.[1] Others, such as Jefferson, were born into families who had been here for generations. Jefferson's ancestors included gentry who settled Virginia in its earliest days.[2]

About half of the Founding Fathers, including Jefferson and James Madison, had college degrees, which were rare at the time. Even finishing high school was not common. Homeschooling was extremely common. For many, formal schooling ended at age ten, followed by an apprenticeship to learn a trade or job from someone who had mastered the trade or skill they wanted to learn.

George Washington never attended college. His formal schooling ended when he was 15, even though his family was far from poor.[3] On the other hand, John Adams was from a relatively poor family but they sacrificed to put him through college.[4]

Ben Franklin's formal schooling ended when he was ten.[5] After that, he was apprenticed to work for his brother and learn to be a printer. He ran away without permission before he finished. This meant that Franklin, one of our most revered Founding Fathers, was a fugitive from justice for a time. However, he never stopped learning and he eventually received multiple honorary degrees, including the title Dr. Franklin. One of his many inventions was bifocal glasses, which people still use today.

ABOUT THE FOUNDING FATHERS

Thirty five of the fifty five Founding Fathers studied law. Some went to law school in England and others were self-taught. Those who were self-taught studied law books without attending formal programs to become lawyers–in short, by apprenticing. People learned much more by either doing or by studying subject-matter books on their own in the past and by apprenticing in their field. This was true for most fields. Doctors, lawyers, jewelers, printers–in the past, almost every field was learned through apprenticeships.

Franklin and Adams, among others, were early supporters of a full and complete break with England–Revolution. Very few colonists truly wanted to leave the British Empire unless they absolutely had to, and support was far less than universal even after the Revolution started.[6] Adams was an early supporter of Revolution as a last-ditch, if-all-else-fails step, but he still defended the British Regulars (soldiers) accused of shooting colonial citizens during the Boston Massacre.[7] He wanted to ensure that they received a fair trial. Emotions were running very high at the time, in part because of the press coverage, which is probably why he was concerned they might not be treated fairly. They were acquitted (found not guilty) and released.

A brawl is a fight, generally a somewhat spontaneous event where it isn't entirely clear who or what started it. The reaction is usually out of proportion to the offense. In short, a brawl is when a group of people over-react to something and start a giant fight.

A massacre is when a large group of innocent people are killed for no particular reason, often quite brutally.

How do you think the name "Boston Massacre" might have influenced people's emotions and opinions of the event?[8] Does it influence your opinion? What do you think happened, based on the name? Would the "Boston Brawl" have the same effect?

Do you think people would have been as upset over the Boston Brawl as they were over the Boston Massacre? Do you think it was an accident that newspapers of the day called it a Massacre instead of a Brawl? They also printed a highly inaccurate image of the event created by Paul Revere (yes, that Paul Revere) that made it look like British Regulars fired on unarmed civilians without any reason, even though that wasn't exactly what happened. Why do you think they might have done this?

Do you think the newspapers that printed the image and used the name Boston Massacre were in favor of doing anything to stay part of England or in favor of Revolution? Why? Do you think it is unusual or common for media (newspapers, TV, internet, etc.) to name or describe things in a way that either helps them get more attention, sell more copies/make more money, or move public opinion in the direction they believe is correct? How and why? Can you think of any examples? How can you know that what you read and see in the news is accurate?

Defending the British Regulars cannot have been an easy or popular thing for Adams to do. This adherence to their own internal moral code, even when it was unpopular, is part of what makes many of the Founders great men. This is far from the only example. Can you think of any examples of this in modern politics or public life?

Can you think of any examples of leaders in any field taking the easy way out or doing what was popular instead of taking responsibility for their actions or of following through on their beliefs, even if it was unpopular or costly? Did they do the right thing? If not, then how should they have reacted? Do you think the increased media coverage in modern life makes it easier or harder to remain true to your own code? How and why?

Other Founders, like John Dickinson, never really wanted to leave the Mother Country.[9] To his immense credit, the day the Continental Congress voted on the Declaration of Independence, Dickinson did not attend.[10] If even one state had voted against signing the Declaration of Independence, it would not have been signed and we would not have declared our independence. Since Dickinson was strongly opposed and could not in good conscience vote for it, he stayed away and allowed the other Pennsylvania delegates to vote for Independence. He knew that not signing it would be unpopular, but he could not sign it and be true to himself. It effectively ended his political career, but he went on to serve in the Continental Army.

Signing the Declaration would have been the easy and popular thing to do, and it would have let him keep political power longer, but he did what he believed was right. That can be a very difficult thing to do, no matter what your age or position in life. Dickinson later wrote actively in support of our Constitution and helped with a lot of the drafting (writing, but not the final version), including the Great Compromise that ensured equal representation for everyone in Congress, citizens in the House of Representatives and states in the Senate, even though he was deathly ill at this time.

Washington, Jefferson, George Mason and other Founding Fathers opposed slavery but were still slave owners. Washington freed his slaves,[11] but not until after he died. Franklin freed his slaves *before* his death and became an active abolitionist (someone working to end slavery).[12] Jefferson wanted to free all his slaves when he died,[13] but he died so deeply in debt that only his house slaves were freed.[14] The rest were sold to repay his debts. He repeatedly tried, but failed, to get the government to abolish slavery. His original version of the Declaration of Independence included text condemning slavery[15] that was removed to ensure a unanimous vote for Independence and Revolution. He also tried to get slavery banned in the US territories west of the Appalachian Mountains[16] but failed again. (His desired ban was part of the Northwest Ordinance, based on his writings.)[17]

John Jay regularly bought slaves and then freed them when he felt they had worked enough that he had earned back what it cost to buy them.[18] It was as if he gave them a loan when he bought them, kept their wages to repay it, and freed them when this had happened. It was similar to being an indentured servant like many early colonists, without the guarantee of eventual freedom. In truth, many African "indentured servants" were never released at the end of their term of service and were simply made slaves. Jay was also a very active aboli-

23

tionist and was instrumental in getting abolition laws passed in the state of New York.

James Monroe,[19] Jefferson,[20] Mason[21] and some of the other Founding Fathers feared that abolishing slavery all at once, as eventually happened, might lead to problems including violence. As a result, they wanted to end slavery more gradually. Jay's New York laws provided a gradual freeing of slaves, as both Monroe and Jefferson preferred.

Only a small number of the Founding Fathers were determined to keep slavery. Even representatives of the slave states were willing to let it end. They were so determined that they refused to sign any document, including the Declaration of Independence and the new US Constitution, that threatened to end slavery. As a result, the majority who wanted to end slavery had to give up that goal so our nation did not split apart before it ever truly got started.[22] This is an important point, so I am going to restate it: **a majority of the Founding Fathers wanted to end slavery, but a small number who were strongly pro-slavery prevented that.**

> *What do you think of Jay's actions? What do you think slaves would have thought of them? What would they have thought about his choice to continue buying and owning slaves while he worked to get slavery abolished? How do Franklin's actions compare? He simply freed his slaves and didn't continue buying and freeing them as Jay did. How powerful do you think either of these examples was at the time?*

Both Monroe and Franklin started out poor and were entirely self-made men. Madison[23] and Jay[24] came from extremely wealthy, socially powerful families, and Washington was born in moderately wealthy. He became much wealthier and more important socially when he married the widow Martha Dandridge Custis.[25] He increased his income a lot more when he went from having one crop on his farm to having a variety of crops and sources of income at his estate of Mount Vernon.[26]

ABOUT THE FOUNDING FATHERS

Most farmers of this time, particularly in the South, only had one crop. Over time, this wears out the soil and farmers earn less money for the same amount of effort and land, which is why his decision to rotate crops was a big deal. In addition to agriculture, Mount Vernon included a mill, distillery, and fishing.

Alexander Hamilton was instrumental in setting the economic and financial policies of our young nation.[27] He rather famously died in a gun duel (a deadly fight between two people with very specific rules to "resolve" a dispute) with another politician named Aaron Burr.[28] Burr was Vice President under Thomas Jefferson.

The possibility that he might die within a few days apparently spurred Hamilton to write a list of who wrote each part of *The Federalist* papers so the secret did not die with him.[29] This list has helped historians, despite some apparent errors. *The Federalist* papers were written to help explain the new Constitution and to convince Americans to support the new, stronger, more centralized government. They were published in newspapers as a series of articles, or papers, and are now more commonly referred to as *The Federalist Papers,* three words instead of two.

Hamilton made many enemies because he had a difficult personality and strong convictions, Burr wasn't the only one. None of this changes the fact that Hamilton was brilliant and a critical Founding Father. He finished an apprenticeship to become a lawyer in three months instead of the normal three years and quickly became a famous lawyer. Washington chose him as the first Secretary of the Treasury and many of his policies remain in place, despite the many enemies they made him. Ironically, Alexander Hamilton, the man who set much of our early national financial course including a determination to pay off our bills and not have a large national debt, died nearly bankrupt. Monroe also died deeply in debt.

Burr also made many enemies. His actions during the 1800 election helped ensure that the 12th Amendment passed, and passed quickly.[30] His duel with Hamilton made dueling socially unacceptable and helped end the practice here. It also ended Burr's political career instead of reviving it as he had hoped. The famous duel, which killed one man and left the other a social outcast with no career, was caused by a political argument. It was a spectacularly unsuccessful way to "resolve" their argument.

Thomas Paine wrote influential pamphlets, such as *Common Sense,* to help convince people to support the Revolution.[31] He was also a key part of the effort to get French money to finance our Revolution. During his life, he was fired from several jobs and several businesses he owned failed.[32] When he died, only six people came to his funeral because his later actions and writings angered so many people.

Washington's inexperience caused him to lead his men to ambush a French scouting party and kill their leader in 1753. Since France and Britain were technically not at war yet, this was considered an act of war and contributed to the start of actual armed conflict. His rash actions, taken without enough thought about or understanding of their consequences, helped start the Seven Years War.[33]

The colonists called it the French and Indian War since they fought the French and Indians for nine years, but it spread beyond North America and was more generally a war between Britain and France that lasted seven years in Europe, which is why it is more properly called the Seven Years War. Of course, the whole situation was extremely complex and Washington's other actions (at the time and later) were brilliant, but even he made mistakes.

The Founding Fathers were not, as a group, Atheists, though some may have privately believed that way. At the time, virtually everyone living here was either a Christian or was very familiar with the Christian religion, and almost all were Protestants. (Protestants are members of Christian churches that broke away from the Roman Catholic Church to protest problems in the church and to try to reform it, or of churches descended from those churches.)

Most who did not regularly attend church or believe in the popular religions of the day were Deists, people who believe in god but do not follow the teachings of a specific church. The Founders prayed regularly at the Constitutional Convention and many other activities. Their actions showed that they believed in God and incorporated him in their daily lives, even if they did not incorporate a *church* into their daily lives.

The Founding Fathers were not always thought well of or remembered kindly when they were alive. They made mistakes. Their actions didn't always match their words, or their beliefs. They agreed to compromises that made things easier at the time but caused problems later. Some were good at getting people to work together and understand a different point of view. Others were firebrands who stirred up people to support and fight for what they (the firebrands) believed was important, but who lacked the skills to create something new after the old was swept aside. Some were brilliant theorists who figured out how to set up the nuts and bolts of running our country, but could not work well with others.

In short, they did great things, but they were also human and flawed with a variety of strengths and weaknesses, just like the rest of us. Their individual shortcomings don't change the simple fact that what they did *together* was more amazing than anything they could have done individually.

What do you think made them great?

A small number of the Founding Fathers were determined to keep slavery. They were so determined that they refused to sign any document, including the Declaration of Independence and the new US Constitution, that threatened to end slavery. As a result, the majority who wanted to end slavery had to give up that goal so our nation did not split apart before it ever truly got started. This is an important point, so I am going to restate it: a majority of the Founding Fathers wanted to end slavery, but a small number who were strongly pro-slavery prevented that.

RESOURCES

1. Alexander Hamilton
www.bioguide.congress.gov/scripts/biodisplay.pl?index=h000101

2. Thomas Jefferson's ancestors
www.monticello.org/site/research-and-collections/jeffersons-ancestry

3. George Washington's formal education
www.xroads.virginia.edu/~cap/gw/gwbio.html

4. John Adams education
www.colonialhall.com/adamsj/adamsj.php

5. Benjamin Franklin
www.ushistory.org/declaration/signers/franklin.htm

6. Loyalists, Fence-Sitters, and Patriots
www.ushistory.org/us/11b.asp

7. Key Figures in the Boston Massacre Trials
www.law2.umkc.edu/faculty/projects/ftrials/bostonmassacre/keyfigures.html

8. Boston Massacre
www.bostonmassacre.net

9. John Dickinson
www.ushistory.org/declaration/related/dickinson.htm

10. John Dickinson skipping the final vote
www.historyhome.co.uk/c-eight/america/dick5.htm

11. Washington freed his slaves
www.gwpapers.virginia.edu/articles/hurrelbrinck.html

12. Jefferson in debt
www.history.org/foundation/journal/winter10/jefferson.cfm

13. Franklin freed his slaves
www.archives.gov/legislative/features/franklin/

14. Jefferson freed his slaves
classroom.monticello.org/kids/resources/profile/263/Jefferson-and-Slavery/

ABOUT THE FOUNDING FATHERS

15. Declaration of Independence condemning slavery
www.vindicatingthefounders.com/library/jeffersons-draft.html

16. Map of Territories west of the Appalachians
www.memory.loc.gov/ammem/collections/continental/territ.html

17. Northwest Ordinance
www.myloc.gov/Exhibitions/creatingtheus/Constitution/Roadtothe
Constitution/ExhibitObjects/NorthwestOrdinanceProhibitsSlavery.aspx

18. John Jay freed his slaves
www.dlc.library.columbia.edu/jay/jayandslavery

19. James Monroe
www.ashlawnhighland.org/jm--slavery.htm

20. Thomas Jefferson and Salary
www.monticello.org/site/plantation-and-slavery/thomas-jefferson-and-slavery

21. George Mason's views on slavery
www.gunstonhall.org/georgemason/slavery/views_on_slavery.html

22. Slavery and the Founders
www.revolutionarywararchives.org/slavery.html

23. James Madison
www.montpelier.org/james-and-dolley-madison/james-madison

24. John Jay
www.newnetherlandinstitute.org/history-and-heritage/dutch_americans/john-jay

25. Martha Dandridge Custis
www.mountvernon.org/george-washington/martha-washington/

26. Mount Vernon
www.mountvernon.org/the-estate-gardens/pioneer-farm

27. Alexander Hamilton's Financial Program
www.digitalhistory.uh.edu/disp_textbook.cfm?smtID=2&psid=2973

28. Alexander Hamilton/Aaron Burr Duel
www.americaslibrary.gov/jb/nation/jb_nation_hamburr_1.html

29. *The Federalist* papers
www.loc.gov/rr/program/bib/ourdocs/federalist.html

30. The Election of 1800
www.socialstudiesforkids.com/articles/ushistory/electionof1800.htm

31. *Common Sense by Thomas Paine*
www.gutenberg.org/ebooks/147

32. Thomas Paine's life
www.thomaspainesociety.org

33. Washington's Role in Starting the Seven Years War
www.history.com/this-day-in-history/lieutenant-colonel-george-washington-begins-the-seven-years-war

CHAPTER 3
IT'S THE OS FOR THE US

Computers are part of everything we do in life today. You cannot avoid computers any more than you can avoid the government and laws. Even if you personally do not use a computer, they control traffic lights, television satellite feeds, systems within our cars–the list is seemingly endless. Each of these computers is controlled by an OS, or Operating System, which is the most basic software program within a computer.[1] Programs, or software, are basically data and codes.[2] Data and codes are not a solid object you can pick up like the monitor or a network server, although the data is often stored on server, or a disc or a thumb drive if it needs to be portable. The parts you can pick up, like a monitor, mouse, or server, are generally called hardware.[3]

Our laws are like the software that runs our country. All the laws for a country, together, are called its legal code, just like computer software is code.[4] According to the House of Representatives' website, "the United States Code...is a consolidation and codification by subject matter of the general and permanent laws of the United States." As colonies, we used a legal code called British Common Law. When we declared our independence, we kept that as basis of our new legal code. Of course, nothing the British added after our independence is part of our current legal system.

UNDERSTANDING HOW COMPUTERS WORK

The most basic system is a single computer operating alone, not in a network. Individual work stations, the laptop or desktop computer each person uses, are often joined together in a "network" that allows them to work more efficiently and do more tasks than they can do alone. It can also give them access to data that isn't available to anyone outside of that network. Office networks often store files and other data employees need to do their work, for example.

Most computer networks are built using one of two designs, called "network architecture." [4] These are peer-to-peer and client-server. A peer is someone who is your equal in status or abilities. Someone who plays in your soccer or gymnastics league is your peer. A peer-to-peer network is one where the computers all have about the same abilities. [5] These are good for small groups of computers that all need to do approximately the same tasks, such as the computers in your home.

Client-server architecture is used when a larger number of computers are networked together or when one central computer or group of computers controls certain functions, most often access outside the network such as the internet and email. [6] The idea is that the server actually serves the client computers by providing services that allow it to function faster and more efficiently than it could alone. A client is someone (or something, in this case) that receives benefits, services, or advice from someone or something else, or is dependent on them.

A computer's OS directs all the other programs and tells them how and when to operate. Our Constitution is like the OS for our country. Without the Constitution, we would have no national government, regulations, or laws. Our nation would not be able to operate, just like a computer cannot run without a functional OS. That is the situation our country was in right after the Revolutionary War ended. We did not have a working national Operating System. We had something called the Articles of Confederation. It operated poorly.

Under the Articles, our government was like a peer-to-peer system. This worked well enough during the Revolutionary War when the states operated independently but after the war, they needed to coordinate a lot more than just military matters. This led them to create a new governing document that uses a system more like client-server architecture. Of course this document is the US Constitution. Under it, most functions are kept at the state or local (city or county) level, just like most computer work is done on individual work stations. Anything that must be the same for and within all the states (trade regulations, currency, the postal system), and all interactions between any part of our nation and any outside organization (treaties, military operations) is clearly reserved for the federal government, just like computer servers control access outside the network.

When our nation was founded, state governments still had most of the power and the federal government had almost no power. The Founders intended the national government to serve the state governments, not the other way around, just as a computer server serves the needs of its users. That is why we are the United *States* of America, not something else like the United *Federation* of America or even simply America.

Unlike a new nation, new computer usually come with the OS already installed. The two basic types of personal computer OSs in common use today are Apple™ and Microsoft Windows™ which runs PCs (Personal Computers), once called IBM™ or IBM compatible. Because the companies that create software, including OSs, know it is virtually impossible to find all the problems in testing, they periodically come out with patches and updates. Companies fix problems as they find them, so new programs need patches to correct problems. As time passes, most of the problems are fixed but other things change and updates (larger changes) are needed.

It is the same with our Constitution. It was a new, never-been-tried-on-a-whole-nation Operating System and the Founders couldn't foresee how everything would work, so they included a way to amend, or change, the Constitution as weaknesses were found. Because of British violations of people's rights, several states demanded a Bill of Rights be added as a condition for ratifying the new Constitution. This resulted in the biggest batch of amendments written at one time. It included the first ten amendments, known as the Bill of Rights, plus the 27th Amendment, which was not ratified until 1992, and one other never-ratified amendment related to the size of congressional districts. These were written and sent to the states for ratification by the first Congress under the new Constitution. The next biggest batch was three amendments written after the Civil War. Times had changed and the long-festering problem of slavery was finally resolved.

Once you have the OS installed and working, the next step is installing the basic software. For most people, these include a word processor, spreadsheet, and presentation program such as Power-Point™. Other programs that are usually installed with the OS are an internet browser, games such as solitaire, utilities like search, and a photo gallery.

After you finish installing those, you need to install more utilities to keep your computer running well[7]. These include a firewall,[8] virus protection,[9] and a cleanup (or defrag/defragmentation) utility,[10] although network servers often take care of these tasks for you. A defrag program cleans up your computer hard drive to make space and to make it easier for the computer to find things, just like you are supposed to clean up your desk. You may also choose to install different programs if you don't like the ones that came with the computer, such as a different internet browser or better photo editing software. That can leave you with duplicate programs, just like the government often has two or more departments with nearly-identical programs.

When all of this is done, then, and only then, you can start installing all the fun programs like your favorite games. Even after that, you may still need to go back and do more work setting up your computer. If you don't have the most recent version of plug-in programs, like Flash™, some websites and games simply won't work until you download and install them.[11] And your virus protection and firewall will both ask you, possibly many times, if you really want to do that.

Computer networks restrict access to those who are part of it or who have met a set of criteria to prove they need access and won't harm the network. Similarly, countries restrict access to those who are part of it (citizens) or who have a reason to be here. In the USA, that's really not hard to do, especially for short periods. Tourists from many countries need nothing more than a passport, and Visas aren't hard to come by either. Access is also granted quite freely to students.

VIRUS PROTECTION/FIREWALLS

Virus protection scans your programs and emails, and warns you (or tries to) before you open something that might infect your computer with a virus that may make it stop working properly, just like a virus makes your body not work properly. The network administrator sets the network rules for which areas the firewall blocks or allows access to.[12]

Most, but not all, networks use firewalls to restrict internet access in some way to keep you from getting a virus online and accidently infecting the entire network. While it can be annoying, this is a good thing because sometimes destructive programs (viruses or worms) automatically download when you aren't paying attention or where you won't notice.[13] The virus, or worm, will then start damaging your computer and infecting the whole network, which can cause a lot of damage and be very expensive to fix.[14]

On a client-server system, such as our government, these are normally done at the server level so everyone has equal protection and restrictions. For example, the federal government controls access to our country by controlling who becomes a citizen and who can enter to visit or work here.

CHAPTER 3

The network sets the rules for outside interactions. Individual desktops cannot over-ride virus protection or the firewall, although individual users can often open attachments that have viruses and accidently infect the system. If the network doesn't have up-to-date virus protection, then the whole system is more open to infection. If access is too restrictive, people may be unable to do their jobs. For instance, if a network will not allow any internet access to prevent people from goofing off watching online videos, they might also prevent them from doing research for their job.

In addition, we have millions of people here with Green Cards and Temporary Worker status. They are people who have retained their citizenship in their home country, but plan on staying here for years, or even the rest of their lives. And of course, we have masses of immigrants and refugees. All of those are people who followed the system and arrived here legally.

The immigration system established by the US government is really not restrictive. Like a computer firewall, it is simply designed to keep the nation and its citizens safe. They check to ensure immigrants are healthy, not enemies of the state (part of a terrorist organization, spies for another country, etc.), or criminals. When this system is bypassed, as is happening today, it becomes increasingly easy for criminals and terrorists to enter the country and stay here.

Illegal aliens, undocumented migrants, whatever you want to call them, a lot of people have moved here without going through even one of the checks necessary to keep us safe. Of course many of them simply want a better life, but their actions still go against current US immigration law. The true problem is that terrorists, gang-bangers, felons, drug lords, murderers, and worse–those who can't come here legally–are using those same paths to come here.

Do you see a link between illegal immigration and national security? Do you think we should throw open our borders, throw out our rulebook, and allow anyone to enter and become citizens? Even hardened criminals? Should we enforce current laws?

The federal government is not just responsible for immigration and visitation. All official interactions between the state or federal government and anything outside our country, including all aspects of treaties, wars, and trade, go through the federal government. It sets restrictions on how states interact with each other and with other nations, particularly in places like harbors where goods and people from other countries can enter ours. This is comparable to the way a computer network controls interactions between work stations and anything outside the network.

Similarly, the federal government is responsible for protecting the states from external dangers and for keeping internal problems and issues from becoming dangers, including issues like slavery. Some nations, particularly those run by dictators such as North Korea and Cuba, allow as little as possible to enter from the outside world.[15] Even Mexico has significantly stricter tighter immigration policies than the USA[16].

Our nation is quite open in what we allow from the outside, whether it is information, goods, or immigrants. While this is generally fine, it can lead to problems. That is why we have passport control at our borders and quarantine animals entering the country to keep them from accidentally bringing in diseases. It is the responsibility of the federal government to prevent, or at least minimize, those problems. The feds set the policies and write the laws but states may help with enforcing them.

Every OS includes a few games and basic utilities like search, a calculator, and the control panel. Most are so basic that we don't think about them, unless we need them and they aren't working. The government also provides services so basic we don't think about them, unless they aren't there or are breaking down, as roads and bridges are wont to do.

At an even more basic level, a government must protect its citizens or it will soon cease to be the government and another will take its place. Have you ever truly been worried that another country will successfully invade the USA? Or that our government might completely stop building and maintaining our roads and schools? Like the search and control panel features on a computer, you don't even think about these unless they stop working. In the US, this includes protecting our borders by setting and enforcing immigration policies, building and maintaining infrastructure such as roads and powerlines, and establishing and maintaining the Armed Services, including the Coast Guard. It also includes protecting individual citizens by protecting their rights as guaranteed by our Constitution and Bill of Rights.

The Constitution makes it clear that the people responsible for ensuring those functions are carried out are in the Legislative branch, with assistance from the Executive and Judicial branches. These people are the ones with the admin rights to our nation's legal code. Just as enabling admin rights ensures that only a few people can add new programs to a computer (even plug-ins), our Constitution limits who can make changes to our legal code. However, just as you do not need admin rights to save bookmarks to your browser or data files (game progress, documents, spreadsheets, etc.) to your hard drive because they are not software (code), federal bureaucracies are able to pass "regulations". These are not part of the legal code but they do become part of system, taking space and using government resources, just as data files take space and use resources on a work station.

Anyone who has admin rights to your computer is generally expected to keep their mouse off your personal (data) files, but they can change other programs without asking. For example, you may go home one night and come back to find out you have a new word processor. The change was made without your knowledge or consent, but might be necessary either to ensure that everyone you work with is using the same program or because the old program wasn't working correctly or was outdated. Your data files should be left untouched by the change, though.

Just as an admin installs new and updated programs for an entire organization, the federal government creates and updates agencies and laws that cover the whole nation. In both cases, they are providing services an individual could not provide that (hopefully) benefit a large number of people at once. They are expected to know what is safe and necessary, and what is not. There are many departments within the federal government that write rules and regulations and implement them without getting approval from anyone outside their bureaucracy, just like you can save data files with your work without asking anyone else. However, unlike your data files, their regulations impact the rest of the nation, for good of for ill.

The USA is large and varied. Some needs are the same for everyone, such as secure borders, safe roads, and a sound currency. These are the responsibility of our federal government, in the service of our state governments, just as a network server takes care of the firewall and storing key programs. State governments are clearly secondary to the federal government, the supreme law of the land under our Constitution, but they provide the majority of the services to our citizens, as the Constitution was originally written, just as individual work stations to most of the work in any home or office.

There is so much variety among our states that it would be somewhere between difficult and impossible for one set of national laws to cover all the rules and regulations for everything for all the states fairly and equitably.

CHAPTER 3

RESOURCES

1. Operating System
www.webopedia.com/TERM/O/operating_system.html

2. Software
www.webopedia.com/TERM/S/software.html

3. Hardware
www.webopedia.com/TERM/H/hardware.html

4. Legal Code
www.uscode.house.gov

5. Systems Network Architecture
www.webopedia.com/TERM/S/Systems_Network_Architecture.html

6. Peer to Peer Architecture
www.webopedia.com/TERM/P/peer_to_peer_architecture.html

7. Client Server Architecture
www.webopedia.com/TERM/C/client_server_architecture.html

8. Utilities
www.webopedia.com/TERM/U/utility.html

9. Firewalls
www.webopedia.com/TERM/F/firewall.html

10. Virus Protection
www.webopedia.com/TERM/V/virus_protection.html

11. Defragging
www.webopedia.com/DidYouKnow/Computer_Science/disk_defragment
ation.asp

12. Plug-ins
www.webopedia.com/TERM/P/plug_in.html

13. Virus
www.webopedia.com/TERM/V/virus.html

14. Worms
www.webopedia.com/DidYouKnow/Internet/virus.asp

15. North Korea Immigration Policy
www.migrationpolicy.org/article/north-korea-understanding-migration-and-closed-country/

16. Mexican Immigration Policy
www.mexperience.com/lifestyle/living-in-mexico/visas-and-immigration/

CHAPTER 4
THE ARTICLES OF CONFEDERATION

O ur Founders were careful to create a new government framework before getting rid of the old, and to leave the colonial/state governments in place. The Declaration of Independence,[1] Articles of Confederation,[2] and Constitution[3] were all drafted by, voted on, and ratified by representatives from colonial/state legislatures, or by the actual legislatures. This involvement helped convince the state governments to participate in the new government. As a result of never being without a government, particularly local governments but national as well, we did not have the problems with lawlessness that France did during and after their Revolution.

On the same day a committee was appointed to write the Declaration of Independence (June 11, 1776), another committee was appointed to prepare some rules or laws to ensure the soon-to-be-independent colonies did not become lawless. The final result was the "Articles of Confederation and Perpetual Union between the States," generally shortened to the Articles of Confederation, or even the Articles. Because the colonies were revolting against a strong national government that gave them little or no power, they made certain the national government was exceptionally weak. Almost all the power stayed with the states under the Articles. They even called them "states", a word that generally refers to a country, instead of the more common term "province." A province is an administrative unit within a state (country).[4]

A country's founding document, such as our Constitution, outlines the nation's basic operating system. Before our revolution, most countries operated on a variation on a monarchy, including aristocracies and theocracies headed by a religious leader. They were generally totally dominated by one person or one small group of people.

This was similar to the old super-computers that predate the personal computers common today. Those old stand-alone supercomputers were made obsolete by modern computers and OSs. Macintosh™/Apple and Personal Computers (or PCs) are currently the two dominant systems, although that has changed in the past and probably will again in the future. The new systems allow more individual control. This makes them more flexible to meet individual needs and faster to respond and update when changes are needed.

From the late 1970s into the 1980s, the Commodore OS was dominant, but Commodore chose not to share their code.[5] They did not let anyone else write software for their computers or use their programs on hardware from other companies. In the same way, the thirteen newly independent colonies chose not to share or cooperate with each other under the Articles of Confederation.

In the 1980s, IBM also had a PC OS. It wasn't as good as the one from Commodore or as user-friendly as the one from Apple, but IBM allowed other companies use their code to run their PCs and run on their programs on the IBM OS. IBM did not let anyone else take the actual OS, but they cooperated with others to create something none of them could have done alone.

Commodore stood alone, as the states initially tried to stand alone. Have you ever heard of Commodore computers? Or seen one in real life? Recently? And that would have been the fate of the states, if they had tried to stand alone. How about a PC or Macintosh/Apple? How often do you use normally one of those?

CHAPTER 4

During the Revolution, the states were all focused on defeating the English soldiers and winning our independence, so the Articles worked well enough. However, when the war ended, the states lost their common enemy and common purpose. It quickly became clear that the country had no real national government since it could not even tax anyone or enforce any laws. That was not a good way to run a country.

Like IBM sharing its code, the Founding Fathers realized that the country would only survive if the states joined together and worked for common goals. The war had left a very large public debt to be paid, as wars usually do, and there was no money with which to pay it, as often happens. The country's trade was broken up and the people were very poor. Congress could make treaties with foreign nations but could not force the states to honor them under the Articles, so of course no one wanted to sign treaties with our fledgling nation. In short, the country and the government were broke and had few prospects for making money.

At this time, Washington wrote, "The Confederation seems to me to be little more than a shadow without the substance."[6] At another time he wrote, "It is a subject of regret that so much blood and treasure have been lavished for no purpose; that so many sufferings have been encountered without compensation; and that so many sacrifices have been made in vain."[7] Clearly, he was concerned about the future of our young nation and could see that change was needed.

Many other important people were actively trying to prepare the public for change. Among the most active were James Madison, "the Father of the Constitution," and Alexander Hamilton, who later wrote most of *The Federalist* papers. (These were a series of articles or essays written after the Constitutional Convention to explain how the new government would operate; they were written primarily to convince American citizens and states to accept the new Constitution.) Finally, their labor was rewarded in 1787 and the public was ready for a change. A convention was called to improve the Articles of Confederation but the delegates were quickly convinced that creating a new document would be better than trying to fix the Articles, so they locked themselves away for several months, in total secrecy, and wrote the United States Constitution.[8]

The Articles allowed each state to create its own legal code, just as programmers create the basic code for individual computer programs, and these state legal codes were not necessarily compatible with one another. Think of it this way: you have a PlayStation™, a computer, and an iPad™. They each run on a different platform, or OS. If you have friends visit, there is no way you can network the different machines together to play a game. The systems simply do not work together. It was the same with the states. Because we lacked an effective basic framework, the states were able to do as they pleased with no restrictions. Each state could, and did, raise money, tax imported goods, print money, and do many other things normally reserved for the central government. This worked about as well as trying to get an Xbox™ game to work on a PlayStation console.

Under the Articles and during the Constitutional Convention, the smaller, weaker states were afraid of the larger, stronger ones and the stronger ones were jealous of each other. Under the Articles, differing state laws sometimes prevented trade between different parts of the country, and they definitely kept the country from functioning as one nation. The states quarreled among themselves and were even prepared to get into wars with one another. That would have been terrible for them.

Despite all this weakness, there was still a national government and its legislature, the Continental Congress, acted to prevent the collapse of our nation before it even truly started. The laws it passed remained in effect after the new Constitution was passed, just as parts of British Common Law remained in force after our Revolution. That was important for keeping everything running smoothly in this country.

For example, the Continental Congress passed the Northwest Ordinance in 1787, also called the Ordinance of 1787.[9] It described how territories and new lands in the territory north-west of the Ohio River could become states. This law was quite revolutionary. Allowing colonies or territories to become a full-fledged part of the nation and its government, equal to the older parts, was unheard of. It makes sense that it would happen here first.

In 1803, Ohio became the first territory to achieve statehood under the terms of the Northwest Ordinance.

What does this tell you about how important these former coloni-als felt about ensuring that colonies/territories would always have a sure, legal path to becoming an equal member of the country?

What affect do you think keeping the past laws (British Common Law and laws passed under the Articles) had on the young nation? Do you think it made it easier, harder, or didn't matter for doing business and running the government? How do you think things might have been different if they hadn't kept the old laws?

RESOURCES

1. The Declaration of Independence
www.archives.gov/exhibits/charters/declaration.html

2. The Articles of Confederation
www.archives.gov/exhibits/charters/charters_of_freedom_4.html

3. The US Constitution
www.archives.gov/exhibits/charters/constitution.html

4. State Defined
en.wikipedia.org/wiki/State

5. Commodore 64
www.oldsoftware.com/history.html

6. Letter from George Washington to James Warren
press-pubs.uchicago.edu/founders/documents/v1ch5s9.html

7. Washington's Circular Letter of Farewell to the Army, 1783
www.loc.gov/teachers/classroommaterials/presentationsandactivities/presentations/timeline/amrev/peace/circular.html

8. The Constitutional Convention
www.teachingamericanhistory.org/convention/

9. The Northwest Ordinance
www.ourdocuments.gov/doc.php?flash=true&doc=8
www.loc.gov/rr/program/bib/ourdocs/northwest.html

CHAPTER 5
THE CONSTITUTION

The Constitution for the USA is not the only constitution in the world. A "constitution" is the highest law of a country and establishes the form of its government and may be either written or unwritten. It tells the form of the government and exactly what power each part of the government has. It is important that every American should understand our Constitution, just as citizens of other countries should understand the constitution or other founding documents for their government. You cannot truly protect and uphold a thing that you do not know or understand any more than you can operate a computer if you do not understand the basics of how it works. In computer terms, this doesn't mean you have to be able to write software or replace a hard drive. It means you need to know how to turn it on and operate the programs you use.

The United States of America has the oldest functioning written constitution of any nation in the world. It established majority rule with strong protections for minorities and equality for all, although that took longer to achieve than some of the Founders' other goals. The men who wrote our Constitution began it with a paragraph called the Preamble, which introduces the Constitution and tells its goals.

<u>We the People</u> <u>of the United States, in Order to</u>

<u>form a more perfect Union, establish Justice, insure domestic</u>
<u>Tranquility, provide for the common defense, promote the gen-</u>
<u>eral Welfare, and secure the Blessings of Liberty to ourselves</u>
<u>and our Posterity, do ordain and establish this Constitution for</u>
<u>the United States of America.</u>

The Preamble very clearly starts with the words "We the People." It does not start with "We the Government" or "We the States," and the extra-large, bold font on those words is from the original document. Our government is meant to be of the people, by the people, and for the people, as Abraham Lincoln stated in the 1863 Gettysburg Address.[1] It is not of the Government, nor of the Political Parties, nor of the States, nor even of the International Community. It is *we the People*–the American people, the American citizens–who give our government power. The Founders clearly did not want us to miss that fact. Our government is most clearly and specifically based on the consent of the governed. We the People are the source of the government's power, and not the other way around. This is the most basic, most fundamental point of the entire Constitution and we must always remember it.

There is a reason that no other text is written as large as those three simple words. Never forget them.

> *Why do you think they were trying to "form a more perfect Union"? What do you think they wanted the Constitution to do that the Articles did not do? Why do you think they chose to start with We the People in such large letters?*

This is why doing your duty as a citizen, including voting, is so important. Those duties and rights are so fundamental to our nation and our government that if people do not exercise those rights, they can be lost and our government will stop working.

CHAPTER 5

The specific tasks the Preamble sets for the government are to establish justice (a court system), insure domestic tranquility (the National Guard, among other things), and provide for the common defense (Armed Services and the Militia/National Guard). Insuring domestic tranquility is far more than simply having Armed Services (Army, Navy, Air Force, Marines) and a National Guard (state militia) to defend us and provide help if the nation or a state needs it. It means making sure the states get along and judging disagreements between or among states, such as border disputes in the early years. In fact, Maryland and Virginia have a dispute over the Potomac River that has continued from the colonial era clear to the present day!

What other actions and powers do you think might be involved in ensuring domestic tranquility?

Providing for the common defense is also more than just having a military. It is having secure borders, which is one reason the federal government is responsible for immigration and naturalization. Without immigration services and with truly open and totally unsecured borders, anyone could enter our country at any time, including not just terrorists and violent criminals but also foreign military and large criminal organizations.

Why are secure borders are important for the common defense? How does the federal government help keep our borders secure? Do states help? How or why not? What else do you think the federal government does to provide for the common defense? How do you think regulating immigration relates to keeping us safe?

The remaining tasks, promoting the general Welfare and securing the Blessings of Liberty, are far harder to define. Posterity means your descendants and the other people who live after you. This means that our government is specifically supposed to consider the effects their decisions will have on future generations.

What does the federal government do to promote the general Welfare and secure the Blessings of Liberty? Is there anything they aren't doing that you think they should do? Is there anything they are doing that they should stop doing?

How much do you think the government and our elected officials do, in fact, consider "our Posterity" when they make decisions? How far past the next election do they think? Is that about right, or too much, or too little? What actions make you think that? Do their words and their actions match?

Our forefathers divided the government into three departments: the Legislative, the Executive, and the Judicial. The Constitution refers to them as departments, but they are usually called "branches" of the government today. Why three? When you hang out with your friends, is it easier to decide what to do if there are two of you, or three of you, or a larger group? Most people find it relatively easy to decide on something with two people, but harder to get three to agree. With three, it is most often a majority decision, or two out of three wanting to do something and the third either going along with it or doing something by themselves. The larger the group, the harder it is to reach a decision, and the more likely that at least some of the group members won't like that decision.

If there were only two branches of government, it would be easier for those two branches to make agreements to do things that benefit them as individuals or the government, but that are bad for the citizens. Having three branches makes that less likely, but having more branches would make it difficult to accomplish anything.

Our system uses something called checks and balances. Just as a hockey player can check, or stop, another hockey player's actions or attempted actions, each branch of the government can check, or stop, actions by the other branches. Two of the three working together can overcome the actions of the third branch so that no one branch becomes too powerful. Operating correctly, it maintains the balance of power among the three branches.

The Legislative department makes the laws and is called the Congress. Congress is composed of two bodies called Houses, although in common usage the House of Representatives is called the "House." Neither house is more powerful than the other, but the Senate has fewer members and its members serve longer terms than members of the House of Representatives. This means individual Senators are generally more powerful than individual Representatives.

In an absolute monarchy, such as England before our Revolution, the same person makes the laws and interprets them. If the monarch (the king or queen) makes a law and afterwards has it brought before him in a way that he did not expect, he can say, "Oh, it does not mean that, but means this instead." The monarch can change the law to suit themselves. In contrast, our government has one branch of the government write the laws and another branch interprets them. In a well-written law, everything will be so clear that it only has one possible meaning.

The Judicial department interprets, or tells the meaning of, laws passed by Congress. Laws do not come to the attention of our Judicial department unless someone has had a problem with that law and chosen to go to court over it. In practice, it takes as little effort to find poorly written, confusing laws as it does to find poorly written glitchy computer programs, and neither one works very well. Bills that are over a hundred or even a thousand pages are not rare.

What type of bill do you think needs to be over 100 pages? Over 1000 pages? Do you think longer bills are more or less likely to be clear and to the point? Or to contain unnecessary provisions?

Do you think unnecessary provisions are more likely to be included in large, important legislation, more routine matters, or equally?

Do you think most bills are probably clear and to the point, or do most include unnecessary provisions? Why do you think that is so?

When the legislature writes the laws poorly, it is hard for the judges to figure out what Congress intended when they make their legal decisions. Badly written laws also let the judiciary interpret the law in a way that they know is contrary to what Congress intended in the law, if Congress did not make that intention clear in the law. This allows judges, many of whom are appointed and not elected, to substitute their opinions and judgments for those of our elected officials. Therefore, all laws should be written, and all judges selected, with great care.

How could the judiciary interpret a law against what Congress wants? Imagine you ask to go out to a movie, and your parents tell you that no, you are not allowed to go out to a movie. You know that they really don't want you to go out at all, but they did not actually say you are not allowed to go out at all. If you then go out to the bookstore with friends (but not a movie), are you following the rule they gave you? Are you following their intention? The same thing can happen with interpreting laws.

The Executive department signs, or executes, the laws. The President of the United States is the highest person in the Executive department and oversees the bureaucracies that implement the law. We will learn more about the powers of each branch later.

Each of these three branches of government has their principal building and many other lesser buildings in the city of Washington, D.C., as do many other departments of our government, such as the Department of Agriculture. There is a very beautiful building called the Capitol Building (spelled with an O instead of an A, the way the word for a capital city is spelled) in which Congress meets. The Judicial Department has the Supreme Court building. The Executive Department has The White House and Eisenhower (formerly Old) Executive Office Building. Because we technically have a government of The People, it is possible to tour any of these buildings.

CHAPTER 5

In 1787, James Wilson, one of the signers of the Declaration of Independence, said , "Regarding it in every point of view with a candid and disinterested mind, I am bold to assert that it is the best form of government which has ever been offered to the world." [2] This was part of a highly influential speech delivered in Pennsylvania to explain the new Constitution and increase support for it. Copies of this speech were more widely read than even *The Federalist* papers. It helped convince both states and citizens to accept the new Constitution.

How does it make you feel that this was written about your country and your government? Do you agree or not? What do you think of the Founders decision to disregard their instructions to improve the Articles of Confederation and instead create a new document? Were they right to do this? Should they have done something else instead?

RESOURCES

1. Gettysburg Address
www.archive.org/details/gettysburgaddres00linc

2. James Wilson's 1787 Speech
www.constitution.org/afp/jwilson0.htm

CHAPTER 6
THE HOUSE OF REPRESENTATIVES

Word processing (Word™) and spreadsheets (Excel™) are the main programs most people use on their computer. Spreadsheets are used primarily for financial documents, although they also work well for anything in a large table.[1] Word processing is used for writing documents such as books and research papers.[2] The two programs have slightly different uses, but both are widely and frequently used in many homes and offices.

Congress is much the same. One of the most basic tasks of any government is writing the laws that form the legal code.[3] Under the US Constitution, the two houses of Congress share that task, although revenue (income) related bills must start in the House.[4] Like budgets created in Excel, House members are updated (put up for election) fairly frequently. Like books and papers created with Word, Senators aren't updated, or changed, nearly that often. Most bills can start in either house, and both must eventually agree on the same exact text before a bill goes to the White House to be signed into law or vetoed. The two slightly different houses, doing slightly different tasks, work together to create the legal code for our nation.

The Constitution lists the exact tasks Congress is expected to carry out. These are Congress's Expressed Powers.[5] Each branch also has

Implied Powers used to carry out their Expressed Powers.[6] For example, Congress was not given the power to start a college or academy to train military officers but it did so to guarantee that we have a professionally trained Officer Corp to staff the Army and Navy, which they are empowered to maintain. Staffing the Army and Navy is an Expressed Power. Starting and maintaining military academies is an Implied Power. Implied Powers do not give any part of the government unlimited authority, just enough to get the job(s) done. Our Constitution limits the authority of each branch of our government and uses checks and balances to maintain those limits.

Each state has its own representatives in Congress. Deciding how many to give each state caused tremendous fighting among the states and their delegates at the Constitutional Convention. The larger states wanted representation based on size, giving them more say, and the smaller states wanted equal representation for all, so the larger states couldn't push them around. The final compromise was that all the states receive two Senators, as the small states wanted, but the number of Representatives is based on population so that the whole population is more evenly represented, as the larger states wanted. This was called the Great Compromise of 1787. It is also sometimes called the Connecticut Compromise because the delegates from the small state of Connecticut argued passionately for it.[7]

This clause is part of the reason we have a Census every ten years—to try to ensure that representation is equal for all. If you do not fill out at least some of the information on your Census form and return it, then your state (and local area) may not get all the representatives it should. Although the Census counts everyone to determine the number of Representatives in Congress, there was, and is, no guarantee in the Constitution for the people to vote directly for any federal official. Let me repeat that: **The United States Constitution does not guarantee anyone the right to vote, anywhere, at any time, for anything, or for anyone.** George Washington did not receive a single citizen's vote to become our first President under the Constitution. He was elected unanimously by the Electoral College.

The Census is similar to disk clean-up software. That software goes through every program and every disk on your computer to find damaged areas and empty spaces. It then moves bits of data around to make sure all the space is being used most efficiently; this is called "defragmenting" because it takes programs that were fragmented, or broken into pieces that were all over the place, and puts them back in the same area so resources are used most efficiently.

The Census does the same thing for our country. It sends workers to check how many people live in each part of the country to track increases and decreases in population, and other demographics changes like which races live where. It makes sure that the federal government sends, and expects to receive, the right amount of tax money, goods, and services to and from each part of the country by making sure the government knows approximately how many people live in each area. States use this information to determine where they need to spend money for schools and other services.

After the census, some states add or lose Representatives, and others may find that they have the same number but people have moved around within the state. In any of these cases, they do something called "redistricting" which means drawing new lines for congressional districts.[8] This not infrequently leads to something called gerrymandering. If you think about how you would divide things up, you probably imagine something like boxes, maybe with some odd pieces to match the edges of towns or counties. In gerrymandering, the district lines are drawn specifically to give one political party as many "safe" seats as possible, while simultaneously giving the other party as few as possible. A "safe" seat is a Congressional district where the majority of voters belong to one party, making it a "safe" bet that they will always win it. These "gerrymandered" districts have very odd shapes. The term originated with a district that was shaped somewhat like a salamander less than thirty years after our Constitution was signed. Governor *Gerry* approved the odd sala*mander* shaped district that benefitted his party, thus the term *Gerrymander*. The federal government has attempted to prevent, or at least reduce, gerrymandering, but has been unable to end it.

THE HOUSE OF REPRESENTATIVES

Article I

Section 1

All legislative Powers herein granted shall be vested in a Congress of the United States, which shall consist of a Senate and House of Representatives.

We have a bicameral legislature, one with two parts, to help ensure equal representation for all parts of our country. Some nations have a unicameral legislature, which only has one house. (The prefix "bi", like bicycle, always means two and the prefix "uni", like unicycle, always means one.) Each Representative in the House represents a specific area, called their Congressional District or, more simply, their District. They have to live in the state they represent, but not in the same District. This means that someone living in New York City could legally represent a New York District near the Great Lakes, but could not represent a Connecticut District, even though it would be closer to NYC. Getting elected is, of course, another matter entirely as people living near the Great Lakes might think someone who lives in New York City wouldn't represent them or their interests well. Whether the candidate lives in outside their District, she must still convince them that she knows the area and its concerns well enough to represent them better than anyone else.

Section 2

The House of Representatives shall be composed of Members chosen every second Year by the People of the several States, and the Electors in each State shall have the Qualifications requisite for Electors of the most numerous Branch of the State Legislature.

When the Constitution was written, some members of the Constitutional Convention wanted Representatives elected for five years but others wanted only one year. Everyone wanted to do what was right and so, sensibly, each gave up a little and it was fixed at two years. This is a short enough time between elections to encourage Representatives to be careful and pay attention to what the people want and to not abuse their power. If at the end of two years a Representative has shown by their actions that they are not fit to represent the people, someone else can be elected to take their place. If they have been just the right person in the right place at the right time, the people can re-elect them for another term.

> *Do you think our politicians still compromise in order to reach the best decision for the largest number of people? If not, what do they do instead? Do you think they pay attention to what the people want or do they focus on something else? If something else, what is it?*
>
> *How often do you think politicians who are doing a poor job are voted out of office? If not, how do they stay in power?*

When the Constitution was ratified, state legislatures selected the Electors for the Electoral College. This gradually changed to citizens electing the Electors over the next several decades. These Electors, along with Congress, actually selected the President as well as Congressmen. For instance, Jefferson was selected as our 3rd President by Congressional voting. By 1828, only Delaware and South Carolina did not have popularly elected Electors, making Andrew Jackson the first popularly elected President of the United States. He was also the first Westerner (from Tennessee, part of "the West" at the time) to occupy the Oval Office.

<u>No Person shall be a Representative who shall not have attained to the Age of twenty five Years, and been seven Years a Citizen of the United States, and who shall not, when elected, be an Inhabitant of that State in which he shall be chosen.</u>

It seems so obvious to us that a Representative must live in the state they represent that it would not even occur to a modern American to require this. Who knows what someone from New Jersey wants and needs as well as a person who lives in that state? No one. However, other countries, including Britain, do not require that representatives live in the area they represent. Britain actually felt that people who lived in Britain and had never even visited America could represent the Colonies as well as or better than someone from the Colonies, since that was the system they used throughout the rest of their Empire. That is why the Constitution says a Representative must live in the state they represent.

How do you think geography and economics might have affected this clause?[9] Do you think a poor farmer could afford to leave his crops to serve in Congress? Do you think the people who could afford to serve in Congress were spread evenly throughout all the colonies, including frontier areas? Do you think all the Districts would have had someone able and qualified to serve in Congress?

What do you think travel was like from frontier areas to the capital? Do you think it was much longer or harder than from established cities such as Boston and Charleston, or from frontier areas like Tennessee and other western areas? How might that have impacted representation if the Constitution required Representatives to live in their District as well as their state?

Our forefathers wisely decided that citizens needed some life experience before being entrusted to such an important position. At the time of our Revolution, the average life expectancy was 35 (thirty five) years old.[10] That means the average person died at age 35, which is clearly much younger than the 78 years an American can currently expect. At a time when many girls were married at fourteen (14) years old, it was probably reasonable to expect a twenty five year old to have formed their character and developed good judgment.

It was also somewhere between unlikely and impossible that someone would serve in Congress for so many decades that they no longer understood the people or place they represented, especially since it was a part-time job. As a result, elected officials did not have term limits. They were discussed but the Founders feared that if representatives did not have to stand for re-election, they would have less reason to stay honest and do their job well.

Given how much shorter most lives were, the Founders could not have imagined someone staying in their position for as many decades as many modern politicians do. They also would not have expected politicians to spend the last year or more of their term focused on being re-elected. This is even more problematic for Representatives than Senators, given their much shorter terms. Some seem to be re-elected for little reason other than because they have been Senator or Representative since before many of the voters were even born. People may even vote for them just because they recognize their name.

> *Do you think the Founders concern that politicians will not do their job well if they aren't standing for re-election is still a strong enough reason to not have term limits? What other reasons do you think might make term limits bad or good? Do you think politicians should be able to be re-elected indefinitely? If not, what limits are reasonable and/or necessary?*

As of 2010, the longest-serving Senator was Robert Byrd of West Virginia.[11] He served in Congress for 57 years, 51 of those in the Senate. He was 28 when he was first elected and 92 when he died, still in office. Because he remained in office for so long, he became a very powerful Senator and brought many benefits to his state.

> *How much do you think Congressmen should focus on bringing the most benefits to their District or state, and how much should they consider what is best for the entire nation? How can/should they balance the two? Is it reasonable to worry that politicians become more concerned with staying in power than with representing their constituents (those who vote for them) once they are in power?*

There is something called "institutional memory." This is when a group of people in an institution or organization follow a set of beliefs, actions, or ways of doing things, and they are always done in largely the same manner. This can be good when it makes things run more smoothly, as when all the older children in a school go through the cafeteria line quickly and efficiently, and the younger ones learn to do the same by watching them. It can also be bad when it makes it seemingly impossible to end bad or outdated practices, such as when women could not get certain jobs because it had not been done before. The skills, education, intelligence, and general ability of any woman did not matter if the institution, government or private, refused to look beyond what it already "knew" from past experience.

How do you think this principal applies to our Congress? Do you think having term limits on Congressmen would lead to losing that institutional memory? Most Congressmen also have staffs, some fairly large. Do you think institutional memory would remain intact if the Congressmen had term limits but their staff did not?

What if term limits were extended to include their staff, not just the elected representative? How and why would that make a difference? Would losing that institutional memory be good, bad, or mixed? Why? What kinds of things do you think that includes? What parts are good and what are bad? How can the good be retained while trying to get rid of the bad?

Representatives and direct Taxes shall be apportioned among the several States which may be included within this Union, according to their respective Numbers, which shall be determined by adding to the whole Number of free Persons, including those bound to Service for a Term of Years, and excluding Indians not taxed, three fifths of all other Persons. The actual Enumeration shall be made within three Years after the first Meeting of the Congress of the United States, and within every subsequent Term of ten Years, in such Manner as they shall by Law direct. The Number of Representatives shall not exceed one for every thirty Thousand, but each State shall have at Least one Representative; and until such enumeration shall be made, the State of New Hampshire shall be entitled to chuse three, Massachusetts eight, Rhode-Island and Providence Plantations one, Connecticut five, New-York six, New Jersey four, Pennsylvania eight, Delaware one, Maryland six, Virginia ten, North Carolina five, South Carolina five, and Georgia three.

CHAPTER 6

The phrase "those bound in service for a term of years" refers to indentured servants. These were people who wanted to come here but didn't have the money to pay for the trip. They agreed to work for someone else without earning any pay for "a term of years" in return for that person paying for their voyage here. It was like a loan that was repaid by being worked off, or like being paid all their wages several years in advance. Indentured servants were often treated badly, so it wasn't exactly the first choice for most people. In later years, many African indentured servants simply became slaves, even though this was not the original condition of servitude they agreed to and was illegal. If this phrase referred to slaves, it would not include the phrase "for a term of years" because slavery was for a lifetime, not a term of years.

"Three fifths of all other persons" does refer to slaves. Today, all citizens are considered equal to each other regardless of color, gender, or national origin but it wasn't always like that. When the Constitution was written, the slave states wanted all of their slaves counted for purposes of determining representation. Of course the slave states had no intention of ever letting them vote freely. In most slave states, it was illegal for slaves to learn how to read or write, which is one reason that education was so very important to freed slaves. Since they could not read, they could not have been sure they were voting for the candidate they wanted if they had been permitted to do so. Their votes would surely have been cast by the slave owner for the benefit of the slave owner.

Counting slaves toward representation gave slave states extra representatives. The more slaves were counted, the more Representatives slave states had, and the harder it would be to end slavery later. Only Georgia, North Carolina, and South Carolina were truly adamant about keeping slavery when our country was founded. (They were not the only slave states, but the others were more willing to move toward ending slavery since it wasn't terribly profitable anyhow.) Counting three out of every five slaves reduced, somewhat, the power of the slave states in the House, compared to allowing them to count all their slaves toward representation.

Knowing all this, the Northern states opposed counting *any* slaves toward representation. The compromise was to require 50,000 slaves per additional Representative instead of 30,000, as was the case with freed men, which was written as "three fifths of all other persons." This is commonly referred to as the "Three-Fifths Compromise" and people often read it as meaning that it means blacks were considered three fifths of a person, less human and less valuable than a white person. It did not mean that a slave was legally considered three fifths of a person. Rather than being a way to show how little they thought of slaves (i.e., they are less human), this was a way to reduce the power, however slightly, of the states that kept them enslaved relative to the free states. The more power slave states had, the harder it was to end slavery and the easier it was to allow it to spread.

It is not hard to misunderstand that passage if you read it quickly, and even easier if you just read a summary. That is one reason it is important to read things yourself. When you rely on a summary or description from someone else (a secondary source), you accept their interpretation and their decision on what is important. They may have a good analysis, but they may not. If you read the document (a primary source) yourself, you may find something they missed or something that is important to you but not to them. The more important it is, the more carefully you need to read it.

A great man named Frederick Douglass had almost exactly this experience. After he escaped from slavery and became free, William Garrison became his friend and helped him in many ways. He taught him that the US Constitution was pro-slavery because of this clause, the acceptance of importing slaves for twenty years after ratification, and some other specific items. Years later, Douglass finally read the Constitution for himself[12]. He, a freed black man with friends and family who were still slaves, felt very strongly that the Constitution, including this clause, was anti-slavery.

Do you think it is primarily pro-slavery or anti-slavery? Why?

Think of it this way: If you go to the movie theater and three-fifths of all persons there have popcorn, are there partial people eating popcorn? No, of course not. It means that if there are 100 people in the theater, 60 of them are eating popcorn. Similarly, if a state had 100,000 slaves, then 60,000 of them would count toward representation instead of the full 100,000, leaving that slave state with fewer representatives to push a pro-slavery agenda.

Even after the Civil War and passage of the 15th Amendment, former slaves were effectively denied the right to vote by measures such as literacy tests and poll taxes. These were part of something called Jim Crow laws.[14] In 1896, the Supreme Court decided for the state of Louisiana in *Plessy v. Ferguson*.[15] They said that separate but equal accommodations for intrastate railroad travel were legal. This was the legal basis that allowed segregation to not simply continue but to flourish and grow seemingly unchecked in many areas until the Civil Rights Movement of the 1960s finally ended it.

When vacancies happen in the Representation from any State, the Executive Authority thereof shall issue Writs of Election to fill such Vacancies.

This means that if a member of the House dies or their seat becomes vacant for any other reason, the Governor of their state should call for an election to fill their place. Our forefathers believed that the state's chief executive, the Governor, would be interested in having the state fully represented and would therefore promptly call an election. The Constitution also provides that each state shall have at least one Representative but cannot have more than one for every thirty thousand people. As our national population changes, the ratio of Representatives to voters changes. As stated before, ensuring fair and equal representation is one reason it is important to answer the Census accurately when it is taken every ten years.

Based on the 2000 census, the average Representative represents 646,947 people. The actual highest number of people represented by one person is in Montana with 905,316 and the smallest only represents 495,304 people in Wyoming. If the number of people per representative was still 30,000 citizens per Representative, then based on the 2010 Census, we would have over 10,000 Representatives instead of 435!

The House of Representatives shall choose their Speaker and other Officers; and shall have the sole Power of Impeachment.

The Speaker of the House presides over the House, determines which bills reach the floor for a vote, and decides when that happens. No one outside of the House approves their choice, so they are independent. In the British system, the Speaker of the House of Commons is a non-partisan position. We cannot truly know what the Founding Fathers intended, but this was the model they were looking at when they included this position so it is logical to assume they hoped it would be non-partisan. In the modern USA, the position of is a highly partisan position most often used to advance the majority party's agenda.[16] The power to decide which bills make it to the floor for a vote gives them tremendous power. They can simply refuse to let the House vote on any bill they don't support, and this has undeniably happened in recent years.

How important do you think this power is? Do you think it is right that one person should have this power to decide what one house of Congress votes on? If not, what do you think should be changed? If so, why?

The Speaker of the House does not have to be an elected member of Congress, but they have all been members of the House.[17]

Many people do not understand what is meant by impeaching an officer. It is simply charging them with committing a crime, such as lying under oath in a court of law, or a misdemeanor, such as not paying taxes, while in office.

Impeachment is very much the same as an indictment by a grand jury.[18] When one person thinks another is guilty of violating the law, they appear before the grand jury. The grand jury hears the charge and if they think the person may be guilty, then they indict that person. It is only then that the case is sent to trial. The person has the right to a fair trial before another jury called the petit or trial jury.

Similarly, an officer (elected official or judge) is impeached by the House, then tried by the Senate, which we shall learn more about in the next chapter. Although removal from office may follow impeachment, an impeached officer is not removed from office unless they are also found guilty. Two Presidents and one Supreme Court Justice have been impeached by the House and all were found not guilty by the Senate.

THE HOUSE OF REPRESENTATIVES

RESOURCES

1. Word Processing
www.webopedia.com/TERM/W/word_processing.html

2. Spreadsheets
www.webopedia.com/TERM/S/spreadsheet.html

3. How a Bill Becomes a Law
www.kids.clerk.house.gov/middle-school/lesson.html?intID=17

4. Revenue Bills Must Start in the House
www.annenbergclassroom.org/page/article-i-section-7

5. Expressed (Enumerated) Powers
www.icivics.org/sites/default/files/On%20the%20Level_0.pdf

6. Implied Powers
www.sparknotes.com/us-government-and-politics/american-government/congress/section2.rhtml

7. The Connecticut Compromise
www.jud.ct.gov/lawlib/history/sherman.htm

8. Redistricting
www.redistricting.lls.edu/index.php

9. Early American Maps
www.publications.newberry.org/frontiertoheartland/items/show/214

10. Life Expectancy Graphs
www.mappinghistory.uoregon.edu/english/US/US39-01.html

11. Senator Robert Byrd
www.bioguide.congress.gov/scripts/biodisplay.pl?index=b001210

12. Frederick Douglass' Own Reading of the Constitution
www.washingtontimes.com/news/2015/feb/11/douglass-and-constitution/
www.teachingamericanhistory.org/library/document/the-constitution-and-slavery/

13. Frederick Douglass' Speech in Glasgow
www.teachingamericanhistory.org/library/document/the-constitution-of-
the-united-states-is-it-pro-slavery-or-anti-slavery/

14. Jim Crow Laws
www.britannica.com/event/Jim-Crow-law

15. Plessy v. Ferguson
www.law.cornell.edu/supremecourt/text/163/537

16. Speaker of the House
www.speaker.gov

17. Electing the Speaker of the House
www.slate.com/articles/news_and_politics/explainer/1998/11/can_anyon
e_be_speaker_of_the_house.html

18. Grand Jury Defined
www.legal-dictionary.thefreedictionary.com/Grand+jury

CHAPTER 7
THE SENATE

<u>SECTION 3</u>

<u>The Senate of the United States shall be composed of two Senators from each State, chosen by the Legislature thereof for six Years; and each Senator shall have one Vote.</u>

State legislators are chosen by the people to make state laws because each state has its own government in addition to sharing in the benefits and costs of the central federal government. In fact, a "federal" government is defined as "a union of states under a central government distinct from the individual governments of the separate states." It is the same in schools where each class has its own rules that the members obey in addition to obeying the rules made by the school principal and the local board of education.

For many reasons, our forefathers really wanted the best men in our land to be elected to our Senate. It is considered the senior and more select of the two houses of Congress. There are fewer members (100 versus 435); they are required to be older (30 versus 25); and they are elected for longer terms of office (6 years versus 2 years). In addition, the Vice President presides over the Senate, not one of its members as in the House.

The Founders were also determined to protect the rights of states, as the rights of citizens are protected, so Senators were selected by states instead of individual citizens. As it is written here, Senators represent state's interests just as Representatives represent individual citizen's interests. Many times states and citizens have the same wants and needs, but this is not always the case. The wants and needs of small states are different from large states, and urban states with more cities differ from more rural/agricultural states. States should look to see what is best for everyone in their state, with their particular needs. Part of this means making sure they can afford to pay for all the things they are required to do, and another part is ensuring they do not violate the rights of one group in favor of another. As we all know, it doesn't always work out that way, but it is nonetheless certain that things look differently from the point of view of a state and the point of view of an individual citizen.

This method of electing Senators was changed by the 27th Amendment so that citizens now vote directly for their Senators just as they do for their Representatives. In theory, this change means that both houses focus more on citizens' wants/needs, and less on states' wants/needs.

Every state has two Senators, no matter how big or small. Rhode Island and Providence Plantations (the full name for the state) has as many Senators as California, which is much bigger (but has a much shorter name). However, California has many more Representatives than Rhode Island, which is fair. The result is that large states have much more voice in the House of Representatives compared to small states and all are equally represented in the Senate.

Immediately after they shall be assembled in Consequence of the first Election, they shall be divided as equally as may be into three Classes. The Seats of the Senators of the first Class shall be vacated at the Expiration of the second Year, of the second Class at the Expiration of the fourth Year, and of the third Class at the Expiration of the sixth Year, so that one third may be chosen every second Year; and if Vacancies happen by

Resignation, or otherwise, during the Recess of the Legislature of any State, the Executive thereof may make temporary Appointments until the next Meeting of the Legislature, which shall then fill such Vacancies.

All members of the House serve for two-year terms and then run for re-election. Since national elections are held every two years and they serve for two years, all the Representatives were all elected at the same time for the same length of time when the Constitution went into effect. This was not the case for Senators, who are elected for six-year terms. If the Senators had all been elected for the same six year term when the Constitution was adopted, then we would only have elections for Senators every six years, not every two years. Instead, one third of the total Senate is up for election every two years, at the same time all of our Representatives are up for election.

In addition, if the Senate adopted policies contrary to what our citizens want, there would be no way to recall any of them until the next election, which could leave them unresponsive to the very citizens they are meant to represent for up to six years. At the same time, because they are elected for six year terms, they are better able to take unpopular actions, such as cutting programs and closing government facilities.

When the first Senators were elected and met in the capital of our country, they were divided into three classes. At that time, only nine states had adopted the Constitution so only eighteen Senators were elected. They were divided into three "classes" of six each. Each new group of congressmen is still called the Freshmen Class until the next election brings in a new "Freshman Class."

According to the Constitution, the term of the first class was set to expire in two years, the second in four years, and only the third would serve the full six year term. Remember, this was only done that one time so that all Senators are now elected to a full six year term, except those elected or appointed to finish a term someone else was unable to complete. So, every two years, one third of the Senators either leave office or run for re-election while the remaining two thirds continue about the normal business of their office.

If a Senator dies or resigns, their state Governor appoints a new acting Senator until either a regular or special election can be held to elect a replacement. Each state has its own procedure and timeline to follow when this happens. The 17th Amendment further modified this section.

<u>No Person shall be a Senator who shall not have attained to the Age of thirty Years, and been nine Years a Citizen of the United States, and who shall not, when elected, be an Inhabitant of that State for which he shall be chosen.</u>

Some of the citizens of our country are *naturalized* citizens. A naturalized citizen has chosen to adopt our country and become a US citizen, and our country has chosen to accept them. They become part of our nation just as an adopted child becomes part of their new family.

Before becoming a citizen, they must promise that when they become a US citizen they will fight for our laws in time of war and do all the other things that a person born a part of our country is expected to do.[1] In addition to taking the Naturalization Oath of Allegiance, they must also demonstrate that they can read, write, and speak English, and basic knowledge of American history and civics; and live here for five years after receiving permanent resident (green card) status.[2]

When they have signed papers promising all this, they are made a citizen, entitled to the same rights and privileges as those who are born citizens, except that they cannot ever be either President or Vice-President of the country. They can even be elected to Congress, once they live here for seven years after becoming a citizen before becoming a Representative and nine years before becoming a Senator.

Other countries don't allow naturalized citizens to hold office or take part in running the government, but the USA embraces our naturalized citizens and welcomes them into even the highest levels of the government. Both Henry Kissinger[3] and Madeleine Albright[4] are immigrants and former Secretaries of State, an extremely high level and important position in the President's Cabinet, and Austrian immigrant Felix Frankfurter was a Supreme Court Justice during World War II.[5]

What do you think of this policy of allowing immigrants to hold such high level positions with high level security clearance?[6] Do you know of any examples where it has created a danger to our country? Do you know any immigrants who served us well?

Becoming a legal citizen takes years and a lot of hard work. It can also be expensive and require a lot of help from lawyers, which is part of what makes it expensive. How do you think this relates to our current problem with illegal immigration? Is there anything you think needs changed about the process?

Those who have been honorably discharged from the United States Armed Services with at least one year of service do not need a declaration of intent and only need to prove one year's residence. If they served during a time of armed conflict, including the one starting on 9/11/2001, there is no minimum residence required. Because many members of our military serve overseas at some time and marry people born there, military families have special provisions making it easier and faster to become a citizen.

What do you think about making it easier and faster for spouses of our service men and women to become citizens?

In the past, immigrants also had to prove they were healthy before entering our country, and many other countries had/have similar rules. This rule helps keep dangerous and highly contagious diseases out of the country, wherever possible, and prevent other countries from dumping their sick people on us so they do not have to care for them. It is no longer realistically possible to keep all people with dangerous contagious diseases out of any country because we can travel between continents in hours instead of months, but no country has, or has ever had, the resources to care for the sick of the entire world.

What do you think about requiring immigrants to prove they are generally healthy? This doesn't mean they can't have the flu, it does mean they can't have an expensive, chronic, and/or highly contagious illness.

If you do not believe one country would deliberately send "undesirables" like carriers of dangerous diseases or criminals to another country, consider Communist Cuba. As part of the 1980 Mariel Boatlift, Fidel Castro sent Cuba's hardened criminals and severely mentally ill persons to the United States to get rid of them.[7] Many of them, but not all, were later found and returned. These were not misunderstood people wrongly imprisoned or political prisoners. They were the worst criminals and most severely mentally ill people in Cuba, and Castro sent them here to simultaneously rid his country of a problem and create a problem here.

The majority of the people who escaped Cuba during the Boatlift were regular people seeking to escape Communist Cuba and come to the freedom of the U.S.A., but Castro used this "opportunity" to rid himself of the most dangerous people he could.

The Vice President of the United States shall be President of the Senate, but shall have no Vote, unless they be equally divided.

If the Senate chose one of its own members to be President of the Senate, similar to the Speaker of the House, then the state that this Senator represented would be deprived of half its representation. Since the President of the Senate can influence the course of legislation, this would simultaneously result in that state having more than its share of power. The ever-thoughtful framers of the Constitution resolved this by making the Vice-President of the United States also be the President of the Senate. The Vice President does not belong to one state but to the people at large, who have already chosen them for a high office. The Vice President has a vote in the Senate because there is always an even number of Senators and this prevents a deadlocked vote, as long as the office of the Vice President is not empty.

In addition, the Vice President has few duties other than being first in line if the President leaves office mid-term and has easy access to the President.

Our first Vice-President was John Adams, a man who believed that the office was "insignificant." [8] Our second was Thomas Jefferson, a man who wanted nothing more than to be out of politics and enjoying his home of Monticello. However, he was a brilliant man and practical politician who decided to use his four years as Vice-President to mold the position; he was also deeply in debt and appreciated the government paycheck.

Jefferson wrote a Manual of Parliamentary Practice which the Senate itself, according to the official website, views as the single greatest contribution of any Vice President.[9] He felt it was necessary to ensure that the Senate did not end up in chaos or tyranny because it lacked a clear, fair set of rules. He was one of the leaders of the minority party of his day. As a result, Jefferson was very particular that the majority could not ride rough-shod over the minority party, particularly by preventing them from controlling all the critical committees. Never adopted as the direct authority on parliamentary procedure in the Senate, this has still been very influential in developing parliamentary procedure in the Senate and the House.

The Senate shall chuse their other Officers, and also a President pro tempore, in the Absence of the Vice President, or when he shall exercise the Office of President of the United States.

Nothing seems to have been forgotten. Just before Congress closes its session, the Vice-President retires and then the Senate elects a President *pro tempore*. If the Vice President becomes President, dies, become ill or disabled, or is otherwise removed from office, having a President *pro tempore* allows the Senate to continue working. The President pro tempore of the Senate is also the third in line if the President dies or is removed from office. The succession is Vice President, Speaker of the House, and then President pro tempore of the Senate, as established by the 25th Amendment. Prior to passage of the 25th Amendment, the Vice Presidency was empty on quite a few occasions, so this was actually an important provision.

The Senate shall have the sole Power to try all Impeachments. When sitting for that Purpose, they shall be on Oath or Affirmation. When the President of the United States is tried, the Chief Justice shall preside: And no Person shall be convicted without the Concurrence of two thirds of the Members present.

It is much easier to call a man guilty of a crime than it is to prove him guilty, which is why our entire judicial system considers us innocent until proven guilty instead of the other way around. "Innocent until proven guilty" comes from British Common Law, the basis for and still part of our legal structure, and is not specifically called out as a right in the Constitution.[10]

Have you ever tried to run a new computer program or website, only to be told you need to update Flash or another plug-in? It doesn't matter that 98% of what you need to run the program is there, one crucial piece is missing, and it cannot run. It is the same with juries trying to determine guilt in a court case. This is often the reason people are found "Not Guilty" of crimes that it seems very clear they committed, based on newspaper and internet coverage. When the jury listened to the evidence brought forth in court, there was some element missing and the jury still had a doubt that maybe, just maybe, they did not commit the crime they are accused of. They might be 98% certain they did it, but that little 2% doubt is still there, and so they must bring in a "Not Guilty" verdict, which is not the same as "Innocent." "Innocent" would imply a higher degree of certainty that they did nothing wrong, and our court system does not include the option for an "Innocent" verdict.

The same is true for impeached officials. If the Senate has any doubt over whether the impeached official did what he was accused of, then they must find them Not Guilty. The Founders gave the House to power to impeach, but the smaller Senate actually tries the cases. This theoretically makes impeaching officials on purely political grounds more difficult, although the impeachment of Andrew Johnson, our 17th President, is generally believed to have been strictly political in nature. In essence, he was impeached for firing a member of his Cabinet without Congressional approval and the law he disregarded was itself later declared unconstitutional.

In Presidential Impeachment trials, the Chief Justice presides in the Senate. If the President is found guilty, the Vice-President becomes President. If the Vice-President presided, they might be tempted to rule in ways that increase their chance of becoming President.

Judgment in Cases of Impeachment shall not extend further than to removal from Office, and disqualification to hold and enjoy any Office of honor, Trust or Profit under the United States: but the Party convicted shall nevertheless be liable and subject to Indictment, Trial, Judgment and Punishment, according to Law.

This means that if an official is impeached and found guilty by Congress, they can be removed from office, but cannot be given further punishment because it is not an actual jury trial. Impeachment and a trial are two separate actions. President Andrew Johnson,[11] President Bill Clinton,[12] and Supreme Court Justice Samuel Chase[13] were all impeached, but none were found guilty.

Richard Nixon resigned before he could be impeached.[14] Had he remained in office, he would have been impeached, but a private citizen cannot be impeached. Impeachment is only for government officials who may need removed from office, and Nixon no longer held an office to be removed from.

If an official is impeached for a criminal offence, they can still be tried in a regular civil court and this is not considered double jeopardy, discussed in the Judicial section, because impeachment is closer to being fired from a job than being tried in court. President Ford gave Nixon a full pardon so he was never tried.[15]

This very clearly states that politicians are to be tried in court following normal legal procedures for their wrong-doings. Historically, for thousands of years, many people have worked hard for their political party, making enemies in the process, only to be sentenced to death for a made-up offence when their side lost power, or when someone on "their side" decided it would help them to let this happen.

Imagine you are taking tae kwon do lessons. You are required to bring your sparring equipment to lessons, but you forget yours one day. After your friend finishes class, you borrow her equipment. Later, the coach comes up and kicks you off the competitive travel team because "you're supposed to bring your own gear." What you did was not actually against the rules but the coach's niece wants on the travel team and kicking you off makes a spot for her. When you go to the owner and argue, they kick you out of the dojo entirely.

Just as you were punished when you hadn't really done anything wrong, many politicians have been punished so other, more powerful people could get something. They may have been guilty of many things, possibly including treason, but that wasn't the reason for their arrest or other punishment. Getting them out of the way of someone more powerful was. We should be very proud that our country was the first in the world to stop such a bad thing from happening legally.

SECTION 4

The Times, Places and Manner of holding Elections for Senators and Representatives, shall be prescribed in each State by the Legislature thereof; but the Congress may at any time by Law make or alter such Regulations, except as to the Places of chusing Senators.

If a state's Legislature becomes disloyal or negligent and fails to call an election, Congress can do it for them to protect the government. If they still don't do it, Congress can set a time and if they do not hold elections then, they lose their representative who was to be elected for that term. In fact, part of the reason for the 17th Amendment, which changed how Senators are elected, is because some state legislatures were not electing Senators in a timely manner.

The Congress shall assemble at least once in every Year, and such Meeting shall be on the first Monday in December, unless they shall by Law appoint a different Day.

Our forefathers feared Congress might not meet some years and that could damage the country, so the Constitution specifies when they must start their new term. How things change! Can you imagine Congress not meeting for an entire year? Nonetheless, having a clearly established start date is good because it ensures that an outgoing Congress cannot stay in power longer by moving the start date for the next Congress later in the year. (The 20th Amendment modified this and the start date is now January 3rd.)

SECTION 5

Each House shall be the Judge of the Elections, `Returns and Qualifications of its own Members, and a Majority of each shall constitute a Quorum to do Business; but a smaller Number may adjourn from day to day, and may be authorized to compel the Attendance of absent Members, in such Manner, and under such Penalties as each House may provide.

This clause was intended to ensure that a disputed election was decided fairly and not by a partisan group who only voted for a candidate because they were of the same party. This clause requires a majority of the Congress to be present to make laws so that a small number of people cannot meet and make bad laws to carry out a scheme of their own. It also reflects the fact that Representatives to the Continental Congress under the Articles of Confederation often simply did not show up and left Congress unable to act because too few members were present.[16] Even important tasks like ratifying the Treaty of Paris with Britain to end the Revolutionary War were delayed because too few Congressmen were present.[17]

The Founders also feared that during a time of high political excitement, such as prior to the Civil War, a majority of one or both houses might stay away to block legislation they opposed. To prevent this, they gave the minority the power to force the majority to be present.

Do you know of any legislation (local, state, or federal) where all or part of a legislature left to avoid voting on one or more bills? What do you think of the way it was handled by the legislature or the government? What was done well and what could have been done better? How did the media cover it? Was the coverage fair? (Google "legislative walkout" for examples.)

Each House may determine the Rules of its Proceedings, punish its Members for disorderly Behaviour, and, with the Concurrence of two thirds, expel a Member.

Each House was created as an independent body. The House follows rules called Parliamentary Law. At one time, the House had a rule that no bill can become law unless it has been read before the House three times and those three readings could not take place on the same day. Clearly, that is no longer true.

Do you think the rule that a bill must be read three times was a wise one? How can someone vote knowledgeably on something they have neither heard nor read in its entirety? At best, they are voting what someone else, generally their staff members, believes and at worst they are voting with no knowledge of what they are voting for or against. What do you think of having such a rule? Is there a better way to accomplish the same thing today?

Each House shall keep a Journal of its Proceedings, and from time to time publish the same, excepting such Parts as may in their Judgment require Secrecy; and the Yeas and Nays of the Members of either House on any question shall, at the Desire of one fifth of those Present, be entered on the Journal.

This is the best way for the people who have elected Congress to ensure that they are truly being represented. The requirement that the actual votes be reported is an important one because it prevents Congressmen from lying about their voting record. Citizens may also attend a session of Congress in person and actually sit in the Chambers, unless it is an Executive (closed) Session. That is when national security issues, such as a war or security measures, are discussed. In some countries, citizens are prevented from being present during *any* debates or voting, even though they are meant to be represented.

Neither House, during the Session of Congress, shall, without the Consent of the other, adjourn for more than three days, nor to any other Place than that in which the two Houses shall be sitting.

Congress meets in the Capitol Building in Washington, D.C. One house cannot decide that they would rather meet on the beach and adjourn there unless both houses agree that the move is right and necessary. The Continental Congress was forced to flee several times during the Revolution and again when the British captured and burnt D.C. during the War of 1812, so this is a wise provision.

There are regularly updated procedures, facilities, and everything the government needs in secure locations in case the government ever needs to flee from an attack on D.C. or other catastrophe again. Little more than that is public knowledge for reasons of national security, which is as it should be. You can, however, visit the Greenbriar Resort in West Virginia.[18] It maintained a secret Congressional Bunker for over 30 years. It is now open for tours.

We cannot know what precautions are currently being taken, but this Bunker met every prescription, medical, and dietary need of every member of Congress. It had full sleeping, working, and medical facilities, some of them hidden in plain sight as part of the resort. Although it is outdated, it gives visitors an idea of the care taken to ensure our government can continue after a catastrophic attack.

SECTION 6

The Senators and Representatives shall receive a Compensation for their Services, to be ascertained by Law, and paid out of the Treasury of the United States. They shall in all Cases, except Treason, Felony and Breach of the Peace, be privileged from Arrest during their Attendance at the Session of their respective Houses, and in going to and returning from the same; and for any Speech or Debate in either House, they shall not be questioned in any other Place.

This is a very important clause. If payment were left to individual states, they could choose to pay different amounts and some might even decide to pay nothing at all, as happened under the Articles. Without this clause, the states could manipulate Congressional pay to try to force the federal government to do things to benefit one or a few states, regardless of its effect on the rest of the country. (Remember, Congress cannot operate if too few members are present.)

Sometimes people argue that we should not pay our Congressmen because some of them have become corrupt or because they believe they receive too much compensation (their paycheck plus other benefits, including travel, health care, free postage, and many others).[19] However, if we did not pay them a reasonable wage with reasonable benefits (free postage makes sense for official government documents but not for holiday cards to friends and family, for example), then either only rich people could afford to represent us or our representatives would have to be supported by some other person or company. That financial supporter could then compel them to vote to their benefit, no matter what the citizens they are supposed to represent want. That is not a good result.

You might argue that they are already beholden to their campaign donors, but as long as the federal government is paying their salary, at least some of them are not. All of them are less beholden to special interests and campaign donors because they aren't entirely dependent on them, as long as the government pays their base compensation.

Our Congressmen must be independent and able to act as their conscience and constituents (the people who constitute, or make up, the district they represent) tell them, not as someone else dictates to them. There does need to be some sort of check to ensure that their wages and benefits are in fact *reasonable,* not excessive.

The 27th Amendment prevents any raises they give themselves from going into effect until the next election, but so many congressmen are re-elected that this is nothing more than a delay and does not address the *amount* of their compensation. In addition, they can and do pass laws that either only apply to them, or that apply to the rest of the country but not to Congress.

What do you think of this? Have you heard of any compensation or perks that you think should be either added or removed from what our Congress receives? Are there other items you think should be added, removed, or modified?

The last part of this clause is important too, not simply an afterthought. If there was a law that some people wished passed but others were equally passionate should not be passed, one side could arrange for several of those on the other side to be arrested for a misdemeanor to keep them away from Congress for the vote to ensure that their side wins. (This was easier when our country was young and Congress was smaller.) In the case of a high crime, then they are not fit to serve in Congress and should immediately be arrested and replaced.

This clause also ensures that our representatives do not have a reason to fear speaking their mind about a law or bill that they are voting on, nor do they need to fear persecution for any reproductions of their speeches, including written and electronic reproductions. Living in the Land of the Free, it is hard to imagine but people have been jailed and worse for simply possessing copies of certain books, letters, and speeches. In some countries, they still are. Even here, prior to Emancipation (freeing the slaves), slaves in most slave-holding states could be punished severely for possessing *any* written documents because they were forbidden to learn reading or writing.

No Senator or Representative shall, during the Time for which he was elected, be appointed to any civil Office under the Authority of the United States, which shall have been created, or the Emoluments whereof shall have been encreased during such time; and no Person holding any Office under the United States, shall be a Member of either House during his Continuance in Office.

In short, no one can create a job while they are serving in Congress and then take that job for themselves. This encourages our representatives to work for the good of their constituents and not just for their own benefit. Unfortunately, it does not stop them from becoming lobbyists after they leave Congress because they didn't create that job and lobbyists are not government employees.

The last sentence means that if someone else holds one office, they must quit before taking another one. They cannot have two government jobs at the same time, which would let them collect two salaries. That is why the new President-elect, who is frequently already either serving in Congress or as a Governor, must resign their other post before taking another position in the government, namely as President. They are not obliged to quit that office to run, however, and most do not, so that the losing candidate still has a job after the election. This is why most people who are running for the office of President officially remain in their position as Senators, Governors, etc., until they win the Presidential election. If they do not win, then they go back to actually doing their job.

> Do you think it is right for candidates to keep their job while they campaign for a different office? How well do you think they will continue to do their current job if they are spending their time campaigning for another office? What will they do if they quit their job and then lose the election, leaving them unemployed? Is that right or fair? Could that make it harder to get people to run for office, or would it not matter? Is there a way to make the system better or more fair?

SECTION 7

All Bills for raising Revenue shall originate in the House of Representatives; but the Senate may propose or concur with Amendments as on other Bills.

Some powers are different in the two houses to encourage them all to remain more honest, such as this one. All bills (a law that hasn't yet been passed by Congress and signed by the President) for raising money and taxation have to start in the House of Representatives. The second part reduces the House's ability to abuse this power.

Every Bill which shall have passed the House of Representatives and the Senate, shall, before it become a Law, be presented to the President of the United States: If he approve he shall sign it, but if not he shall return it, with his Objections to that House in which it shall have originated, who shall enter the Objections at large on their Journal, and proceed to reconsider it. If after such Reconsideration two thirds of that House shall agree to pass the Bill, it shall be sent, together with the Objections, to the other House, by which it shall likewise be reconsidered, and if approved by two thirds of that House, it shall become a Law. But in all such Cases the Votes of both Houses shall be determined by yeas and Nays, and the Names of the Persons voting for and against the Bill shall be entered on the Journal of each House respectively. If any Bill shall not be returned by the President within ten Days (Sundays excepted) after it shall have been presented to him, the Same shall be a Law, in like Manner as if he had signed it, unless the Congress by their Adjournment prevent its Return, in which Case it shall not be a Law.

This clause is intended to make it more difficult to pass bad laws, but it also means that there are more opportunities to put unnecessary items in to secure the necessary votes to get a bill to pass, and this has been done since the very first days of our nation. These items are commonly called "pork" (short for "pork barrel projects") or earmarks.[20] Both houses and the President must all agree before a bill becomes a law, which is part of our system of checks and balances.

Every Order, Resolution, or Vote to which the Concurrence of the Senate and House of Representatives may be necessary (except on a question of Adjournment) shall be presented to the President of the United States; and before the Same shall take Effect, shall be approved by him, or being disapproved by him, shall be repassed by two thirds of the Senate and House of Representatives, according to the Rules and Limitations prescribed in the Case of a Bill.

Without this clause, Congress could effectively pass laws without the President's signature and approval by simply calling them something else, like a Resolution, in the manner that the President can sign Executive Orders and bypass Congress, as FDR did when he used and Executive Order to intern Japanese Americans.[21] (Either Congress or a future President can easily revoke or change Executive Orders far more easily than they could a law.) That would allow the Congress to bypass an important part of our checks and balances system.

The President has the power to veto a bill and prevent it from becoming a law, which is a check on the power of the Congress. If the Congress leaves and goes on recess less than ten days after passing a bill, the President can simply not sign the bill and it will not become law. This is called a pocket veto. "Veto" is from Latin and means "I forbid."

However, this section provides a check on that Presidential power by providing a way for Congress to over-ride a Presidential veto. If 2/3 of both houses vote to over-ride the veto, then that bill become a law without the President's approval. Initially passing the law only requires a simple majority (more than 50% voting for it). This prevents one person, the President, from totally over-riding the will of the entire American people by simply vetoing bills that they want but the President does not want.

A computer firewall is part of your computer software that protects your system from viruses and other problems, but it is much firmer than virus protection. Virus protection warns you of a danger or potential danger but a firewall stops access completely to place and files its programming says are unsafe. Depending on your firewall settings, you may not be able to access websites for shopping, entertainment (games, videos), or other categories that the administrators decide are not necessary for your work or may be dangerous.

Certain kinds of websites are known to be massively and routinely infected with viruses, making it dangerous to your computer's continued functioning if you visit them, even accidentally, so they are often blocked. A firewall's settings can, however, be changed or over-ridden to allow access to once-forbidden places, or to forbid access to once-permitted places. The firewall can even be turned off, although that is rarely a good choice.

A Presidential Veto is like a firewall. When the President is presented with a bill they believe may be bad for the country or our citizens, they Veto it so it doesn't move from Congress into our legal code at all. Like a firewall, it can be overcome. Congress can re-pass the same bill and it will become a law without the President signing it, if two thirds of Congress votes for it during this second vote.

Recently, the media has talked about getting a "veto-proof majority" for various bills. This is a bit of a nonsense statement. There is no guarantee that someone who votes for, or against, a bill once will do the same thing if it comes up for vote a second time. None. Most will, but people change their mind all the time about how they will vote, and there is nothing–not a single thing in the whole world–to keep that from happening between when a President vetoes a bill and when Congress votes to over-ride the veto. They don't have a second vote on every bill that is vetoed, so it might never make it that far.

CHAPTER 7

RESOURCES

1. US Citizenship Naturalization Test
www.uscis.gov/us-citizenship/naturalization-test

2. Naturalization Oath of Allegiance
www.uscis.gov/us-citizenship/naturalization-test/naturalization-oath-allegiance-united-states-america

3. Henry Kissinger
www.nobelprize.org/nobel_prizes/peace/laureates/1973/kissinger-bio.html

4. Madeleine Albright
www.notablebiographies.com/A-An/Albright-Madeleine.html

5. Felix Frankfurter
www.history.com/topics/felix-frankfurter

6. All About Security Clearances
www.state.gov/m/ds/clearances/c10978.htm

7. Mariel Boatlift
www.uscg.mil/history/articles/USCG_Mariel_History_1980.asp

8. Quotes from John Adams
www.americanhistory.about.com/cs/johnadams/a/quoteadams.htm

9. Thomas Jefferson's Manuel of Parliamentary Practice
www.constitution.org/tj/tj-mpp.htm

10. "Innocent Until Proven Guilty"
faculty.cua.edu/Pennington/Law508/InnocentGuilty.htm

11. The Impeachment of Andrew Johnson
www.andrewjohnson.com/

12. The Impeachment of Bill Clinton
www.historyplace.com/unitedstates/impeachments/clinton.htm

13. The Impeachment of Samuel Chase/Sedition Act Trials
www.fjc.gov/history/home.nsf/page/tu_sedbio_chase.html

14. Impeachment and Richard Nixon
www.historyplace.com/unitedstates/impeachments/nixon.htm

15. President Ford Pardons Nixon
watergate.info/1974/09/08/ford-pardons-nixon.html

16. Requiring Congressional Attendance
prologue.blogs.archives.gov/2012/05/14/no-quorum-no-constitution/

17. Ratifying the Treaty of Paris
msa.maryland.gov/msa/educ/exhibits/treaty/treaty.html

18. The Congressional Bunker at the Greenbriar
www.greenbrier.com/the-greenbrier/play-here/the-bunker.aspx

19. Congressional Salaries and Allowances
library.clerk.house.gov/reference-files/112_20120104_Salary.pdf

20. Earmarks
www.phrases.org.uk/meanings/earmark.html
www.akdart.com/pork3.html

21. Executive Orders: A Blueprint for Dictatorship?
standeyo.com/News_Files/Exec.Orders/EOs.Blueprint.for.dictator.html

CHAPTER 8
WHAT CONGRESS HAS THE POWER TO DO

The Congress shall have Power To lay and collect Taxes, Duties, Imposts and Excises, to pay the Debts and provide for the common Defense and general Welfare of the United States; but all Duties, Imposts and Excises shall be uniform throughout the United States;

U nder the Articles, Congress lacked this power. The government was so weak it couldn't even pay its own bills. As a result, no one wanted to sell us anything, including services and work, because they might not be paid. Getting the first tariffs (taxes) approved by Congress was very difficult and only happened because of the very real threat of the nation not being able to pay its bills.

How do you think this compares to our current financial situation? Is Congress reluctant to change how much or the way (different tax brackets, for instance) it taxes citizens or businesses? Is there a real threat of the nation being unable to pay its bills?

When our nation was founded, our military was tiny and other services were few because the government was too poor to pay for them and the Founders did not want to impose a heavy tax burden to do so. How has this changed? Do you think it is for the better?

Requiring duties (taxes on imported goods) to be the same through-out the country is only fair. If the port in New York City, NY and the port in Newark, NJ had different tariffs applied to them, it would have a huge impact on the two ports. They are very close to each other, but in different states. Goods would simply flow through the one with lower taxes, leaving the other port and state worse off economically. One state could have a low rate so that everyone built their facilities and infrastructure (warehouses, roads, cranes, etc.) there. The other port might close or remain as a smaller, less success-ful port with poor infrastructure, leaving the port with the lower rate without any (or much) competition. The low-rate port could then increase their rates. In either case, the other port, city and state would lose a lot of income.

Congress also approves the budget, submitted by the President.[1]

To borrow Money on the credit of the United States;

During the War of 1812 and also during the Civil War, this proved to be a wise provision because Congress would not have been able to carry on the wars and our country might have ended. Congress and our government do not always seem to exercise this ability wisely, but that does not mean they should not have it at all.

Do you think there should be limits placed on it? If so, what should they be and how should they be updated and changed? Do you think bills related to borrowing should be required to start in a specific House the way bills for raising revenue must originate in the House of Representatives? Which one? Why?

The government has few ways to "earn" money to pay for services it provides. They are limited to charging fees, such as for National Parks and toll roads; borrowing money; and levying taxes. Because no one likes to see taxes raised, politicians often borrow money to pay for services they know will make voters happy without having to raise taxes, which they know will make them unhappy. This lets them end up with happier voters, who then vote to re-elect them. It also leads to ever-increasing amounts of debt, if they just keep spending more and borrowing more every year.

Fees cannot be charged for everything. How would you assess a fee for military protection, for example? No one likes to pay taxes, and the same question applies there. How would you levy it? It isn't like sales tax where each person buys a certain amount of protection. It is a service provided to all. What is the best way to cover the cost of these services?

Do you think our politicians and government are behaving responsibly with their spending/borrowing? When it adds new programs does it find revenue to pay for them first? Is raising taxes and fees every time they want to add a new program a good idea? What else could they do? (Hint: You have more money when you earn more, or save more.) What do you think is the best solution?

How does your family find money to do things? Do they keep borrowing money? Will the bank let your family borrow past what they think you can pay back?

Do you sometimes have to change one thing to afford another, such as getting a cheaper cable TV package to pay for a faster internet connection or stopping sports lessons to have a nice vacation? Do you sometimes need to buy fewer things so you can buy more expensive, nicer ones, or can you buy just as many of the expensive item as the cheaper one?

How do you think your family's reality translates to the government and politicians? Do you think they do the same things, or do they just keep spending citizen's money and borrowing more with-

out trying to balance the federal government's budget the way your family balances their budget? A budget is an estimate of how much money a person, family or organization expects to receive or spend for a set period of time. Governments and businesses usually create budgets for one to five years, and they do this every year.

Could taxes become so high that people no longer have an incentive to work hard and earn money? Do you think any people already feel that way? How might this affect how Congress governs and acts? How else could the government find money for new programs?

To regulate Commerce with foreign Nations, and among the several States, and with the Indian Tribes;

This is called the Interstate Commerce Clause because it gives Congress the power to regulate commerce (business) both between states and between our nation (including the individual states) and foreign nations. It also means that Congress makes the rules that other nations must follow to trade with us, and they are free to make different rules for different countries. The result is that some nations have "Most Favored Nation" status while others are under embargo and cannot legally trade with us at all. Under the Articles of Confederation, other nations could place restrictions on us, including embargoes against us, but Congress had no power to do the same for them. We were at the mercy of foreign nations.

In 1824, the United States government established the Bureau of Indian Affairs (BIA), a descendent of the Committee on Indian Affairs established by the Continental Congress, to help negotiate treaties and govern trade with the Indian tribes, as indicated in this clause.[2] The tribes are now, and have always been, treated as independent nations—at least in theory. That doesn't mean they have always been treated well, fairly, or consistently, but the US government has recognized that they have their own laws and leaders. The BIA still exists and its mission is now working with tribes.

CHAPTER 8

To establish an uniform Rule of Naturalization, and uniform Laws on the subject of Bankruptcies throughout the United States;

If each state created their own laws regarding naturalization (the process of a citizen of another country becoming a US citizen), this would lead directly to a lot of problems because you are not a citizen of Missouri or Tennessee or any other state, you are an American citizen.[3] A naturalized citizen is an immigrant who has become an American citizen by meeting a standard set of requirements that are equally stringent or lenient across the entire nation, not someone who is an American citizen by birth.

> *Some states have made it easy for people here illegally and other non-citizens to receive driver's licenses/state IDs. These are one of the most basic forms of identification used to prove a person is a US citizen, particularly for voting. When you move to a new state, it has been fairly easy to exchange one state license/ID for one in your new state, although this may have changed.*
>
> *How do you think this difference among the states might create problems? How could they be alleviated? Should citizens and non-citizens have licenses/IDs that look the same?*

Our nation is fairly unique in that everyone here is an immigrant or descended from immigrants. Even the "Native Americans" technically migrated from Asia during the last ice age by crossing the Bering Strait and then heading south through Alaska and Canada.[4] Each group has added something to the Great American Melting Pot. While all the nations in both North and South America are in the same situation in that everyone in an immigrant, the USA is different because there is no single culture the majority of our citizens are from. In Europe, most citizens in Germany have traditionally had 100% or nearly 100% German ancestry. People in Korea have been Korean, in Saudi Arabia they have been Saudi Arabian, and so on. (That is changing in many countries for a variety of reasons, including the fact that travel is much faster and easier than in the past.)

Do you, personally, even know someone whose family has been here more than one or two generations who knows for sure that their ancestors are all from the same country? Do you know people who have no idea where their ancestors are from, and don't care?

If you know any immigrants or someone who is first generation (the first generation of their family born here), is it the same or do they know exactly where their ancestors lived? Are their ancestors all from the same country, or even the same town or province?

The 2011 HBO™ documentary "Citizen USA: A Fifty State Road Trip" interviewed newly naturalized citizens and asked why they chose the USA as their new home. They also interviewed long-established immigrants including former Secretary of State Madeleine Albright. Her story shows how unusually welcoming the USA is for immigrants.

During WWII, her family fled from Czechoslovakia to London and then to the United States. She summarized her experience of the difference between being a refugee in a European country and the USA as follows. In Europe, citizens said, "Your country has been taken over by a terrible dictator, what can we do to help you, but when are you going home?" When her family arrived in the U.S.A., citizens said, "Your country has been taken over by a terrible dictator, what can we do to help you, and when will you become a citizen?"

Just as an adopted child becomes part of a new family, a naturalized citizen becomes part of our country. This is why ICE (Immigration and Customs Enforcement) is a federal department.[5] All issues related to immigration, legal or otherwise, are referred to the federal government, not handled by states. They coordinate everything for the entire nation, even issues that come up in other countries. They do this through our system of embassies and consulates.

When states find illegal immigrants, they hand them over to ICE, they do not keep them in local facilities, and ICE decides what to do with them, generally either deporting them back to their home nation or simply letting them go. Citizenship assumes that you will obey the law, pay taxes, serve jury duty, and fulfill all the other duties that come with the rights of citizenship, including serving in the military if you are asked.[6] This is like following the rules in a game, paying your monthly fees, completing quests, and helping your clan or faction make decisions, something illegals are not doing. (This is neither a judgment nor an opinion: If they were following the rules they would be legal, not illegal.)

Becoming a citizen is like joining a massively multiplayer online game like World of Warcraft™. You can hack into it and join without paying–illegally–but that isn't very fair to those who paid the price, followed the rules, and joined legally. Just as logging into a computer game with your user name and password proves you have the right to be there, citizenship papers (birth certificate, naturalization papers, driver's license, passport, social security card–there are a variety of them) prove you are a citizen or legal resident and that you have earned the benefits that come along with it, or one of your ancestors earned them for you.

To coin Money, regulate the Value thereof, and of foreign Coin, and fix the Standard of Weights and Measures;

If money had different values in different states, there would be constant confusion. Can you imagine a trip from Los Angeles, CA to New York City, NY with a layover in Denver, Colorado, and arriving into Newark, New Jersey? You would need four different currencies!

Now, imagine that you and three friends are baking cookies and each of you measure one cup of sugar. Each one has an ever-so-slightly-different amount. Now imagine that one of each of these cups is put in a container and sent to the four different cities in the example above, probably spilling a bit in the process and maybe adding in a bit to try to correct for spillage, so that the amount in each of the four are just a bit more "different" from each other. Those cups are now used as a standard for how much is in "one cup." In those cities, more people measure "one cup" based on this and go to other cities and the process is repeated, with the amount changing a little bit in every city or town.

It's like when you play the game "telephone" and whisper a message in the ear of the person next to them. It doesn't take long for the message to become so garbled you can barely tell what the original was. It's the same way with weights and measures. It wouldn't take very long for weights and measures to vary wildly in different areas without one national, now international, standard of weights and measures. This is why our forefathers had Congress create one standard set of weights and measures for the entire country. And that is why if you took the trip in the paragraph above and bought a 16 oz. bottle of water in each city, they would all have the same amount.

To provide for the Punishment of counterfeiting the Securities and current Coin of the United States;

This is an offence against the national government, not state governments, and so it is right that the federal government has the power to punish it. If people could print their own bills just like the US Treasury Department prints our federal currency (there is no state currency), our money would quickly become worthless, and that hurts everyone in the nation. Therefore, this is a federal and not a state issue.

The Federal Reserve, or simply "The Fed", is the central bank for the US and was created by Congress in 1913.[7] It is a bank for banks and for the nation, and has twelve branches called Federal Reserve Banks.[8] The Fed sets interest rates, distributes the US currency, and oversees other banks to make sure they are safe places for people to put their money. Congress delegated, or gave, responsibility for our currency to the Fed. It is not part of our Constitution, and so can be changed, modified, or even removed without touching the Constitution. In fact, a few months before he was assassinated, President Kennedy issued Executive Order 11110 to begin stripping the Federal Reserve of some of its powers and begin returning them to the federal government, but it was never fully implemented.[9]

CHAPTER 8

To establish Post Offices and post Roads;

"Snail mail" seems like an unimportant after-thought when you can send a text message or email anywhere in the world almost instantly without ever being touched by a postal carrier, but it isn't.[10] The same routes that carry the mail also carry packages, including Christmas cards (even the ones with checks) and presents. Even more importantly, many of our major roads started out as the post roads that carried letters and goods. Post roads were the equivalent of major highways and they made frontier life here a little easier.[11]

The original Articles of Confederation authorized the creation of Post Offices, but not the Post Roads on which to carry the mail and goods. In the days before the internet, physical communication was critical. Actual letters with written messages; news; cash, gold, and bank letters of credit; election results; new laws, regulations, and tariffs; goods…*everything* traveled by road, and there weren't enough of them.

When the first colonists arrived here, there were only deer paths and Indian trails, and not a lot of those. The colonists enlarged these existing "roads" and created new ones, but there still weren't very many. Believe it or not, some of these are still in use, although time and usage has changed their paths a bit. An old north-south Algonquin and Iroquois route the colonists renamed the Carolina Road[12] is now part of US Route 15 and the historic Journey through Hallowed Ground route, for example.[13]

As useful as these were, there were not enough of them to fill the new country's needs, and they weren't always in the places our young country needed them. We needed the federal government to establish and maintain more of them, especially as new areas were developed.

A canal system opened in New York in 1825,[14] followed quickly by the first railroad in Quincy, Massachusetts in 1826.[15] The Transcontinental Railroad was completed in 1869.[16] The Eisenhower Interstate Highway System long-haul truckers use to carry goods was started in 1956.[17] Air shipment of freight and mail is a more gradual development that did not become a big part of the postal system until even more recently. As these new forms of transportation were added to our transportation system, they were also designated as "post roads" because our entire transportation system works together to move goods and information around our country. Removing even one section of one part of it can create massive transportation problems throughout the country.

Can you think of a time when part of our transportation system was not working, even if it was only for a few days? The most common reason is a natural disaster such as a volcano, hurricane, blizzard, flood, or tsunami, but terrorist activities can be a factor as well. How did it impact you? When and if it happens again, how do you think it will affect your family?

Think about your town, your city, and the places your family drives to visit. Now imagine all the highways and freeways are gone. And all state roads and turnpikes. And finally, all the four lane roads (two lanes in each direction) are gone as well.

How easy would it be to get around? How would this change shopping, including online and catalog shopping? How about FedEx and UPS shipping, especially things that have to be shipped the entire way across the country? Big 18 wheel trucks aren't designed for small roads.

Many people commute to work on highways. How do you think not having highways would affect where people live and work? Or visiting family?

How do you think it would affect your diet?[18] Without the full transportation network, how easy would it be to ship perishables like juice, fruit, and meat long distances before they went bad? Could you still have orange juice for breakfast or fruit in the winter? Could you have a hamburger or a glass of milk? (Are there cows or orange orchards near your home to supply these?)

The importance of the postal system in our national development is made clear by one simple fact: the Postmaster General was a Cabinet position from 1829 until 1971, when it stopped being a government department and became a semi-independent agency. The first Postmaster General, appointed by the Continental Congress, was Benjamin Franklin.

To promote the Progress of Science and useful Arts, by securing for limited Times to Authors and Inventors the exclusive Right to their respective Writings and Discoveries;

The government regulates many aspects of our lives, just like the OS regulates how computers operate, but it also provides many services, such as the immense resources of the Library of Congress and of the Patent and Copyright Office.[19] Think about the information available in the books in your local library, and contrast that to how incredibly much is available on the entire internet. Before the internet, the mind-bogglingly large information source in that comparison would probably have been the Library of Congress.[20] The knowledge and information stored there has been an amazing resource since the earliest days of our country, and no other institution can match it, even today.

The Patent and Copyright Office protects our inventions and helps the creator keep the profits from their hard work by granting copyrights, for books and movies, and patents, for all manner of inventions, such as the bifocal glasses Benjamin Franklin invented. Because this power ultimately resides in Congress, copyrights and patents are equally valid in all parts of the United States.

A copyright gives the author the sole right to print and sell their work in the United States for a set period of time, which may be continued for another period of time when the first ends. The exact length of time has changed over the years. That's one reason why you can't simply copy something written by someone else when you write a paper, and also why you can't copy or publicly show someone else's movies without permission. Once that protection ends, that item is considered "in the public domain" and can be used by anyone without paying the author for its use or asking them for permission. Anything written before 1922 is now in the public domain.

Similarly, an inventor's patent gives them the sole right to make, use, or sell their invention in the United States for a set span of time, which may also be extended. Once a copyright or patent expires, or ends, that item is also considered "in the public domain."

Inventors sometimes chose to keep their invention secret instead of registering it. Their reasoning is that once it is registered, other companies can look at the information on file in the Patent Office and copy it, changing it just enough to avoid violating the patent. Others can also easily duplicate it when the patent does expire. Coca Cola is an example of how this works.[21] They never registered the formula for Coke because they didn't think anyone could figure it out and duplicate it. (They didn't, and Coke has been around so long now that it doesn't really matter–the brand is extremely strong.) If they had, it would be in the public domain by now and anyone could make "Coca Cola."

On the other hand, if you don't register it, then you don't have the legal protection of a patent. Eli Whitney's cotton gin was so simple that it very easy to reverse engineer, so he needed a patent to protect himself.[22] Reverse engineering happened when his rivals bought one of Whitney's cotton gins, figured out how it worked, and then made their own versions.

Whitney's cotton gin was one of, if not the, earliest super-successful patents in this country.[23] Because it was one of the first, there were still loopholes, ways to legally avoid following a law, and he didn't profit much from it. The lawsuits and problems brought about by his invention led to closing loopholes in the original law and to improvements in the patent system. Whitney's patent a mere five years later for machine-manufactured muskets with interchangeable parts (the start of mass production) was far more profitable.[24]

It also helped the North win the Civil War.

To constitute Tribunals inferior to the supreme Court;

The federal government sets up the federal courts (or tribunals), in-cluding a system of courts below and feeding up to the Supreme Court, which is our supreme court.[25] If you notice the capitalization in the text of the Constitution, there is no actual name for this "su-preme Court." We simply took the description and used it as the name.

The federal trial courts are called United States District Courts (94 judicial districts and two specialty courts) and they feed into the ap-pellate courts called the United States Courts of Appeal (13 total). Each district also has bankruptcy courts. The Courts of Appeal feed into the United States Supreme Court (only one).

Very few cases ever make it to the Supreme Court, which has nine Justices and no jury. In federal court, only District Courts can have juries, although they don't always have them. The US Supreme Court can also hear cases on appeal from state Supreme Courts. A few oth-er federal courts, such as military courts and tax court, exist outside the main judicial system.

To define and punish Piracies and Felonies committed on the high Seas, and Offences against the Law of Nations;

If a United States citizen is found guilty of piracy or felony on the high seas, foreign governments could hold our government generally responsible for it and not one state. Therefore, the government has the power to punish them.

Piracy here refers to sailing vessels (boats, ships, etc.) and people like Blackbeard and Captain Jack Sparrow (Pirates of the Caribbean), not people violating copyrights by making illegal copies of movies and other copyrighted materials.

To declare War, grant Letters of Marque and Reprisal, and make Rules concerning Captures on Land and Water;

If the government grants Letters of Marque and Reprisal, that means citizens may seize the property of an enemy at war with us. If citizens do the same things without a Letter of Marque and Reprisal, they will be considered pirates if they are captured by the enemy and treated as such. If they have them, then they are supposed to be treated as prisoners of war.

The modern USA has one of the largest militaries–Army, Navy, Air Force, Marines–on the planet. The 1700s USA didn't exactly have the same resources. Although they knew a navy could be very important, the Continental Congress and the USA in general were flat broke, and their biggest problems were to the land-locked west, not the coastal east. They sold the last ship from the Continental Army two years after the Revolution ended. As a result, and as memorialized in this part of the Constitution, they had to rely on seafaring citizens with Letters of Marque and Reprisal to keep our waters and shipping safe.

In the mid-1790s, pirates from the Barbary Coast in North Africa began to attack US merchant ships in the Mediterranean often enough that Congress decided to establish a small navy In 1794, they authorized building six (6) ships.[26] And in 1796 they put the whole project on hold and left the partially constructed ships mothballed until the Department of the Navy was created in 1798 by John Adams, our second President. Construction on a total of thirty ships was authorized by 1800.[27] World events ensured that we have maintained a navy ever since, despite our initial reluctance to have one and concerns about paying for it.

To raise and support Armies, but no Appropriation of Money to that Use shall be for a longer Term than two Years;

The Founders did not want or approve of more than a token (tiny) standing army.[28] A standing army is an army kept by a nation when they aren't at war with another country.[29] Under the Confederation, Congress decided how many troops it needed and told each state how many to send. It did not have the power to raise an army itself and was utterly dependent upon the states to do so. Our Constitution improved the situation but we still did not maintain a sizable standing army until after World War II because they are expensive, and the Founders and former colonists didn't trust them. This provision clearly shows that preference and distrust because money can only be appropriated, set aside specifically, for the military for two years at a time. That is a very short time for any government to fund anything.

The War of 1812 finally made it clear that this was inadequate and we needed to maintain at least a small standing army. The militia could not drill regularly enough or assemble rapidly enough to be a true national defense force, but our standing army remained small until after World War II.

To provide and maintain a Navy;

Britain ruled the seas and even the Founders could see that we needed some form of navy, although, as discussed above, it was initially so small it sometimes disappeared entirely. Comparing the US Navy in the years after the Revolution to European navies of the same time is like comparing the free solitaire program that comes with the basic computer OS to a massively multiplayer online game. They are so far apart that they aren't even in the same galaxy.

To make Rules for the Government and Regulation of the land and naval Forces;

The President is the Commander in Chief of the military, but Congress makes the rules and regulations for how the military operates.

To provide for calling forth the Militia to execute the Laws of the Union, suppress Insurrections and repel Invasions;

The statement is that the Militia, now the National Guard, and not the Army must be "called forth." This implies that the Founders expected and desired that the federal Armed Forces (standing army) would normally be a small force, not a large standing army, and would need the Militia to have enough strength and numbers to fight. It also shows that they expected state militia to be an important and integral part of the national defense force. This is discussed more with the 2nd Amendment.

It also seems clear that state-based Militias, not the federally-controlled Army, is given any military tasks within our national boundaries. This does not, however, mean that the groups cannot work together. For much of our history, we did not maintain a large standing army in part because Congress had this power, but also because standing armies are expensive and tend to lead to involvement in wars, which are always expensive.

Why do you think the Founders believed this requirement was important? Do you agree? Why would they say that state-based soldiers and not those controlled by the national government should respond to domestic problems (within our national borders, not within someone's home)? What dangers or problems can you think of if federal troops respond? What if the National Guard responds instead? Does that create a different set of dangers or problems?

Who do you think will get there more quickly? Which organization is more likely to know the terrain (land) and local resources and issues better? Is one more likely to be better trained or better equipped? Do you think it would be better today to have federal troops respond instead?

What examples can you think of from our history or from other countries to support your opinion that it is better to have either federal troops or the National Guard respond?

To provide for organizing, arming, and disciplining, the Militia, and for governing such Part of them as may be employed in the Service of the United States, reserving to the States respectively, the Appointment of the Officers, and the Authority of training the Militia according to the discipline prescribed by Congress;

This shows that the Founders expected our standing army to be small and the Militia to be the key force in national defense. If the Militia was not to be part of our national defense force, they would not have had the federal government be so strongly involved in the critical matters of organizing, arming, and disciplining the Militia, particularly since arming any military force is now and has always been expensive.

> *We take the existence of a large, powerful American military very much for granted today. How do you think the Founders and early American citizens felt about a national Army and/or Navy, based on all the clauses preceding this related to the Armed Services? Why do you think they felt it necessary to be so specific about Congressional powers relative to our Armed Services?*
>
> *What do you think their reaction would be to our modern Armed Services? What, if anything, do you think they might want to change?*

To exercise exclusive Legislation in all Cases whatsoever, over such District (not exceeding ten Miles square) as may, by Cession of particular States, and the Acceptance of Congress, become the Seat of the Government of the United States, and to exercise like Authority over all Places purchased by the Consent of the Legislature of the State in which the Same shall be, for the Erection of Forts, Magazines, Arsenals, dock-Yards, and other needful Buildings;--And

This is the only place in the Constitution that allows the Federal Government to own land, and that is for the specific purposes of forts, magazines, arsenals, dock-yards, and other needful buildings. "Other needful buildings" is a nebulous term that can encompass any federal building from the Capitol and Supreme Court Buildings to passport control booths at border crossings. All of the others are in support of the military.

Forts are, clearly, places where the military lives, works, and trains. The term "base" is used more commonly today, but it serves the same purpose. Just as a "magazine" holds the ammunition used by an individual rifle, a military "magazine" holds the ammunition used by a group of soldiers or sailors. (Ships have magazines on board.) An arsenal is a place where weapons are manufactured, repaired, and stored. A dock-yard is a place where ships are manufactured, refitted, and repaired.

The "Bureau of Land Management" (BLM) is part of the Department of the Interior. BLM administers public land (land controlled by the Federal Government), all of which is in Western states (Alaska, Arizona, California, Colorado, Idaho, Montana, Nevada, New Mexico, Oregon, Utah, and Wyoming). While BLM can trace its roots to the Northwest Ordinance, the 1862 Homestead Act and 1872 establishment of the National Park Service (NPS) were changes in how the government treated land. (NPS is also part of Interior.)

BLM officially took large tracts of Western land from Native Americans. They encouraged some of them to reclaim their by adopting European ways and simultaneously encouraged Americans and European immigrants to settle the land. This wasn't terribly different from past practices that encouraged the government to return land to citizens. BLM originally oversaw the homesteading process whereby settlers claimed land in newly opened territories. Alaska was the last of these to become a state in 1959.

> *BLM still controls over 80% of the land in Nevada. (It is less for other ten states it operates in, with the lowest being 30% of Montana.) What do you think about that? To put that in perspective, it's more land than all of the New England States combined. How would you feel if they owned 80%, or even 30%, of your state?*
>
> *Why do you think BLM retains control of so much land? What do you think should have been done with unclaimed land after each territory became a state?*

The real change happened after NPS was established in 1872. The first National Park, Yellowstone, was formed from part of the Wyoming and Montana territories. Their mission has always been keeping large areas of national history and scenic beauty in trust for everyone to enjoy now and into the future. BLM's original mission was to move huge tracts of land (entire territories) from the government into the hands of the people. NPS permanently removed land from private hands (or kept it from ever being privately owned), but in a highly curated, highly focused way.

After NPS was established, BLM started to keep land "for the public" instead of actively working to put it back in private hands. The varied uses of the 245 million+ acres under the modern BLM include ranching, mining, energy, and recreation, although all of this is strictly regulated and most definitely not freely available to anyone and everyone. BLM continues to acquire new land, often in large chunks.

> *Do you think BLM land should remain under federal control, be given to states, be sold to citizens, or a combination? Why? Does it make sense for them to keep buying land?*
>
> *Every state has its own system of parks and recreational areas. Does it seem efficient to have BLM, NPS, and the states all administer public parklands? Where might their missions overlap? How could they be combined?*
>
> *Every state and former territory from the Founders' era controls all the land within its borders except small areas fitting the criteria listed here (forts, jails, etc.), even though most had large areas of unclaimed land in the late 1700s. What does this tell you about who the Founders thought should control land within state and territory boundaries? Does their requirement that states approve any boundary changes affect your opinion?*
>
> *When BLM buys land, it is considered an "eminent domain" purchase, basically meaning it's for the greater good, so the existing land owners really cannot either refuse or effectively negotiate the selling price. Do you think that's right or fair?*
>
> *Under what circumstances does eminent domain make sense?*

In 1916, President Woodrow Wilson combined all the assets (parks, monuments, historical buildings, etc.) from all the federal agencies under the umbrella of the NPS, marking the real start of the agency most of us know today. NPS remains one of, if not the, most popular federal agencies. They have preserved places ranging from Presidential birthplaces to trails to the Grand Canyon itself.

No Europeans had seen Yellowstone or the Grand Canyon in the 1700s, but they had seen smaller wonders like Natural Bridge in Virginia. What do you think the Founders would have thought of our modern NPS? What do you think they would think of BLS? How might they change either agency?

To make all Laws which shall be necessary and proper for carrying into Execution the foregoing Powers, and all other Powers vested by this Constitution in the Government of the United States, or in any Department or Officer thereof.

The District of Columbia (Washington, D.C.) did not yet exist when this was written, but that is what it refers to. It was called "The Territory of Columbia" with "The City of Washington" inside it until the 1870s. Like so many other things, its location was a source of conflict for the Founders. In the past, the head of state (king, sultan, emperor, etc.) simply chose a location they liked. That city generally either was or became a major center of commerce and finance as well as a political center. Once again, our young nation chose a new and different path and created a city where there was nothing as our capital.

In choosing a new capital for our new country, geography dictated somewhere generally in the center of the country because of travel time and distance, not in far southern Georgia or far northern New England.[30] New York City, Philadelphia, Annapolis, and Baltimore were all existing cities that were generally in the middle, and all had already served as the capital at some point.

The North naturally preferred to keep the capital in the north and the South naturally preferred to move it farther to the south. New York was the current capital when the Constitution was written and Philadelphia had been the capital for much of our very brief national history, making them both strong contenders.

At the same time, there was a separate issue called Assumption. The Southern states had paid off most of their debts from the Revolutionary era and the Northern states were struggling with their debts, which they wanted the federal government to assume. (The war started and many of the battles took place in the North.) Of course the Southern states opposed Assumption because they had paid off their debts. They had nothing for the federal government to assume. The entire benefit would go to the Northern states.

An agreement was finally reached whereby the capital was moved temporarily to Philadelphia with a permanent location on the Potomac River, the boundary between Maryland and Virginia, under the Residence Act.[31] In return for the Northern states agreeing to this relatively Southern location, the federal government took over, or assumed, the Revolutionary debt of all the states under the Assumption Bill.[32] The Residence Act specified that the new location, to be chosen by the President, had to be ready in 1800. That was a mere ten years to create a new city and have it ready for occupancy in an area that was wilderness at the time.

Northerners probably thought this could not be done and the capital would simply stay in Philadelphia once it moved there "temporarily." It might have, except that the Residence Act also gave the President the power to make most decisions related to the new capital so that it did not need to go in front of Congress, or be delayed by Congressional politics, once the bill passed. Even in our first years and the first decisions that needed made, Congress could make any decision long, drawn-out, and painful to participate in. That is not a new development.

At one time during the Congress of the Confederation, under the Articles of Confederation, Congress was meeting in Philadelphia and was surrounded by a mob of mutineers from the Continental Army who were angry that they had not been paid for months because the government had no money.[33] (When the Marquis de Lafayette came here with French aid, it included gold so the government could again pay its bills.) The Pennsylvania Governor was so slow to defend

Congress that it adjourned to Princeton, New Jersey. If Congress had possessed the power over its meeting place that it does now, then the mutineers might have been stopped at once. These experiences undoubtedly influenced the Founding Fathers' decision to create a separate Capital City for our new nation.

Putting the capital on federal land, not controlled by any state, removed a potential source of state control over the federal government. The states of Maryland and Virginia each gave a tract of land along the Potomac River to the federal government to create The Territory of Columbia. If one or both had kept control of "their" land, then they could have used that power to force the government to take, or not take, actions, based on what benefitted their state rather than the American citizens.

As a result, our capital depends on the federal government, not a state, for infrastructure needs such as road upkeep and security. D.C. cannot raise much money from taxes because most of the city is federal land, federal offices, and foreign embassies, which cannot be taxed the way private lands and businesses are.

Because most manufactured goods were shipped here by boat (airplanes not having been invented), access to a good port was a critical consideration. When the Territory was founded, Alexandria, Virginia, was already a major slave trading center and the largest town/port in the area at the time.[34] Georgetown, Maryland, a much smaller port, was also included in the boundaries of the new capital.[35]

George Washington's insisted on including Alexandria, despite the fact that the Residence Act had to be modified to allow its inclusion. This was controversial at the time because Washington's home, Mt. Vernon, is nearby, and he owned land in Alexandria. The Amendment to the Residence Act of 1791 that allowed the capital to be slightly farther east, to include Alexandria, also required that all public (government) buildings be built on the eastern shore of the Potomac–land that was formerly part of Maryland.[36] This was partially to keep Washington and his family members who owned land in Alexandria from profiting from the capital's location.

Why do you think Washington insisted on including Alexandria? How could his familiarity with the two ports (as a nearby land-owner) have influenced his conviction on this? Or was it personal?

How might port access and Alexandria's status as a slave trading center have impacted the debate on where to put the capital? Do you think states looked at how they might benefit from having the main capital city port?

Since no federal government buildings were permitted to be built on the Virginia side of the Potomac, and no states were responsible for any upkeep including roads, things fell into disrepair and the area suffered economically. This is part of the reason that the County of Alexandria, as the Virginia portions of the Territory of Columbia were called at the time, wanted to be retroceded, returned to the Commonwealth of Virginia.

A movement to ban slavery in our nation's capital started in Maryland in the 1830s but the slave trading city of Alexandria opposed it.[37] As a result of this impasse, or situation where the two sides would never agree, Maryland accepted retrocession and the portions south of the Potomac successfully petitioned to be retroceded to Virginia in 1847.[38]

When that happened, the South gained two more Representatives (DC residents are not represented in Congress) to help counter increases in Representatives from non-slave holding states and it became easier to end slave trading in the capital. All the land that is currently part of D.C. was originally part of Maryland.

In the 1870s, the name officially became the District of Columbia (D.C.).

RESOURCES

1. Budget and Accounting Act of 1921
lcweb2.loc.gov:8081/ammem/amrlhtml/dtbudact.html

2. Bureau of Indian Affairs
www.bia.gov/WhoWeAre/index.htm

3. A Guide to Naturalization
www.uscis.gov/us-citizenship/citizenship-through-naturalization/guide-naturalization

4. Bering Strait Theory
www.native-languages.org/bering.htm

5. Immigration and Customs Enforcement
www.ice.gov/

6. Citizenship
www.usconstitution.net/consttop_citi.html

7. The Founding of the Fed
www.newyorkfed.org/aboutthefed/history_article.html

8. Federal Reserve Bank
www.federalreserve.gov/otherfrb.htm
www.federalreserve.gov/pf/pf.htm

9. Executive Order 11110
www.archives.gov/federal-register/executive-orders/1963-kennedy.html

10. Snail Mail
www.webopedia.com/TERM/S/snailmail.html

11. Transportation in America's Postal System
www.fhwa.dot.gov/infrastructure/back0304.cfm

12. The Carolina Road
www.loudounhistory.org/history/carolina-road.htm

13. Journey Through Hallowed Ground
www.hallowedground.org

14. The Erie Canal
www.eriecanal.org

15. The First Railroad in America
thomascranelibrary.org/legacy/railway/railway.htm

16. The Transcontinental Railroad
www.blm.gov/ut/st/en/fo/salt_lake/recreation/back_country_byways/transcontinental_railroad/transcontinental_railroad.html

17. The Eisenhower Interstate Highway System
www.fhwa.dot.gov/interstate/homepage.cfm

18. The Impact of Refrigerated Railcars
www.history-magazine.com/refrig.html

19. Patent and Copyright Office
www.uspto.gov

20. Library of Congress
www.loc.gov

21. Understanding Intellectual Property Law through Coca Cola
zvulony.ca/2010/articles/intellectual-property-law/understanding-intellectual-property-law/

22. Reverse Engineering
en.wikipedia.org/wiki/Reverse_engineering

23. Eli Whitney's Patent for the Cotton Gin
www.archives.gov/education/lessons/cotton-gin-patent/

24. Eli Whitney and Interchangeable Parts
study.com/academy/lesson/eli-whitney-and-interchangeable-parts-definition-history-quiz.html

25. About Federal Courts
www.uscourts.gov/about-federal-courts

26. Barbary Pirates
history1800s.about.com/od/americanwars/tp/barbarywars.htm

WHAT CONGRESS HAS THE POWER TO DO

27. A Brief US Naval History
www.usna.edu/USNAHistory/

28. Founders Desired a Small Standing Army
newhistories.group.shef.ac.uk/wordpress/wordpress/why-americas-
founding-fathers-would-not-recognise-the-country-they-created/

29. A Standing Army defined
en.wikipedia.org/wiki/Standing_army

30. The Nine Capitals of the United States
www.mentalfloss.com/article/22848/quick-9-nine-capitals-united-states

31. Agreement on the Capital
www.pbs.org/wgbh/amex/hamilton/peopleevents/e_dinner.html

32. The Residence Act
www.loc.gov/rr/program/bib/ourdocs/Residence.html
www.gwu.edu/~ffcp/exhibit/p12/p12_1.html

33. Pennsylvania Mutiny of 1783
www.forgottenhistory.us/pennsylvania-mutiny-1783

34. Alexandria Slave Trading
edu.lva.virginia.gov/online_classroom/shaping_the_constitution/doc/slave
pen

35. Georgetown's Hidden History
www.washingtonpost.com/wp-
dyn/content/article/2006/07/14/AR2006071401398.html

36. DC's Early Boundaries
www.boundarystones.org/

37. Ending Slavery in DC
emancipation.dc.gov/page/ending-slavery-district-columbia

38. Retrocession of the Virginia Parts of DC
www.virginiaplaces.org/boundaries/retrocession.html

CHAPTER 9
WHAT CONGRESS AND THE STATES CANNOT DO

SECTION 9

The Migration or Importation of such Persons as any of the States now existing shall think proper to admit, shall not be prohibited by the Congress prior to the Year one thousand eight hundred and eight, but a Tax or duty may be imposed on such Importation, not exceeding ten dollars for each Person.

Worms are a rarely-discussed danger to your computer. They are as bad as that sounds gross. If a computer or network gets a worm, it can burrow its way into the systems and just sit there until another computer, program, or preset date or activity triggers it. You probably won't even know it is there until it is triggered and starts doing what it was designed to do. Worms are extremely difficult to completely get rid of, and often even detecting them can be hard.

For our nation, slavery was a like a computer worm, and it was at least as difficult to get rid of. It sat there relatively quietly (in terms of national politics, there were always some fighting to end it) most of the time, but slavery reared its ugly head and threatened the Union whenever it was threatened. This was true from the earliest days of the Revolution until the Civil War finally ended slavery. Even after actual slavery ended, problems related to and caused by slavery have continued in different forms. These included poll taxes, racism, and separate-but-equal policies, to name a few.

While this clause may sound like it's simply talking about immigration, it is really saying that states may continue to import slaves from other countries until 1808 and may charge slavers up to $10 per slave, which was a lot of money at the time.

> *The standard meaning of a "dollar" at that time was one silver Spanish milled dollar.[1] The Spanish dollar was an internationally recognized unit of currency just as the US Dollar is today and, as such, the US Government could not change its value in any way.*
>
> *Milled coins have grooves on the outside, like a modern quarter, which prevent the historically common practice of shaving bits of silver off the side of a coin to keep, thereby decreasing its value.*

Having seen pictures and movies like *Gone With the Wind* with beautifully dressed people enjoying parties at huge estates with hundreds of slaves toiling to support their lavish lifestyle, it is hard to realize that slavery as an institution wasn't very profitable in the 1780s.[2] Growing cotton and other crops with slaves was simply too labor-intensive before the Industrial Revolution. Slaves also incurred expenses including housing, food, and health care on even the worst farms and plantations. Even when slaves were too old or sick to work, their owners still had to feed, clothe and care for them.

Since many of the Founding Fathers were slave owners and/or businessmen, they were undoubtedly aware of this financial reality. Even without considering the moral side, slavery really did not make good business sense at the time. Regardless of how they felt about the financial viability of it, the Founders were far from united in support of slavery. Only a few were truly determined to keep "the Peculiar Institution."[3] While some wanted it ended immediately, others wanted it ended gradually, fearing chaos if it was too abrupt. They may have believed this clause was the first step in doing that.

If you think this is wishful thinking to make our Founders seem "better" with no basis in history, please Google Frederick Douglass's 1860 Glasgow speech on whether the US Constitution is pro-slavery or anti-slavery. He was a freed slave and a brilliant man born a mere forty years after it was written, and this is part of what he discussed. Unlike any living person, he and his family and friends were affected by it in the most personal ways possible, and Frederick Douglass's view is that the Founders expected ending the importation of slaves to lead to the end of slavery.

Unfortunately for this hope, and for the slaves, in 1794 Eli Whitney invented the cotton gin mentioned above as a labor-saving device.[4] It was the first of a series of inventions, including spinning and weaving machines used in Northern mills, that combined to start the Industrial Revolution and make slave-based cotton plantations profitable. It also ensured that slavery continued long past 1808.

Because slavery led to so many arguments among the Founding Fathers, it was effectively unsolvable at the time and they ultimately chose not to address the issue further. Opponents of slavery, including Thomas Jefferson, tried to include a paragraph condemning it in the Declaration of Independence but were forced to drop it so all the colonies would sign the Declaration and declare open rebellion against Britain. We cannot know if they were right, but their first priority at that time was to get everyone to agree to Revolution.

The Founders believed we could not secure our continued freedom from Britain if we continued trying to reach a solution because a few states simply refused to even consider ending it for any reason. Their first priority when drafting the Constitution was to quickly get a functioning national government so that we did not descend into lawlessness or disintegrate into separate little nations. Either of those would have allowed Britain to re-conquer us. They included a method for amending the Constitution in Article V because they knew that in their quest to finish things quickly they were going to miss or ignore important points. They also knew the issue of slavery would need resolved eventually.

> *Do you think they were right to secure our independence first and leave slavery for later? Do you think they could have done both? Do you think they should have forced the issue when they were working on the Constitution? How could they have succeeded with that? If not, why do you believe those efforts were destined to continue to fail?*

The Privilege of the Writ of Habeas Corpus shall not be suspended, unless when in Cases of Rebellion or Invasion the public Safety may require it.

In the United States, we have something called the *writ of habeas corpus* (Latin for "you may have the body").[5] It prevents unjust imprisonment of our citizens. If a writ of habeas corpus is not sued out before a judge and a good reason given for it, then the accused person is set free. In addition, our jails are cleaner, safer, and provide better care, including health care, for prisoners than is true in many other countries. Americans should be very proud of this law.

In some countries, people are kept in prisons year after year until they get sick and die, even though they may not have committed any crime that justified being imprisoned in the first place. This happened to Mahatma Gandhi in India. He was an important leader in improving conditions in his country and securing their independence from Britain, but he and his wife were both arrested and imprisoned for their leadership in this, even though all their efforts were non-violent.

No Bill of Attainder or ex post facto Law shall be passed.

A "Bill of Attainder" is an act of legislature that imposes the death penalty *without trial* on citizens thought to be guilty of high crimes.[6] Once again, ours was the first government to forbid acts of attainder.

An ex post-facto law is one which renders an act punishable after it was done, even though it was legal when you did it. Imagine that you are on a trip with your family. Grandpa decides that he doesn't want to go through the airport scanner because he has shrapnel (little bits of metal) from the Korean War in the 1950s stuck in him and it would show up and cause a ruckus. So, Grandpa gets a pat-down and away you go on your trip.

A few days later, the government decides that only Bad People would want to avoid the scanner, so they come and arrest Grandpa. Now Grandpa's stuck in jail in another state, Grandma doesn't want to leave him, so she's trying to figure out how to stay near him, and the rest of you really have to get home to go to school and work. Grandpa's choice was perfectly legal and sensible when he made it, but that doesn't matter with an ex post facto law. It's hard for us to really imagine this because it is illegal in this country. We should all be proud of that.

No Capitation, or other direct, Tax shall be laid, unless in Proportion to the Census or enumeration herein before directed to be taken.

The 16th Amendment modified this so that the federal government can levy an income tax, something that the Founding Fathers were absolutely opposed to.

> *Why do you think the Founders opposed an income tax? Do you think they would approve of our modern income tax?*

No Tax or Duty shall be laid on Articles exported from any State.

This is why there is no sales tax on items you order from another state and have delivered out of state without taking possession of before the items are shipped, including online purchases. Some large stores, such as those in big theme parks, can ship purchases directly to your home for you. If they provide this service, then you will have to pay shipping when you check out but you won't have to pay sales tax. You also won't have your items between when you pay and when they arrive at the shipping address; they go directly from the cash register to shipping. If, on the other hand, you take those items back to your hotel room first, you will have to pay sales tax on them when you buy them because they are no longer a direct export, and you will then pay separately to ship them, if you choose to do that.

No Preference shall be given by any Regulation of Commerce or Revenue to the Ports of one State over those of another; nor shall Vessels bound to, or from, one State, be obliged to enter, clear, or pay Duties in another.

During Colonial times, England passed a law that forbade the colonies from importing anything unless it was shipped from an English port on an English ship, no matter where it originated from. This clause is a direct result of that. It also closes a loophole states might have used to charge each tariffs on goods from other states, or to charge import duties more than once on goods from other countries.

No Money shall be drawn from the Treasury, but in Consequence of Appropriations made by Law; and a regular Statement and Account of the Receipts and Expenditures of all public Money shall be published from time to time.

This clause protects the public money.

If actual expenditures were never published, do you think politicians would be more or less careful of how they spend money? If they could spend money on anything they think is a good idea without having to get approval first, in the form of a law, how do you think they would spend the money?

No Title of Nobility shall be granted by the United States: And no Person holding any Office of Profit or Trust under them, shall, without the Consent of the Congress, accept of any present, Emolument, Office, or Title, of any kind whatever, from any King, Prince, or foreign State.

CHAPTER 9

In our country, all people have equal rights, so there should be no titles of nobility. If foreign nations could confer titles of nobility on our officers, then these might be offered as bribes.

Section 10

No State shall enter into any Treaty, Alliance, or Confederation; grant Letters of Marque and Reprisal; coin Money; emit Bills of Credit; make any Thing but gold and silver Coin a Tender in Payment of Debts; pass any Bill of Attainder, ex post facto Law, or Law impairing the Obligation of Contracts, or grant any Title of Nobility.

If Congress was forbidden from doing things like passing Bills of Attainder but states were not, then they wouldn't really be forbidden.

Recent Revolutionary-era experiences with states creating their own money, collecting import duties at the expense of the federal government, etc., are clearly evident in this clause. The currencies created at this time were fiat currencies. The hyperinflation of the Revolutionary period was caused in part by this use of fiat currency.[7]

Fiat currency is printed on or stamped from something that has little or no value in and of itself, such as paper.[8] The government that issues it also declares its value, and declares it to be "legal tender" which must be accepted for all debts within that country. Sometimes there is gold or silver in a vault, such as Fort Knox, to back the currency and give it some value.

If more money is printed or some of the gold or silver backing it is sold, stolen, or otherwise lost, then the currency loses its value and inflation begins. If less money is printed, or more gold or silver are discovered or bought, then the currency is worth more.

Hyperinflation is the extreme end stage of this. Twentieth century examples of hyperinflation include Weimar Germany in the 1920s, Eastern Europe in the 1990s, and Argentina around 2000.

Instead of fiat currency with nothing but promises giving it value, currency can be made from or fully backed by precious metals such as gold and silver.[9] This money is said to be on a gold standard or silver standard.[10] If they are fully backed by precious metals, that means you can take a $1 bill and exchange it for $1 of the metal backing it. Gold and silver each have intrinsic value, which means that the metal they are made from has a value no matter what its form. It does not matter if it is shaped into coins, jewelry, spoons, or dog bowls, gold and silver are still valuable.

When Lafayette came to the United States from France, he brought his knowledge, his skills, French troops, and French gold. The gold is not discussed as much as the others, but it was absolutely critical in our ability to continue fighting the Revolutionary War because our troops needed to be fed, clothed, paid, and cared for when they were sick, and we were out of money. Our fiat currency was worthless, until French gold gave it value. As mentioned above, at one point our troops were rioting and threatening the Continental Congress because they had not been paid.

No State shall, without the Consent of the Congress, lay any Imposts or Duties on Imports or Exports, except what may be absolutely necessary for executing it's inspection Laws: and the net Produce of all Duties and Imposts, laid by any State on Imports or Exports, shall be for the Use of the Treasury of the United States; and all such Laws shall be subject to the Revision and Control of the Congress.

This section prevents states from abusing their power to put duties (taxes) on imports since Congress has the right to revise and control these.

No State shall, without the Consent of Congress, lay any Duty of Tonnage, keep Troops, or Ships of War in time of Peace, enter into any Agreement or Compact with another State, or with a foreign Power, or engage in War, unless actually invaded, or in such imminent Danger as will not admit of delay.

CHAPTER 9

This forbids states from having their own private armies and navies, other than state militias. It also forbids one state from dragging the whole country into a war, although it does allow states to defend themselves if they are attacked without requiring them to first get Congressional Consent, which could easily have taken weeks or even months in the early years of our country.

RESOURCES

1. Spanish Milled Dollar
www.columbiagazette.com/smd.html

2. Growth and Entrenchment of Slavery
www.pbs.org/wgbh/aia/part3/3narr6.html

3. The Peculiar Institution
en.wikipedia.org/wiki/Peculiar_institution

4. How the Cotton Gin Started the Civil War
www.asme.org/engineering-topics/articles/history-of-mechanical-engineering/how-the-cotton-gin-started-the-civil-war

5. Writ of Habeas Corpus
legal-dictionary.thefreedictionary.com/writ+of+habeas+corpus

6. Bill of Attainder
www.techlawjournal.com/glossary/legal/attainder.htm

7. Early American Finance
history.state.gov/milestones/1784-1800/loans

8. Fiat Currency
www.investopedia.com/terms/f/fiatmoney.asp

9. Gold Standard
www.investopedia.com/terms/g/goldstandard.asp

10. Silver Standard
www.investopedia.com/terms/s/silver-standard.asp

CHAPTER 10
THE EXECUTIVE DEPARTMENT

Programs to create presentations/slide shows (PowerPoint™) are not designed to write long documents or to create budgets. They are used to present information, usually a lot of it, in a way that helps people understand and remember that information. It may also explain something new, review something, or even try to persuade people to believe something. Presentations can have an impact by convincing people of, or teaching them about, something. By themselves, these programs don't really do much.

The Presidency is much the same. Because we had just revolted against a powerful monarch, the Founders were very careful to ensure that our President does not have much direct power.[1] He, and they have all been men so far, is our national leader. This gives him a great deal of influence and contact with other world leaders, but that is a different type of power called indirect power.

The President exercises his direct power when he vetoes bills, negotiates treaties, drafts and submits the budget to Congress, or writes Executive Orders. Considering he is the chief executive for one of the biggest countries on earth, the office really has very little direct power. Many other countries have or have had dictators with absolute power who can do many things in their country, such as torturing and killing citizens, that no US President can ever do.

The President's power has increased a great deal over the last 200+ years, particularly his indirect powers.[2] In addition to being the head of the armed services, the representative of our citizens both at home and abroad, the highest ranking person in his party, and responsible for proposing some legislation, he is the head of the Executive Branch. In the 1790s, this didn't amount to much. That has changed–a lot. The Executive Branch now includes many regulatory departments in addition to all the cabinet departments.[3] These departments interpret and implement federal laws.

Executive branch departments can also write new regulations. These often have the effective force of laws without having to go through the process of being introduced by one or more legislators whose names are attached to the bill, going to committee, being debated, being voted on by both houses of Congress, and then (if they pass) sent for Presidential signature. Congressional bills have a clear record of who introduced them, who argued for or against them, and who voted for or against them. Regulations have none of that, and the top bureaucrats are appointed by the President, not elected.

How do you think the power of these departments impacts the checks and balances system the Founders so carefully set up? Is there anything else that has happened that also affects the system? What do you think they would think of it?

The President is the person who represents our nation at home and abroad. They go in front of the nation on television today, on the radio before that, and in speeches reprinted in newspapers before that, to encourage and lead us, and to promote their plans for the path and policies we should follow.

They provide a vision of who we are and where we want to go not just to our citizens but to the rest of the world as well, just as a PowerPoint presentation presents a vision of what someone wants you to know and believe. They also meet privately with other leaders both domestic and foreign for diplomatic reasons, and give speeches (presentations) to convince us all that their policy is the right one. They meet with leaders of different nations and different political groups to help them reach agreements and move forward on political, economic, and other issues.

They can push whatever items they think are important, sometimes rather forcefully, but the President cannot start a bill in Congress without the help of Congressmen. They must work together with Congressmen to get bills the President wants introduced and passed, which is another place they can use their indirect power.

The President submits a budget to Congress by the first Monday in February because the *Budget and Accounting Act of 1921,* not the Constitution, requires it.[4] The President also negotiates treaties and interacts with foreign nations, including choosing Ambassadors to other countries. As part of our system of checks and balances, Congress must approve those treaties and ambassadors, but they are not primarily responsible for either.

In short, the President is the Chief Executive Officer for the country. He leads us but does not control our citizens or our Congress, although he does have a lot of indirect power. The President presents the information to us and works with Congress and others to craft plans, but he cannot govern without Congressional consent and participation. Congress, on the other hand, can pass laws even without the consent or participation of the President by over-riding his veto, if necessary.

But Congress is not where we look for a leader to provide guidance in a crisis. When things go wrong, the President is the one we turn to for information and a plan of action. The President is the one who stands behind a podium, or sits behind a desk, and gives a speech to reassure and guide us.

Article II

SECTION 1

The executive Power shall be vested in a President of the Unit-

ed States of America. He shall hold his Office during the Term of four Years, and, together with the Vice President, chosen for the same Term, be elected, as follows:

Each State shall appoint, in such Manner as the Legislature thereof may direct, a Number of Electors, equal to the whole Number of Senators and Representatives to which the State may be entitled in the Congress: but no Senator or Representative, or Person holding an Office of Trust or Profit under the United States, shall be appointed an Elector.

Did you know that when citizens vote for the President, they are voting for people called Electors who vote for the President? This is called an indirect election because the voters don't vote for the President directly. This is why each state has a number assigned to it (the number of Electors) that is much smaller than the number of citizens it has.

The number of Electors is equal to the number of Representatives the state has in both houses of Congress combined. That is why the number of Electors for states often changes slightly after each Census. Population changes, and that changes how many Representatives and Electors a state has when the increase or decrease is large enough.

Electors are not Constitutionally bound to vote for a particular candidate, although in practice they always vote for the candidate they are pledged, or promised, to vote for. The Electors base their votes on who won their state and they all normally vote for the same candidate. Most states do have laws to punish "faithless" electors who do not vote for the promised candidate. (The rules are different for primary elections, which are where each party chooses their candidate for the general presidential election.)

Nebraska and Maine split their electoral votes between candidates based on the number of votes for each candidate, something called the Congressional District Method.[5] The states are divided into Districts and each District selects on Elector. Two Electors are awarded to the state winner of the popular vote. Maine adopted this system in 1972 and Nebraska adopted it in 1996.[6]

What do you think of this system? Do you think winner-takes-all is better or the Congressional District Method? If there was wide-spread voter fraud, under which system could it do the most damage?

Consider a swing state. What happens if there is massive voter fraud in only three or four relatively small districts? Under winner-takes-all, that could tip the entire state for one winner. Do you think that is a realistic scenario?

When our nation was founded, it was difficult for people to get information across the whole country. It wasn't until the twentieth century that it became possible for people to learn a lot about candidates and their views before voting for them. In times when citizens did not have much information or fast information, this system made sense. In fact, it was not until 1828 that our first president was elected by popularly elected Electors instead of Electors chosen by the state legislatures.

In the early years, the delay between when the citizens and Electors voted meant that the people actually voting for President had extra time to learn about the candidates. This reduced, however slightly, the chances of someone not eligible, including criminals, being elected. There is no way to know if this was part of the reason for the delay between the two sets of votes, but the Founders did many things to insulate the government from short-term, popular (but not necessarily wise) desires.

Although we have access to massive amounts of information instantly now, the Electoral College still makes sense because it forces Presidential candidates to pay attention to states they would otherwise simply fly over on their trips between the East Coast and West Coast. When you read about "flyover states" in the news, this is what they are talking about–roughly speaking, the states that aren't on either coast that politicians often just "fly over" when they are going between large cities on the two coasts. They pay attention to these flyo-ver states because they cannot win just with the votes from a few big coastal states, and they have to work to get the voters in those rela-tively less populated states to vote for them.

Some states vote reliably for one or the other of our parties, election after election, because the majority of its citizens are members of that party. The citizens of other states are more divided, with some of them voting for one party and some for the other party. These are called "swing states" because they swing from one party to the other at elections. Politicians concentrate their time and attention on the states that are politically divided, not the ones who reliably vote for the same party election after election, particularly since the winner does take all the electoral votes for every state except Nebraska and Maine. This makes these states more of a focus for Presidential can-didates.

Running for office is expensive and most candidates cannot afford to waste to money. If they know a state will vote for them, then they do not see a need to spend a lot of time and money convincing voters who already agree with them. Likewise, if they know most of the vot-ers disagree with their views, they won't spend much time there be-cause they are unlikely to convince enough people to vote for them to win the state. However, in swing states where the vote is close, they might manage to swing enough people to vote for them to win.

A candidate can win a state by one vote or 100,000 votes, and they still get the same number of Electoral College votes from that state (except Maine and Nebraska). This means they get a greater return for their time and campaign money in these states. This also makes it possible for a President to win the popular vote but lose the election, although this is rare.

When we vote, we chose the people who write our laws. They have the admin rights to our nation's legal code. When you are legally eli-gible to vote, it is your responsibility to vote to ensure that our gov-ernment has and funds the programs you think are important, and not the ones you don't want.

If you watch the news coverage of politicians, especially near an election, you will see and hear a lot of things that really are not related to their ability to do a good job in elected office are discussed—a lot. These are like pop-ups when you go online because they distract you from what you really need to know and do. The presence of lots of irrelevant and even flat-out wrong information doesn't mean you can't learn enough to make an educated decision. You just need to ignore the distractions and go research the facts for yourself. Yes, it is more work, but isn't your freedom worth it? It doesn't always seem like it, but each vote really does matter.

What kinds of things are important in a President or Congressman? Are the things they own (houses, cars) important, or are their values important? Are statements by people who have worked with them or are their friends helpful? What kinds of things make you question or feel confident of a candidate's values?

How could an extra-marital affair (or habit of sleeping around) be relevant? How about a person who isn't rich but likes to buy expensive things? (This is one way the things they own may be important.) What could a candidate's health have to do with their fitness for office? If they have a life-threatening condition? If their memory or brain functioning is being altered?

The Electors shall meet in their respective States, and vote by Ballot for two Persons, of whom one at least shall not be an Inhabitant of the same State with themselves. And they shall make a List of all the Persons voted for, and of the Number of Votes for each; which List they shall sign and certify, and transmit sealed to the Seat of the Government of the United States, directed to the President of the Senate. The President of the Senate shall, in the Presence of the Senate and House of Representatives, open all the Certificates, and the Votes shall then be counted. The Person having the greatest Number of Votes shall be the President, if such Number be a Majority of

the whole Number of Electors appointed; and if there be more than one who have such Majority, and have an equal Number of Votes, then the House of Representatives shall immediately chose by Ballot one of them for President; and if no Person have a Majority, then from the five highest on the List the said House shall in like Manner choose the President. But in choosing the President, the Votes shall be taken by States, the Representation from each State having one Vote; A quorum for this purpose shall consist of a Member or Members from two thirds of the States, and a Majority of all the States shall be necessary to a Choice. In every Case, after the Choice of the President, the Person having the greatest Number of Votes of the Electors shall be the Vice President. But if there should remain two or more who have equal Votes, the Senate shall chose from them by Ballot the Vice President.

This clause is not carried out as it was originally written because it was quickly determined that the original plan wasn't working out terribly well and the 12th Amendment was passed. Remember, this was a new form of government that had never been tried before so some problems were inevitable. Our first Vice President, Federalist John Adams, was elected as our second President and Democratic-Republican Thomas Jefferson was elected as his Vice President. They were both great men, but they didn't like or trust each other; they had different views of how the new government should operate; and they didn't work well together.[7]

This was technically the only time in our history when the President and Vice President were from different parties. In reality, it happened a second time when Republican Abraham Lincoln selected Democrat Andrew Johnson as his Vice President on a "National Union" ticket (technically making them the same party) for his second term.[8] This was a deliberate choice by Lincoln to gain support from pro-war Democrats during the Civil War.

In the 1800 election, Jefferson and Aaron Burr intended to run and be elected as President and Vice President, similar to a modern "ticket" but this clause, as written, didn't separate votes for President and Vice President. The person with the most votes became President, and the second most votes became Vice President. Jefferson and Burr received the same number of electoral votes, which led to the House choosing. Alexander Hamilton, a staunch political foe of Jefferson's, lobbied in favor of Jefferson because he hated and distrusted Burr even more. After the House voted 36 (thirty six) times, Jefferson was finally declared the President and Burr the Vice President, just as the original ticket was intended and almost certainly because of Hamilton's efforts. The 12th Amendment was passed soon after.

Because Burr had refused to take his name out of the running for President, despite having agreed to be Vice President, Jefferson no longer trusted him. This made working together rather difficult and Jefferson selected George Clinton as Vice President for his second term. It also made the political rivalry between Hamilton and Burr worse and their eventual duel more inevitable. Hamilton died several years later at Burr's hands, which made dueling less socially acceptable and ended Burr's political career. Ironically, Burr had hoped that he would win the duel and it would revive his political career.

How would you have felt if you were Jefferson? Would you trust anything Burr said? Was this a good change? Why do you think Burr did not stay with the original agreement? What do you think you would have done if you had the chance to be President?

Think about any recent election and imagine the current President as President and the Presidential candidate from the other party as Vice President. This is what happened with Adams and Jefferson. The Jefferson-Burr debacle happened at very next election. As a result, rather than the two candidates with the most votes being President and Vice President, we vote for a "ticket" with one President and one Vice-President on it. Once a candidate wins the primary and knows they are The Candidate for their party, they select a Vice-Presidential running-mate from the same party. They are elected as a pair, even though the Vice Presidential candidate from one ticket might be less popular or less qualified than the Presidential or even Vice Presidential candidate from the other ticket. Letting the Presidential candidate pick his potential Vice-President also makes it much more likely they will work together well.

The House of Representatives chooses the President if the Electoral College does not, as happened in 1800. This is because it is and always has been directly elected by the people, and because its members more closely reflect our population distribution. This was particularly true before the 17th Amendment changed the way Senators are elected.

In fact, our 6th President, John Quincy Adams, did not receive as many popular or electoral votes in the 1824 election as Andrew Jackson did. Because no candidate won a majority, the vote went to the House. One candidate withdrew and gave his support and Electors to Adams, allowing him to win and become our 4th President. Jackson was understandably upset by this and went on to win the next election and become our first popularly elected President.

The Senate elects the Vice President if the Electoral College does not because the Vice President becomes their presiding officer.

The Congress may determine the Time of choosing the Electors, and the Day on which they shall give their Votes; which Day shall be the same throughout the United States.

Electors are chosen in late November, a few weeks after Election Day, in order to allow enough time to count all votes, including absentee ballots, and permit any recounts that are needed. The Electoral College votes the following January, approximately three months after the election. In the past, this was necessary just to allow enough travel time for everyone. Today, it is a formality.

No Person except a natural born Citizen, or a Citizen of the United States, at the time of the Adoption of this Constitution, shall be eligible to the Office of President; neither shall any Person be eligible to that Office who shall not have attained to

the Age of thirty five Years, and been fourteen Years a Resident within the United States.

The phrase "natural born citizen" has not been clearly and fully de-fined by our government.[9] It definitely means that the President must be a US citizen but nothing further is explicitly clear. While scholars do have some rather firm opinions on the matter, the meaning has not been defined in either the Constitution or the US legal code. The 1874 Supreme Court case *Minor v. Happersett* addresses this issue in passing but does not fully resolve it.[10] There is no requirement that a candidate prove they are a natural born citizen, and therefore eligible, before they either run for or assume the office of President.

If the Founders had believed that someone born in and raised a citi-zen of another country was a natural born citizen, then they would not have needed to state that anyone who was a citizen when the Constitution was adopted was eligible. They would not have made that exception if being a citizen and being a natural-born citizen meant the same thing, and *Minor v. Happersett* confirms this. Natural-born and naturalized are not the same thing. There were no people who were natural born citizens who were old enough to hold elected office at the time, so an exception was made for those who were here before the USA existed.

What do you think "natural born citizen" means? Does it require being born on US soil? What if you grow up in another country? Can you have dual citizenship? This means that you have citizen-ship in, and loyalty to, two different countries. How could having a Commander in Chief with dual citizenship be a problem?

Do you think this is a wise requirement or not? Why?

Candidates make a lot of information public when they run for of-fice. This usually includes birth certificates and a wide variety of other personal, educational, and professional information that is normally protected by the Privacy Act, but it is not required of them.[11] This material normally also proves where they are a legal resident. Candidates often provide health and medical information to reassure the public that they are of sound (healthy) mind and body.

Having a minimum age ensures the President has at least some life experience, just as it does for Congress.

In Case of the Removal of the President from Office, or of his Death, Resignation, or Inability to discharge the Powers and Duties of the said Office, the Same shall devolve on the Vice President, and the Congress may by Law provide for the Case of Removal, Death, Resignation or Inability, both of the President and Vice President, declaring what Officer shall then act as President, and such Officer shall act accordingly, until the Disability be removed, or a President shall be elected.

This entire clause has been replaced and clarified by the 25th Amendment.

The President shall, at stated Times, receive for his Services, a Compensation, which shall neither be increased nor diminished during the Period for which he shall have been elected, and he shall not receive within that Period any other Emolument from the United States, or any of them.

Without this clause, Congress could maneuver the President into doing what they wanted with the promise of a generous pay raise, bonus, or other large gift, or with the threat of a large pay cut. Since they cannot change the current President's salary, they lose this potential power. This also prevents the President and other officials from keeping large gifts from other governments. Any gifts they receive are government property. The President cannot take them with him when he leaves office any more than he can keep Air Force One.

Before he enter on the Execution of his Office, he shall take the following Oath or Affirmation:--"I do solemnly swear (or affirm) that I will faithfully execute the Office of President of the United States, and will to the best of my Ability, preserve, protect and defend the Constitution of the United States."

The President specifically swears to preserve, protect, and defend the *Constitution*, not a political party, a set of interests, or anything other than the *Constitution*. Their first duty is to protect this nation and *our Constitution*, not to protect other countries, citizens of other countries, businesses, international interests or organizations, or anything else, unless protecting them also serves to protect the United States.

What do you think of this Oath? Are you surprised by how short and simple it is? How do you think recent, or not-so-recent, Presidents have done in fulfilling this task? Do you know of any times when Presidents have done something they knew, or strongly suspected, was unconstitutional?

The most famous example of this was when Thomas Jefferson approved the Louisiana Purchase in 1803. He himself had serious doubts about whether it was Constitutional, but securing access to the Mississippi River and out into the Gulf of Mexico was critical for the future of our country and this achieved that goal. He thought a Constitutional amendment would be necessary to do this but his advisors convinced him otherwise.

Can you think of any other time(s) the President did something that violated the Constitution, or might have? Were they right to do it? Why? Were there any consequences to their actions? Do you think Jefferson was right and there is nothing in the Constitution that gave him the authority for that purchase, or was he wrong and the Constitution did allow for his actions?

Throughout the Constitution, it says people are to "swear (or affirm)" various things.[12] This is because it went against the beliefs of certain Christian denominations to swear at all, for any reason, at any time. The Quakers in particular took the Biblical injunction in The Sermon on the Mount "do not swear at all" very literally.[13] In modern life, it is not just Christian groups such as Quakers who use the option to affirm. Atheists and others who are opposed to, or simply not comfortable with, swearing to God also use this option.

THE EXECUTIVE DEPARTMENT

<u>SECTION 2</u>

<u>The President shall be Commander in Chief of the Army and Navy of the United States, and of the Militia of the several States, when called into the actual Service of the United States; he may require the Opinion, in writing, of the principal Officer in each of the executive Departments, upon any Subject relating to the Duties of their respective Offices, and he shall have Power to grant Reprieves and Pardons for Offences against the United States, except in Cases of Impeachment.</u>

The President is the Commander in Chief of the Army and Navy, but Congress has the power to declare war, set the budget, and establish rules and procedures for the Armed Services. The War Powers Resolution (or Act) of 1973 clarified the President's ability to put troops into action without waiting for Congressional approval, although they are required to seek that approval promptly.[14]

It gives the President the ability to act quickly when there is an immediate threat but keeps him from involving us in a foreign dispute without Congressional authorization. This is yet another example of the checks and balances the Founders established. Both the Executive and Legislative branches have a say in how, when, and where our Armed Services are used.

The President has the power to pardon criminals as a way of righting potential injustices.[15] The President does not have this power for impeachment because it might allow them favor their political friends and allies, no matter what their offences might be.

Although it is not named in the Constitution, Presidents rely on their Cabinet, which is made up of "the principal Officer in each of the executive Departments" as mentioned in this section.[16] It is an advisory group for the President. The Constitution specifically says that these advisors can be required to give their opinions in writing because the Founding Fathers believed that this would make them more careful.

CHAPTER 10

Do you think people are more careful of what they say if they put it in writing, if they are speaking, or equally careful (or careless) either way? Which is true for you, personally? What are the benefits and drawbacks of writing versus speaking?

The next section details how the President's Cabinet has grown from four department heads to fifteen plus six other Cabinet-level positions, not including the Vice President who is also a member.[17] It is not meant to bore you, even though it is not exactly exciting, but rather to show you how easily something can grow from small to large with one small addition at a time. This is what has happened with much of our government.

George Washington's Cabinet included four department heads–the Secretaries of State (concerned with relations with other countries, not our individual states), Treasury, and War, and the Attorney General. John Adams added the Secretary of the Navy since he added a Navy. In the 1800s, Andrew Jackson added the Postmaster General, Zachary Taylor added the Secretary of the Interior, and Grover Cleveland added the Secretary of Agriculture.

In 1913, Teddy Roosevelt added the Secretary of Commerce and Labor, which Warren Harding then split into the Secretary of Commerce and the Secretary of Labor in 1921. No new departments were added until after Kennedy's death in 1963, although the Secretary of War was combined with the Secretary of the Navy and renamed the Secretary of Defense under President, formerly General, Eisenhower.

Under Lyndon Johnson, the Cabinet added the Secretaries of Health, Education, and Welfare; Housing and Urban Development; and Transportation. Richard Nixon removed the Postmaster General from his Cabinet when the Postal Service was changed to a semi-independent federal agency. Jimmy Carter added three Cabinet members, the Secretaries of Health and Human Services; Education; and Energy. These did not replace the Secretary of Health, Education, and Welfare, but were in addition. Health, Education, and Welfare was removed from the Cabinet by Ronald Reagan. George Bush added the Secretary of Veterans Affairs. George W. Bush added the Secretary of Homeland Security.

As of 2010, the President's Cabinet includes the heads (Secretaries) of fifteen executive departments: Agriculture, Commerce, Defense, Education, Energy, Health and Human Services, Homeland Security, Housing and Urban Development, Interior, Labor, State, Transportation, Treasury, and Veteran Affairs, and the Attorney General. On top of that, there are six more cabinet-level positions: the White House Chief of Staff, United States Trade Representative, United States Ambassador to the United Nations, and the heads of the Environmental Protection Agency, Office of Management & Budget, and Council of Economic Advisers. Full Cabinet meetings now include 23 members, with the President and Vice President.

Imagine you are working on a group project. How would that be different with four people, fourteen people, or twenty one people? Each has benefits and problems. You would have more opinions and information with more people, but in larger groups, people often choose not to speak, which can decrease the real discussion.

This may be because they know others will disagree and they don't want to argue, or it may be because they want the meeting to end so they can do something else, or it may be something else entirely. In smaller groups, everyone's thoughts are more likely to be heard, but you may not get very many different opinions or ideas, and that can also be bad. How do you think this might relate to the President's Cabinet?

George Washington had only four departments in his Cabinet. There were seven during the Civil War and Reconstruction. There were ten during World War I and II. Today, there are twenty one people in the President's Cabinet. Which, if any, do you think should be removed or combined?

What do you think would be the best number of members for the President's Cabinet? Why?

Each Cabinet level position represents an entire section of bureaucracy within the federal government. Going back to the idea of our Constitution as the OS for the US, imagine that each department is a different program running on your computer. Some might be very small, like the built-in calculator. Others are very large, like playing a massively multiplayer online game.

> *How well would your computer work if you had two or three windows open with different massively multiplayer online games running, plus a window where you were writing a paper, another with your music playing in the background, and your email in another?*
>
> *Each of these programs uses a lot of resources and makes the others run a little bit slower because there is less free memory, until you get to the point that you have no more memory or bandwidth and everything just...stops. Your computer is frozen. Do you think this could happen to the federal government? Do you think it would? What might cause it to happen or not happen?*
>
> *How much do you think it is possible for the President, or any other person, to keep track of? What limits, if any, do you think there are on what the federal government can effectively keep track of and maintain?*

In addition to the Cabinet, Presidents have appointed special advisors that report only to them and provide information on very specific areas since the earliest days of our country. When our country was young, Presidents did not have many special advisors, or indeed much staff at all. Many handwrote their own speeches and letters. The number of these special advisors exploded in the twentieth century, when they also received the nickname "czar."

By 2010, there were more than three dozen, although the position is so poorly defined and so hidden within the budget and framework of the executive branch that even trying to figure out how many czars there are can be difficult. Details of what the government provides to each modern czar in staff, facilities, and other expenditures are not available to the public. Descriptions of what they actually do are not available either. Some of them, if not all, almost certainly have larger staffs than most pre-twentieth century Presidents.

Unlike Cabinet heads, Congress does not need to approve their appointment and cannot recall them, which makes them controversial. Each modern czar is a government position, generally with a paid government staff, offices, and other benefits. Unlike Czars, most Presidential and Judicial Appointments above a certain level are approved, or not, by Congress. The requirement for Congressional Approval is another aspect of our system of checks and balances.

Do you think czars, or special advisors, can affect the balance of power? How? Should they require Congressional approval?

Plug-ins are a special type of "accessory" software for your computer that lets another program do something it couldn't do by itself. Many of the most popular (Flash, Java™, Adobe Reader™) work with a wide variety of programs. They can be added, deleted, and updated without changing the programs that use them. For instance, if you delete all three of these programs, your internet browser will still work, but many website features (and entire websites) will no longer work because the plug-ins they need are gone.

Parts of our government are like this. They are not necessary, and are not specifically included in the Constitution, but they make things run more smoothly. The President's Cabinet and joint Congressional committees are examples. They do not create policy or write legislation. They advise the President and both houses of Congress when they do. By allowing information to flow between groups that might not otherwise communicate directly, these groups help the process run a bit more smoothly and efficiently.

He shall have Power, by and with the Advice and Consent of the Senate, to make Treaties, provided two thirds of the Senators present concur; and he shall nominate, and by and with the Advice and Consent of the Senate, shall appoint Ambassadors, other public Ministers and Consuls, Judges of the supreme Court, and all other Officers of the United States, whose Ap-

pointments are not herein otherwise provided for, and which shall be established by Law: but the Congress may by Law vest the Appointment of such inferior Officers, as they think proper, in the President alone, in the Courts of Law, or in the Heads of Departments.

The President is expected to be familiar with foreign affairs, so the power to make treaties is placed in their hands. Congress should also be expected to be familiar with foreign affairs, but treaties often require secrecy and a large group like Congress cannot keep a secret. Once the treaty has been agreed upon, however, it must be ratified by Congress, so the President cannot make a treaty that is against our national interests. This is checks and balances at work, once again.

In 1867, President Johnson negotiated a treaty with Russia to purchase some land they had claimed in North America because he believed it was important to expand our territory.[18] His Secretary of State, William Seward, did much of the negotiating and presented the treaty and their arguments for it to the Senate, which barely passed the treaty. The President did not have the power to do this without Congressional approval. They could have stopped the entire deal.

The territory was known as Seward's Folly or Seward's Icebox because it was widely believed to be a waste of resources.[19] It has since proven its value many times over, starting when gold was found there in 1898. While purchasing the area now known as Alaska has definitely proven to be the right choice, it could have been the foolish choice it first looked like, which is why the Senate must be involved in approving all treaties.

Ambassadors are ministers to foreign countries at the highest level. They represent their government and manage its interests. Consuls are government agents in foreign countries who look after and protect the rights, commerce, merchants, and other duties that are given to them. The President has the power to fill vacancies in these and other departments so that all the government departments are always in working order. This clause is often used to fill judicial and other positions when Congress is in recess ("recess appointments").

In our modern government, there are over 1,000 positions that each new president must fill and Congress must approve. This process literally takes years, in no small part because it is so highly partisan. In other words, many politicians only vote according to what their political party or party leader tells them to do rather than looking at each case individually and making their own judgment. The President often considers candidates' political views instead of deciding strictly based on their qualifications.

Recess appointments are used so that departments and courts continue to function despite this partisanship.[20] Sometimes just one or two Representatives or Senators can block an appointee from moving forward in consideration, which can cause departments and committees to grind to a halt because they lack a department head, a quorum, or simply a member to vote as a tie-breaker.

Although not as historically obvious as slavery, partisan politics is also a like a computer worm that eats away at our government's effectiveness. When our representatives will not listen or talk to each other about issues if they are part of a different political party, it hurts our government. When they delay confirming a nominee, such as a Supreme Court Justice, because of party affiliation, it damages our nation. When our representatives and citizens are unwilling to ever work together on anything, it hurts our government and our nation.

Realistically, political parties are unavoidable. Having political parties isn't the problem. The problem starts when people (politicians, newscasters, regular citizens, it doesn't matter) refuse to listen and do not try to understand either people with a different point of view from them or facts they don't like, and it is not a new problem.

The President shall have Power to fill up all Vacancies that may happen during the Recess of the Senate, by granting Commissions which shall expire at the End of their next Session.

This is called a recess appointment and happens often, partially because Congress moves so slowly and is so partisan in the approval process. On the other side, Presidents make partisan nominations they know Congress is unlikely to approve. They also take a long time to nominate people for all the positions, some of which is undoubtedly because they have more urgent issues. It is not unusual to read in the news that the President waited until Congress left for some break, even one of only a few days, and immediately used this power to appoint someone to some position.

> *How can this power be used positively? How can it be used negatively? Do you think anything about it should be changed? What and how?*

He shall from time to time give to the Congress Information of the State of the Union, and recommend to their Consideration such Measures as he shall judge necessary and expedient; he may, on extraordinary Occasions, convene both Houses, or either of them, and in Case of Disagreement between them, with Respect to the Time of Adjournment, he may adjourn them to such Time as he shall think proper; he shall receive Ambassadors and other public Ministers; he shall take Care that the Laws be faithfully executed, and shall Commission all the Officers of the United States.

George Washington gave this information on the state, or condition, of the nation (Union) as a speech,[21] but in 1801 Thomas Jefferson decided to present the information as a written message called "The President's Message."[22] Jefferson was a writer, not a speaker, and was far more comfortable giving a written message than a spoken one. He also said that giving it as speech seemed too monarchical. This concern is reasonable since it was based on the Speech from the Throne given by the British monarch during the opening of Parliament.[23] The information was presented as a written message from then until President Woodrow Wilson returned to giving a speech in 1913. It can still be presented as a written message but the last President to do so was Jimmy Carter in 1981.

Every January, the President gives the annual State of the Union Address to a joint session of Congress held in the House of Representatives' Chamber. Because so many senior members of our government attend, at least one member of the President's Cabinet and some Congressmen deliberately do not attend so that if the site of the State of the Union speech is attacked, we will still have someone left to serve as President.

The President normally tells Congress and the nation what his legislative priorities are for the year during this speech. Since it is broadcast live to the nation, it is also an appeal to the people to support what he cares about and a chance to explain to citizens and legislators alike why his priorities matter.

If something truly urgent comes up when Congress is not in session, the President can recall one or both Houses to deal with the crisis. If the two Houses cannot agree when they should adjourn, or end their current session, then the President may decide for them.

When Ambassadors and other officials come to the United States, the President receives them. This is why foreign heads of state (Presidents, Queens, etc.) primarily visit the White House, not Congress, on their visits here, and why State Dinners are hosted at the White House and not at a Congressional facility.

Section 4

The President, Vice President and all civil Officers of the United States, shall be removed from Office on Impeachment for, and Conviction of, Treason, Bribery, or other high Crimes and Misdemeanors.

This plainly tells officers the reasons they can be impeached to guarantee that they can't be impeached and removed from office by an ex post facto law or some flimsy, politically-inspired charge. It also clearly states that if they are convicted, then they must be removed from office and not given a lighter punishment.

If you read back through all of this, you may find something missing. There are no duties for the Vice President. The only duty listed in the Constitution for the Vice President is to be the President of the Sen-

149

ate. As Vice President John Adams complained to his wife Abigail, "My country has in its wisdom contrived for me the most insignificant office that ever the invention of man contrived or his imagination conceived." [24]

Adams was Vice President under George Washington. He became our second President and first one-term President when Washington retired. As our second Vice President under John Adams, Thomas Jefferson, later our third President, wrote to Benjamin Rush, "a more tranquil and unoffending station could not have been found for me." [25] Jefferson did not really want public office at this time, particularly the Presidency, which is why he was pleased with the position.

Why do you think they did not list any particular duties for the Vice President? What do you think of what Adams and Jefferson each said? Which one do you think was happier to serve as or more interested in actually being Vice President? Do you think the Vice President should have more responsibilities today?

How do you think the modern position of Vice-President could be updated to make the position less "insignificant," without taking on any unconstitutional authority or responsibility? Would the fact that the Constitution says so little about the Vice President and their duties make it easier or harder to change them?

Consider the Presidential Cabinet's growth since George Washington. What does that tell you about the early Presidents' responsibilities, and what he was expected to oversee and know about? How does that compare to what modern Presidents are expected to oversee and know about? Which one could use more help from the Vice President for day-to-day governing?

RESOURCES

1. Presidential Powers: An Introduction
law2.umkc.edu/faculty/projects/ftrials/conlaw/prespowers.html

2. 11 Reasons Why Presidential Power Inevitably Expands and Why it Matters
www.bu.edu/law/journals-archive/bulr/documents/marshall.pdf

3. 3 Branches of US Government
www.usa.gov/branches-of-government

4. Budget and Accounting Office
www.gao.gov/about/history/articles/working-for-good-government/01-introduction.html

5. The Congressional District Method
archive.fairvote.org/e_college/me_ne.htm

6. Why Do Nebraska and Maine Split Votes?
mentalfloss.com/article/13017/why-do-nebraska-and-maine-split-electoral-votes

7. President Adams and Vice-President Jefferson
www.homeofheroes.com/profiles/profiles_jeffadams.html

8. "National Union" Party
www.lincolncollection.org/collection/curated-groupings/category/election-of-1864/

9. Natural-Born Citizen Defined
www.federalistblog.us/2008/11/natural-born_citizen_defined/

10. *Minor v. Happersett*
www.law.cornell.edu/supremecourt/text/88/162

11. The Privacy Act of 1974
www.hhs.gov/foia/privacy/index.html

12. The Difference Between "Swear" and "Affirm" in an Oath
www.wisegeek.org/what-is-the-difference-between-swear-and-affirm-in-an-oath.htm

CHAPTER 10

13. Full Text of The Sermon on the Mount
www.archive.org/stream/sermononmount00findiala/sermononmount00fin
diala_djvu.txt

14. The War Powers Resolution (or Act)
www.loc.gov/law/help/war-powers.php

15. Pardon Information and Instructions
www.justice.gov/pardon/pardon-information-and-instructions

16. The Presidential Cabinet
www.whitehouse.gov/administration/cabinet

17. Cabinet Members, Election Results, and more for Presidents
    from Washington to Obama (not updated after Obama)
www.ipl.org/div/potus/

18. Presidential Cabinet Members
www.infoplease.com/ipa/A0101184.html

19. Treaty with Russia for Purchase of Alaska
www.loc.gov/rr/program/bib/ourdocs/Alaska.html

CHAPTER 11
THE JUDICIAL DEPARTMENT

C omputer virus protection and firewalls have built-in criteria
they use to judge if a program is probably safe or probably
unsafe to download, but the system administrator can adjust those
based on what their group needs, including blocking certain actions.
For example, in a client-server system individual users are almost always unable to install new programs (including plug-ins) on their
computer. System administrators (admins) are responsible for installing programs and keeping them updated, most particularly including virus protection.[1]

Virus protection scans programs and files, and warns you when it
sees something that may be infected with a virus. Computer viruses
make computers "sick" so that they don't function properly just as
regular viruses make the human body sick so it doesn't function
properly. Virus protection updates are usually automatic because they
are frequent and small. New computer viruses are created all the
time, just like there are new flu viruses every year, and it's important
to have virus protection that stays up to date to protect you from
these new threats.

The federal government, particularly branches such as the Department of Defense (DoD), Immigration Control and Enforcement

(ICE) and Homeland Security protect our nation from outside dangers such as nuclear or terrorist attacks, but the Judiciary is our primary "virus protection." It is responsible for keeping our legal code healthy.

After Congress and the President transform a bill into a law, the Supreme Court can still declare it unconstitutional and remove it from our legal code. Judges, mostly at the state level, use their knowledge of the US legal system and Constitution to judge whether something might be unconstitutional. (US District Courts are not a primary part of this.) If a law seems like it may be unconstitutional, then it is passed up to the Supreme Court for final judgment. The Congress can only overcome a Supreme Court decision by passing a Constitutional Amendment, which must also be ratified by the states.

Congress writes the bills and the President signs bills into law, but it is the Judicial department that interprets and applies those laws. The rights of the people depend more upon the ability and honesty of judges than upon any other department of the government.

Imagine that you are a little kid. Your parents go out to dinner and your grandparents stay with you. Your parents give you permission to stay up late and play a new game while they are out. Five minutes after they leave, your grandparents tell you they're turning off your new game because you aren't "wasting your time" while they're in charge and you can only stay up an extra five minutes.

They made a judgment about what your rights are that goes against the clear intent of the rules your parents established, although they technically followed the rules by letting you play briefly and stay up for a few minutes. Does it matter that your parents gave you permission, or the right, to play the game while they were gone, and to stay up late? Not really because you couldn't enjoy it.

It is the same with the government. It doesn't matter if the Congress confirms your right to do things if the Judges say you do not, particularly if Congress does so with poorly worded or easily misinterpreted laws. Judges who confirmed that actions were just when they knew they went against the law (or were simply wrong) helped the Nazi's seem more legitimate and law-abiding when they were seizing control of Germany in the 1930s. Some of these judges were corrupt, some were Nazis who believed in what the Nazi party was doing, and some were frightened men trying to keep their own families safe.

Their motivation and the legality of what they did or did not do don't matter, though, because the end result is the unbelievable death and destruction caused by the Nazis and World War II in general. This is, of course, an extreme example, and the historical reality was complex, but it is an important point to understand. A just and impartial judiciary is critical for freedom.

Similarly, it didn't matter that the 15th Amendment said no one could be denied the right to vote based on their race or color when judges ruled that poll taxes and other means could be used to keep blacks and other groups from voting. The 24th Amendment corrected this particular problem.

In fact, the Civil Rights Act of 1875 stated, "That all persons ... shall be entitled to full and equal enjoyment of the accommodations, advantages, facilities, and privileges of inns, public conveyances on land or water, theaters, and other places of public amusement." Separate but equal is a very clear violation of this federal law.[2]

The Judiciary branch is the branch that can declare a law "unconstitutional", which means that law says something that goes against our most basic and fundamental law, the Constitution. Any law that is "unconstitutional" is no longer enforced, although it is still "on the books" just as the 18th Amendment, repealed by the 21st Amendment, is still on the books. The only way to over-ride a Supreme Court decision is with a Constitutional Amendment, as the 13th and 14th Amendments over-rode *Dred Scott v. Sandford*.[3]

In 1833, the Supreme Court ruled in *Civil Rights Cases* (five similar cases considered as one issue by the Supreme Court) that the 14th Amendment only protected black citizens from discrimination by the states, not by individuals or businesses and declared the Civil Rights

Act of 1875 unconstitutional. Shortly after this, Southern states began enacting segregation legislation and the US Supreme Court upheld those laws as Constitutional.[4] The Supreme Court used its power to over-rule Congress and set back Civil Rights for over 80 years.

What do you think of this? Is it right that the nine Supreme Court Justices, who are selected not elected, should be able to over-rule the elected members of Congress? Contrariwise, what advantage do you see to having people who are not elected as a check to our elected officials? Can you think of examples where this has helped our country and where it has hurt it?

Do you think it should take a Constitutional amendment for Congress to over-rule a Supreme Court ruling? Is there a better way to do this?

The Constitutionally protected rights of blacks, backed by legally passed legislation, did not matter because the Supreme Court made a decision contrary to what Congress clearly intended. They were able to do this because many citizens agreed with the Supreme Court and Congress had barely passed the original legislation. It took over half a century to begin to undo the damage after the Supreme Court reconfirmed this position in the ruling for *Plessy v. Ferguson,* which legitimized separate-but-equal in 1896.[5]

History has also shown that there can be no prosperity in a government without justice. For this reason, the Founding Fathers made the Judicial department independent from the Congressional and Executive branches and gave judges lifetime tenure, although the fact that many judges are nominated by the Executive branch and confirmed by the Legislative branch has blurred that safeguard somewhat. Longer lifetimes have also made lifetime tenure seem like a more questionable choice. Simply look at the process of getting someone new in or someone old to retire from the Supreme Court for proof of this. They also did this to make it harder for our government to become corrupt.

Article III

SECTION 1

The judicial Power of the United States shall be vested in one supreme Court, and in such inferior Courts as the Congress may from time to time ordain and establish. The Judges, both of the supreme and inferior Courts, shall hold their Offices during good Behavior, and shall, at stated Times, receive for their Services a Compensation, which shall not be diminished during their Continuance in Office.

This clause prevents politicians from decreasing either the pay or benefits of our judges. This keeps judges more independent of our political parties because politicians can't use the threat of cutting their pay to force them to decide a certain way.

It also makes it clear that they cannot be removed unless they break the law. If they do break the law, then they can be impeached by the House, tried by the Senate, and possibly removed from office. This gives them "lifetime tenure" in an attempt to keep them above and separate from partisan political concerns.

In colonial times, judges were appointed by the King and he could dismiss them at any time, for any reason—or for none at all. If the King had a servant named Christopher who spilled a drink on the King and made him angry, and later that day a judge named Christopher was brought to the King's attention, the King might have fired the judge because he was angry at anyone named Christopher. It would have been perfectly legal. A day earlier or later, and the judge would not have been fired because there was really no cause for it. American judges have been kept safe from this worry.

The Supreme Court of the United States established by this clause is currently composed of one Chief Justice and eight Associate Justices. The Constitution does not set a number and the number of justices has been as low as six in the past. It started out with only two Justices, before staffing was finished. It was not exactly considered a desirable job in the early years of our country.

The Justices make Supreme Court decisions. There is no jury. The US Court of Appeals hears appeals and they don't have juries either. Appeals are requests to reconsider a case after a guilty ruling and require proof of a reason for a new trial, beyond the person wanting to be found not guilty. (If they were found innocent, there can't be a second criminal trial because that would be "double jeopardy" and is illegal.) US District Courts have original, not appellate, jurisdiction and may or may not have juries, depending on the case.

In 1937, President Franklin Delano Roosevelt (FDR) attempted to add six Justices to the Supreme Court in order to "pack" it.[6] "Packing the court" was meant to ensure that a majority of the judges would vote the way FDR wanted them to. When you pack a suitcase, you fill it up with things you think you will need or want while you are gone. Packing a court fills it with people who will vote the way you need or want them to. FDR was very unhappy because the existing court had declared many parts of his New Deal legislation unconstitutional.

Specifically, FDR wanted to appoint one judge to serve jointly with every serving judge who was over 70 years old and refused to retire. Six of the nine serving at the time were over 70. The older justices "just happened" to be the ones opposed to FDR's policies. These six new judges added to the ones who already voted for him would have given his views a majority. Because our Founding Fathers were wise, Congress had the power to prevent President Roosevelt from doing this, and they did.

Forcing the old Justices to retire seems reasonable, which makes what FDR was doing seem reasonable at a quick glance.[7] After all, it isn't hard to find examples of Supreme Court Justices, congressmen, and other government officials who are so old or ill that it is hard to believe they can still do their jobs. However, if it was really about judges staying in office past when they could really do their job, his proposal would have targeted retirement age in general, not just the Supreme Court Justices who voted against his legislation.

The Constitution did not include term limits or retirement because people did not live very many decades when our country was founded, and because the Founders feared the negative effects of term limits, primarily that those near the end of their term wouldn't have a reason to do their job well.[8] In addition, serving in the national government was often viewed as a hardship and citizens truly chose to do so as a service to the nation, not as a decades-long career path.

> How do you think this has changed? What caused this change? Is it a change for the better? What, if anything, do you think we should do to make serving in the national government more about serving our nation and less about being a career?
>
> What do you think about term limits–limiting how long people can serve in office, instead of allowing them to serve indefinitely? Do they seem like a good idea or not? If they seem like a good idea, how many terms or years do you think they should be limited to? What jobs should have them? If you don't think it is a good idea, why not?
>
> What benefits are there to having the same people in office for many years and to permitting people to continue in office past the time they would otherwise be forced to retire?
>
> Do you think citizens should be able to serve in government offices past the regular retirement age? Retirement age is generally 60-65 years old at the present. Think about your own older family members. Do you think any of them are mentally and physically healthy enough to serve? Do you think other retired people are fit enough to serve well in our government? What would be the risks or benefits to having retired people serving in Congress or the Judiciary? Do you think there should be a mandatory retirement age? What should it be?

If the majority of members of any court or other group are appointed by the same person, which would have happened under FDR's court-packing scheme, then they will probably all have similar political opinions and their decisions may reflect that. It may even be possible to figure out their decisions before cases reach them simply on the basis of their politics. There is nothing illegal about this, but it is unfortunate when all the members of any court or decision making body, including the President's Cabinet, have very similar political beliefs, no matter which party they belong to, because it does not encourage critical thinking on the issues before them.

Do you have a hard time explaining to your friends why you want the latest video game? You probably don't need to, because they want it too. How about your parents and grandparents? They probably don't play many video games, so all the games may look alike to them. Explaining how New Super Mario Bros is different from Super Paper Mario (and, of course, why you need *both*) to your parents will require you to think about it a lot more critically than explaining it to a friend who also wants both.

It's the same idea with the courts. If everyone on a court believes that a thing should be allowed or forbidden, they probably won't talk about it much and will give an opinion quickly. If they have different views, then they will be forced to spend more time thinking about it and trying to convince the other judges. In doing this, they may either better understand the reasons for their original conclusion or they may reach a different conclusion. Sometimes two things look similar on the surface, like Super Mario Galaxy and Super Mario Galaxy 2, but are different enough in the details to lead to a different conclusion *if you stop and really think about them* and do not assume that you already know the answer.

The other officers of the national courts are the Attorney-General (appointed by the President and a member of every President's Cabinet), the District Attorneys, the Marshalls, and the Clerks, each of whom has their own particular duties to perform.

Section 2

The judicial Power shall extend to all Cases, in Law and Equity, arising under this Constitution, the Laws of the United States, and Treaties made, or which shall be made, under their Authority;--to all Cases affecting Ambassadors, other public Ministers and Consuls;--to all Cases of admiralty and maritime Jurisdic-

tion;--to Controversies to which the United States shall be a Party;--to Controversies between two or more States;-- between a State and Citizens of another State,--between Citizens of different States,--between Citizens of the same State claiming Lands under Grants of different States, and between a State, or the Citizens thereof, and foreign States, Citizens or Subjects.

This clause gives the United States Courts (that is, federal courts) jurisdiction, or authority, in the nine listed subjects.

Imagine that State A decides to coin money and put it into circulation. When they offer it to pay State B for goods or services, State B refuses to take it but State A won't pay with any other money. This case can easily be brought before a Federal Court because it is clearly unconstitutional for a state to coin their own money, so it has no value. Constitutional issues go to the Federal Courts.

If a US citizen visits another country and smuggles goods, this would also be tried under the Federal Courts. Imagine we have a treaty with Fredonia to prevent exporting weapons to Badlandia. If the smuggled goods were weapons for Badlandia, this case would have arisen under a treaty, not just our laws, but the trial would still be in the US under US laws.

If the United States is at war and captures a ship at sea that it believed at the time of capture belonged to the enemy, but the enemy claims doesn't belong to them, a US court will decide the question under the Admiralty section of this clause. If a railroad or other country buys United States land but doesn't pay for it, the federal government can bring a suit and force payment to protect their rights. Questions of states boundaries, such as a long-standing dispute between Virginia and Maryland regarding the Potomac River, may also be settled in Federal Court.

In all Cases affecting Ambassadors, other public Ministers and Consuls, and those in which a State shall be Party, the supreme Court shall have original Jurisdiction. In all the other Cases before mentioned, the supreme Court shall have appellate Juris-

diction, both as to Law and Fact, with such Exceptions, and under such Regulations as the Congress shall make.

The Ambassador and other members of diplomatic missions stationed in the US are not subject to our laws, just as our diplomats are not subject to the laws of other countries when they are stationed there. Instead, they remain subject to the laws of their own country. The fact that they are not technically "under the jurisdiction" of the US government is the reason their children are not US citizens even if they are born here.

Members of the Foreign Service (diplomats) are normally only stationed in a country for a few years before they move to another country or back to their homeland. Because they move often and laws differ widely among countries, Ambassadors and other Foreign Service members are not expected to remember the laws of their host country. They have something called Diplomatic Immunity. Even though there are some laws, such as murder, that all countries have, Diplomatic Immunity means they are not subject to the laws of their host nation and cannot be tried in a court of law there, except under specific circumstances both governments agree to. Any case related to a diplomat and their actions is tried before the Federal Courts.

"Original jurisdiction" means the case starts, or originates, with the Supreme Court. "Appellate jurisdiction" means the decision of a lower court is taken to them on appeal. Very few cases originate in the Supreme Court and most of these have to do with the general government, such as a disputed Presidential Election.

The Supreme Court's primary purpose is to review cases from lower courts. Once the Supreme Court has ruled, there are no further appeals because there is no higher court in our country. Of course, Congress may over-ride a Supreme Court decision with a Constitutional Amendment, as they did when the 15th Amendment was passed to over-ride the *Dred Scott* decision, but that is extraordinarily rare.

The Trial of all Crimes, except in Cases of Impeachment, shall be by Jury; and such Trial shall be held in the State where the

said Crimes shall have been committed; but when not committed within any State, the Trial shall be at such Place or Places as the Congress may by Law have directed.

No one can be convicted of a crime unless all the jurors agree he is guilty. The verdict must be unanimous, either guilty or not guilty, or it's called a "hung jury" because they have gotten stuck and are unable to reach a unanimous decision. It is similar to when you get "hung up" at work or school—you are stuck and unable to move on with your day. They are stuck and unable to move on to a decision.

If a unanimous verdict cannot be reached, there is a new trial in the same state. If a trial could be held anywhere, then a more powerful, wealthier, or better connected person could make sure it was somewhere that the opposition's witnesses couldn't get to for the trial or where prospective jurors would be biased in their favor, although there are protections against this as well.

There are some places, such as air space and certain waterways, that are clearly part of the US but that are not clearly part of a specific state. If a crime is committed in one of these places, then Congress may decide where the trial shall be. In the early days of our nation, there were also territories and much larger areas that were claimed by two or more states and so were not clearly within any specific state.

CHAPTER 11

RESOURCES

1. System Administrators
www.webopedia.com/TERM/S/system_administrator.html

2. Civil Rights Act of 1875
chnm.gmu.edu/courses/122/recon/civilrightsact.html

3. Dred Scott v. Sandford
www.loc.gov/rr/program/bib/ourdocs/DredScott.html

4. Civil Rights Cases
www.4lawschool.com/conlaw/crc.shtml

5. Separate but Equal: Plessy v. Ferguson
landmarkcases.org/en/landmark/cases/plessy_v_ferguson
www.ourdocuments.gov/doc.php?flash=true&doc=52

6. Packing the Supreme Court
www.authentichistory.com/1930-1939/2-fdr/5-courtpacking/index.html

7. Forcing old Supreme Court justices to retire
xroads.virginia.edu/~MA02/volpe/newdeal/court.html

8. Term Limits
www.termlimits.org/the-founders-and-term-limits-jefferson/

CHAPTER 12
MISCELLANEOUS PROVISIONS

SECTION 3

Treason against the United States, shall consist only in levying War against them, or in adhering to their Enemies, giving them Aid and Comfort. No Person shall be convicted of Treason unless on the Testimony of two Witnesses to the same overt Act, or on Confession in open Court.

Throughout history, people have been tortured until they confessed to treason (whether they were guilty or not), and then tortured some more. This section was designed to prevent that from happening here. The most famous traitor in American history, General Benedict Arnold, was still a fresh memory for the Founders.[1] Before he became a turncoat, he was one of our most famous Revolutionary War heroes, well-known to all the Founders, and false statements against him was part of what led him to commit treason.

After winning the critical Battle of Lexington, General Arnold was held in such high regard by the people he was considered equal to General Washington. Unfortunately, some of his fellow officers falsely accused Arnold of wrong-doing and their political allies supported them. These were the start of a campaign by his enemies designed to keep him from getting promoted in the Army. They did not want him to have more rank or responsibility and he was skipped over for a promotion shortly after this.

That was part of a series of coordinated petty little actions that made him feel unvalued. This led to his eventual decision to commit treason by handing over the critical defensive fort at West Point (the future site of the US Military Academy) and join the British Redcoats, despite having served the Colonial Army with great honor before that. It was very difficult for people of that time to believe he had turned traitor. He was valued by many people, but he couldn't see it because they were not the ones he interacted with the most. Of course, today he is only remembered for being a turncoat.

What do you think of this? Do you think it is fair to ignore Arnold's contributions as a Patriot and only discuss his treason? Do you think it would be right to do the opposite and discuss his history as a Patriot and ignore his treason?

Life and history are complicated. There are many reasons for things happening. They cannot all be contained in any one conversation, book, newspaper, or article, which is why his life is often simplified to his treason. What lessons do you think we could learn from what happened to Benedict Arnold both during his lifetime and in historical portrayals of him?

The Congress shall have Power to declare the Punishment of Treason, but no Attainder of Treason shall work Corruption of Blood, or Forfeiture except during the Life of the Person attainted.

"Corruption of Blood" disinherits a person's children and other descendants, which means they cannot inherit anything from the traitor. Citizen B is convicted of treason. Their father, Citizen A, is wealthy. After B is executed for treason, A dies. Citizens C and D are B's children. Corruption of Blood would prevent them from inheriting their grandfather's possessions, even though they did nothing wrong and probably knew nothing of their parent's treasonous actions. This is hardly fair, and it is definitely not the American way.

With an Aristocracy, Corruption of Blood was a way to remove noble families who were plotting against the throne in an attempt to become the monarch themselves. For much of history, nobles were expected to keep their own small, and sometimes not so small, armies to protect their lands. The King would call them all up to protect the kingdom, if needed, much as our government may call the National Guard to help the Active Duty Armed Services in an emergency.

Many royal lines started out with nobles who rebelled against their king and became the new King. Other times, rebellious nobles were killed but their children inherited their title and continued the rebellion. Thus, "Corruption of Blood" protected kings like King George III. We don't have kings here, so we don't need this type of law.

ARTICLE IV

SECTION 1

Full Faith and Credit shall be given in each State to the public Acts, Records, and judicial Proceedings of every other State. And the Congress may by general Laws prescribe the Manner in which such Acts, Records and Proceedings shall be proved, and the Effect thereof.

Each state must believe that all the other states are acting properly and legally. This helps prevent people from bringing the same lawsuit in multiple states. It also means that states must share information with each other, and shows that all states are equal within the Union.

SECTION 2

The Citizens of each State shall be entitled to all Privileges and Immunities of Citizens in the several States.

We are citizens of the United States of America, not an individual state, and have the same rights and privileges in every state.

CHAPTER 12

<u>A Person charged in any State with Treason, Felony, or other Crime, who shall flee from Justice, and be found in another State, shall on Demand of the executive Authority of the State from which he fled, be delivered up, to be removed to the State having Jurisdiction of the Crime.</u>

This clause prevents people from committing a crime in one state and fleeing to another state, where they would be free. If they flee to another country, they can be sent back here if we have an extradition treaty with that country.[2] An extradition treaty is when one country agrees to send convicted or suspected criminals back to the country they originally came from upon request.

We do not have extradition treaties with every country, so criminals can flee to a country where we do not have an extradition treaty. They will still be arrested if they are caught coming back to this country or to another country we do have an extradition treaty with. This clause means that an extradition treaty is not necessary if a criminal goes from one state to another.

<u>No Person held to Service or Labor in one State, under the Laws thereof, escaping into another, shall, in Consequence of any Law or Regulation therein, be discharged from such Service or Labor, but shall be delivered up on Claim of the Party to whom such Service or Labor may be due.</u>

While slavery comes to mind first for a modern person reading this clause, it does not specifically say slavery and so also applies to all people "held to service or labor," such as indentured servants and apprentices. This clause is now irrelevant because indentured servitude, apprenticeships, and slavery are relics of the past, but it meant that an escaped slave, indentured servant, or apprentice would be sent back to their master if they were caught, no matter what state they were in.

Do you remember from the section on the Founders that Ben Franklin was a fugitive for a time because he ran away while he was an apprentice? That is in part what this was referring to. Escaping or running away was *not* the same as earning, buying, or being given freedom from a contract or from slavery, which is why Ben was considered a criminal when he ran away and would have been returned to his master. And yes, an apprentice would have called the master craftsman who was teaching him a trade his "master."

SECTION 3

New States may be admitted by the Congress into this Union; but no new State shall be formed or erected within the Jurisdiction of any other State; nor any State be formed by the Junction of two or more States, or Parts of States, without the Consent of the Legislatures of the States concerned as well as of the Congress.

The Congress shall have Power to dispose of and make all needful Rules and Regulations respecting the Territory or other Property belonging to the United States; and nothing in this Constitution shall be so construed as to Prejudice any Claims of the United States, or of any particular State.

When the country first formed, firm boundaries were drawn for states that didn't already have them. Many states had boundary disputes because the generally vague colonial boundaries were drawn up by different countries, at different times, with different goals, and with little attention to the actual geography.

When many of the colonies were first chartered, Europeans did not know what the Atlantic Coast of North American looked like or how far away the Pacific Ocean was. It was a very long time before they realized you had to go the whole way around the southern end of South America to get from one to the other. In short, they had no idea at all what the continent's geography was truly like but still attempted to give the colonies geographical boundaries.

As a result, these Colonial borders were based on guesswork, some scouting expeditions and colonist's exploration, and probably some Native American knowledge. Mostly, though, the countries the colonists came from wanted to get as much land and natural resources in

North America as they could, so they worded colonial charters vaguely (e.g., "from sea to sea"). This theoretically kept other countries from claiming that land, although in reality Spain claimed everything west of the Mississippi River.

By our Revolution, many, but not all, boundaries were fairly well established for the original thirteen colonies. Most of these were natural boundaries such as rivers, the Great Lakes, and the ocean. Almost all of them looked very much like they do today.

A natural boundary is one that nature provides, such as an ocean or a lake. A political boundary is decided by governments and the politicians within them.

One exception to this was Massachusetts, which included all the territory of what we know as Maine. In 1820, Maine was carved out of Massachusetts as part of the Missouri Compromise, but the northern (Canadian) boundary had never been agreed upon in that area.[3] The new state of Maine did not like the proposed new boundary that the US and Canadian governments agreed upon so the treaty could not be ratified because states have to agree when their boundaries are changed or established. The boundary was finally set in 1842.

Other states had charters that said their western boundary was the edge of the continent, although in practice they were considered no farther west than the Mississippi. Smaller states like Delaware wanted clearly set boundaries for these states. They were afraid that if the size of these states wasn't reduced with clear boundaries, then those few states would eventually dominate the government. After the Revolution, the new western edge of these states was generally placed in the Appalachian Mountains. The remaining land to the west was given to the federal government to hold and develop into new territories, which in turn became new states.

This section also kept the federal government from carving up states to suit itself or other states. On four occasions, states have been formed from part of another state, with Congressional approval. In 1792, portions of Virginia became the new state of Kentucky.[4] In

1796, Tennessee was made from part of North Carolina.[5] In 1820, as part of the Missouri Compromise, Maine separated from Massachusetts. Under the Missouri Compromise, Maine was admitted to the Union as a free state and Missouri was admitted as a slave state so the balance of slave versus free states was maintained, and slavery was outlawed north of the 36° 30° latitude line in the rest of the Louisiana Purchase. Finally, in 1863, the western parts of Virginia did not want to be part of the Confederate States and chose to form their own new state (West Virginia), which Virginia did not agree to until after the end of the Civil War.[6] Virginia is the only state that has been split into three states–Virginia, Kentucky, and West Virginia.

We have also had states join that were independent sovereign countries before they joined the United States. Vermont became the 14th State in 1791, but had been its own nation since 1777.[7] New York also claimed this land, so it could not join the United States as its own state until this territorial dispute was resolved. Because of this, it can also be considered a fifth instance of one state formed from parts of another. This dispute was an important reason for including this provision in the Constitution. In 1845, Texas also entered the United States having been a sovereign nation after it left Mexico in 1836.[8] Hawaii was a sovereign kingdom before becoming a US territory in 1900 and a state in 1959.[9]

The United States has never been an Empire that regularly goes out in search of new territories to conquer, but it has still acquired them. Manifest Destiny was a nineteenth century belief that the United States was destined to expand from the Atlantic to the Pacific in North America, so we have searched out new lands in that sense.[10] However, we do not regularly go in search of new territories to conquer to add to our country, and we have *always* had a path for territories/colonies to follow to become fully part of our nation.

In fact, we have willingly given areas that we controlled, such as the Philippines, their independence.[11] In the case of the Panama Canal Zone, we controlled one specific part of another country but later returned control.[12]

Other than the states discussed above, most states started out as territories. A few territories, most notably Puerto Rico, have chosen to remain that way and not become states.[13] Guam,[14] Northern Marianas Islands,[15] and the U.S. Virgin Islands[16] are also currently American territories.

Under President Jefferson, we completed the Louisiana Purchase, in which we purchased France's claim to a large area of North America.[17] This effectively doubled the size of the country overnight and, more importantly at the time, guaranteed US access to the Mississippi River through the Port of New Orleans, even more vital for trade and shipping at that time than it is today. As mentioned before, it was considered a potentially unconstitutional act even by President Jefferson, the President whose administration concluded the deal.

The purchase was completed because it was considered so vital to national security. Territorial boundaries had to be set for this large territory and every other new territorial acquisition we have had. This was easier for some, such as Seward's Folly, than for others.[18] All of the sparsely populated, isolated territory of Seward's Folly simply became Alaska.

SECTION 4

The United States shall guarantee to every State in this Union a Republican Form of Government, and shall protect each of them against Invasion; and on Application of the Legislature, or of the Executive (when the Legislature cannot be convened), against domestic Violence.

This principal that the federal government will protect each and every state is the reason they help the states when there is a natural disaster or if there was an uprising—if the state **asks**. If a state does not **request** *assistance*, the federal government cannot legally do anything. Areas are declared disaster zones to speed up access to federal aid.

If the federal government could simply come in with troops, supplies, and whatever else it wanted anytime it felt that an area was unsafe or needed help, any part of our country could technically end up under martial law (military control) at any time for little or no reason. Clearly, that is something the Founding Fathers would have opposed, and equally clearly that is not something Americans want today.

> In 2005, Hurricane Katrina hit the city of New Orleans and the state of Louisiana. The federal government did not arrive with aid for several days. Why do you think this was? What do you think they were waiting for, or were they just slow? Who is responsible for aiding and requesting aid for an area that is hit by a natural disaster? Do you think this system makes sense? Why do you think it was set up this way? What, if anything, do you think should be changed about it?

This clause also assures that the states will have a Republican government, not a dictatorship or anything except a Republic.

ARTICLE V

The Congress, whenever two thirds of both Houses shall deem it necessary, shall propose Amendments to this Constitution, or, on the Application of the Legislatures of two thirds of the several States, shall call a Convention for proposing Amendments, which, in either Case, shall be valid to all Intents and Purposes, as Part of this Constitution, when ratified by the Legislatures of three fourths of the several States, or by Conventions in three fourths thereof, as the one or the other Mode of Ratification may be proposed by the Congress; Provided that no Amendment which may be made prior to the Year One thousand eight hundred and eight shall in any Manner affect the first and fourth Clauses in the Ninth Section of the first Article; and that no State, without its Consent, shall be deprived of its equal Suffrage in the Senate.

The Founding Fathers knew they were creating a new form of government and things wouldn't necessarily go the way they expected. There had been republics and democracies in the ancient past, but never one for a country as large as the original thirteen colonies.

Therefore, they added this clause as a way to correct problems by changing, or amending, the Constitution.

If an amendment is later determined to be undesirable, the only way to change it back is with a new amendment. This happened with 18th Amendment, commonly called Prohibition because it forbade or prohibited the manufacture, sale, or transport of any "intoxicating liquor"–alcohol. It was repealed by the 21st Amendment.

Beginning with the 18th Amendment in 1917, most (but not all) amendments have included a deadline of seven years for their ratification by the states, after which the process must be started again. The never-enacted Equal Rights Amendment is an example of this.

The majority of amendments, including any prior to 1917, have no deadline. For example, the Congressional Proportionment Amendment proposed as part of the original Bill of Rights is technically still open to be ratified. It is the only one of the original twelve amendments sent to the states by the first Congress that was never ratified, and it's virtually certain that it never will be because it is outdated.

Before they become part of our Constitution, amendments must be ratified by three fourths of the states, not all of them. If an amendment is already ratified when a state becomes a state, that state never needs to ratify it. The same is true for the remaining one quarter of the states once the first three quarters ratify. It simply does not make a difference at that point if they ratify or not, so they often do not.

In Article V, the Founders also specifically required that every single state, not three fourths of them, must agree before representation in the Senate can be changed from the agreed upon format of every state having the same number of Senators, no matter what size it is. This is the *only* section of our Constitution that requires unanimous consent to be amended.

They Founders provided two different ways to amend the Constitution. One begins in Congress and goes to the states for ratification. The other starts with state legislatures requesting a Constitutional Convention to amend the Constitution and ends with the state legislatures ratifying amendments (or not). Congressional involvement is limited to calling the Convention when two thirds of the states have applied for it. This is also called an "Article V Convention" or, more recently, a "Convention of States" because it is entirely driven by the states, not the federal government.

The federal government (Congress) is not involved in this second process, except to be required (not asked—required) to call the convention, and their approval is most certainly not required to pass amendments in this way. The states' approval via ratification, on the other hand, is mandatory for any amendment to the Constitution, under any circumstance.

An Article V Convention was included as a fail-safe because Founders such as Thomas Jefferson, James Monroe, James Wilson (a member of the first Supreme Court and signer of both the Constitution and the Declaration of Independence), and Samuel Adams knew that despite the best of intentions, governments have always, throughout history, been corrupted over time.

"Corrupt" has two meanings. Common usage implies bribery and other illegal, or at least unethical, activity. The other is "made inferior by errors or alterations" (like a computer file), per dictionary.com. Over time, either type of corruption makes the corrupted object stop working properly. Although they hoped for the best, the Founders also planned for the worst. They included the mechanism to have an Article V Convention so states could reign in an out-of-control federal government, if and when it became necessary.

If an Article V Convention is called, it could theoretically pass one or more amendments that entirely replace the existing Constitution (a "runaway convention", discussed more below). As long as they keep equal representation for all states in the Senate (as mentioned above), only three fourths of the states would need to ratify a proposed amendment, including one replacing the Constitution, for it to become law.

Please go back and re-read that paragraph. It states that "only" three-fourths of the states must ratify an amendment for it to become law. Now consider the red state/blue state maps on the news and around elections. Consider news reports on the partisan divide in Washington. For that matter, think about political "discussions" you see online and how often people from different parties are able to chat politely, much less agree.

Think about the last time both political parties were able to agree on anything–anything at all. Include items like "it's not hot outside" in reference to an Alaskan winter, if you think they could agree on that. When was the last time they agreed on anything that really mattered?

> *How easy do you think it is to get "only" three-fourths of the states to agree to anything? Do you think enough states would ratify an amendment radically changing the structure of our government for it to pass?*
>
> *Could one group "pack" an Article V Convention to force an outcome they want, even replacing the Constitution? How might they do that? What could be done to prevent it? How does the current highly partisan nature of politics affect your opinion? Do you think many states would ratify any radical amendments?*
>
> *If you focus on what happened in 1787 instead of current events, does it change how you feel? How is the current situation the same or different? How would that impact the outcome of any attempt to have an Article V Convention?*

If we ever do have an Article V Convention, it could result in literally no changes *at all* if three quarters of the states can't agree to pass any amendments.

> *What kinds of amendments do you think could pass? Popular proposals (among citizens) include term limits for Congress and requiring a balanced federal budget. Why do you think these proposals are popular with citizens but not Congress? (Congress could have passed an amendment years ago, but they haven't.)*

MISCELLANEOUS PROVISIONS

An Article V Convention has never been held and no one really knows how it would proceed if it ever is. Do all the requesting states have to submit identical requests? Perhaps, or perhaps not, but it would certainly make it impossible for Congress to not call one if they do. Can a state rescind the request once it's made? Some states have tried, but the legality is questioned. Can they restrict it to a single purpose, such as a balanced budget amendment or term limits? No one really knows the answers to these questions.

The biggest concern most people have with this possibility is a "runaway convention" that entirely replaces the Constitution with something new, as the original Constitutional Convention replaced the Articles in 1787. What those arguments fail to take into account is one simple fact: the Articles hadn't really established much of anything, which is why they were so easily swept aside. They didn't even have a standard currency, and the state governments had a lot of variety, including in state religions.

Today, the Constitution is the tiny tip of a Mt. Everest-sized iceberg of bureaucracy, government, habit, culture, and more. The physical structure of our government alone makes it impossible to simply sweep it aside. The habits of all the people in the nation make it impossible to simply sweep it aside. And perhaps most importantly, there are 50 states under it with governments modeled on it that will not be changing their Constitutions.

On top of all that, everyone in our government–including elected officials and the military–has taken an oath to the Constitution. While an Article V Convention could create legally binding changes to that, the simple truth is that an attempt to toss out the Constitution in favor of an entirely new form of government might result in the governmental equivalent of a mutiny. Even more likely, the Supreme Court could immediately throw it out as invalid before it ever had a chance to be enforced at all.

Do you think an Article V Convention is a good idea or not? Why? What are the benefits and risks? Do potential benefits out weigh potential risks? If you knew your state legislators were voting on an Article V Convention, what would you tell them to do and why?

Are there any amendments you or people you know would like to see passed? Do you think Congress would pass them or would they need to start with the states?

The following series of quotes gives you an idea of just how concerned the Founders were that our government might be corrupted, and just how wide-spread and long-lasting this concern was among them. It is clear from reading them that they did not fear one specific thing but rather knew that the danger could come in many different guises, most of them seemingly innocuous until it was too late. This worry was included in public speeches as well as private letters, which shows it was either shared by regular citizens or they wanted them to guard against it.

"If ever the Time should come, when vain & aspiring Men shall possess the highest Seats in Government, our Country will stand in Need of its experienced Patriots to prevent its Ruin."

Samuel Adams, letter to James Warren, October 24, 1780.

"We have more to apprehend from the union of these branches than from the subversion of any; and this union will destroy the rights of the people. There is nothing to prevent this coalition; but the contest which will probably subsist between the general government and the individual governments will tend to produce it. There is a division of sovereignty between the national and state governments."

James Monroe, Virginia Ratifying Convention speech, June 10, 1788.

"Allow me to direct your attention, in a very particular manner, to a momentous part, which by this Constitution, every citizen will frequently be called to act. All those in place of power and trust will be elected either immediately by the people, or in such a manner that their appointment will depend ultimately on such immediate election. All the derivative movements of government must spring from the original movement of the people at large."

James Wilson, 4th of July Speech in Pennsylvania, 1788.

"The germ of dissolution of our federal government is in the constitution of the federal judiciary; an irresponsible body, working like gravity by night and by day, gaining a little to-day and a little to-morrow, and advancing its noiseless step like a thief, over the field of jurisdiction, until all shall be usurped from the States, and the government of all be consolidated into one."

Thomas Jefferson, letter to Charles Hammond, 1821.

ARTICLE VI

All Debts contracted and Engagements entered into, before the Adoption of this Constitution, shall be as valid against the United States under this Constitution, as under the Confederation.

The Founding Fathers could have said that any debts, or money owed, that were from the time of the Articles of Confederation were the fault of the old government and not their responsibility. If they had done this and refused to pay our debts, it would have been hugely unfair to those who had lent us money to help us become independent. It would also have made it very unlikely that anyone else would lend us money again anytime soon. We were far too small, weak, and poor to survive without outside assistance. Most of the debts were incurred buying supplies for the Continental Army, including food, clothing, weapons, ammunition, tents, medical supplies, horses, wagons, and all the other things an army needs.

Did they do the right thing? What would you have done in their place? Do you think this was easy for them or popular with the people?

This Constitution, and the Laws of the United States which

shall be made in Pursuance thereof; and all Treaties made, or which shall be made, under the Authority of the United States, shall be the supreme Law of the Land; and the Judges in every State shall be bound thereby, any Thing in the Constitution or Laws of any State to the Contrary notwithstanding.

If the federal government says that an action is either legal or illegal, no state government can pass a law that says otherwise. If they do, that law is null and void, which means it is like it never existed. State governments are also forbidden from saying something in their state Constitution that runs contrary to federal laws. Federal treaties are binding on states whether they like them or not. Federal law is supreme over state law. This is why Constitutional Amendments and federal law were able to end slavery and segregation in the Southern states, whether those states liked it or not.

Can you think of anything the federal government regulates that you think should be left to the states? Is there anything the federal government leaves to the states that you think it should regulate?

The Senators and Representatives before mentioned, and the Members of the several State Legislatures, and all executive and judicial Officers, both of the United States and of the several States, shall be bound by Oath or Affirmation, to support this Constitution; but no religious Test shall ever be required as a Qualification to any Office or public Trust under the United States.

This is related to the 1st Amendment because it deals with religious freedom. Other countries prohibit people from serving in their government if they are not part of a specific religious group. It is also important that they are bound to serve the *Constitution,* full stop. They are not bound to serve the President, or any branch or department of the government, but rather to our founding document and its ideals.

Similarly, members of our Armed Services (the military) take an oath to protect and serve the *Constitution.* Their oath is not to a politician, a political office, a political party, or anything except the Constitution. If you look at the text of the Oaths of Office in Appendix III, you will see that they are all to the Constitution and our country. They are not to a particular person, office, or political party.

ARTICLE VII

The Ratification of the Conventions of nine States, shall be sufficient for the Establishment of this Constitution between the States so ratifying the Same.

The Constitution was adopted when nine states ratified it. They did not wait for all thirteen colonies to sign it. The actual governing document for the country at the time, the Articles of Confederation, required unanimous decisions, so this was a bold move. It was a good one, though, because one of the biggest flaws with the Articles was the requirement for unanimity. The Founders were determined to keep that from continuing to plague our government.

As noted above, few of the Amendments passed after the Bill of Rights have been ratified by all the states, so this was a very wise choice. Even if they had all chosen to ratify any or all of them, it still would have taken much longer. This path also led to the first class of Senators having 18 members, not 26, since not all of the new states had ratified the Constitution yet. This permitted them to start the new government much more quickly.

Without this provision, we would have had a government everyone knew was going to be replaced at any time, a lame duck government, for months or even years. The members of the government would not have had any reason to work hard or carefully, and other governments would not have been comfortable making agreements with a government they knew would soon be gone. All in all, this would have been a very dangerous position for any government to be in, and so much worse for a weak young government with few friends.

The Word, "the," being interlined between the seventh and eighth Lines of the first Page, the Word "Thirty" being partly

CHAPTER 12

written on an Erasure in the fifteenth Line of the first Page, The Words "is tried" being interlined between the thirty second and thirty third Lines of the first Page and the Word "the" being interlined between the forty third and forty fourth Lines of the second Page.

Attest William Jackson Secretary

done in Convention by the Unanimous Consent of the States present the Seventeenth Day of September in the Year of our Lord one thousand seven hundred and Eighty seven and of the Independence of the United States of America the Twelfth In witness whereof We have hereunto subscribed our Names.

Signatories and our Capital.

Washington, D.C. is the capital of the United States of America, but it hasn't always been. Philadelphia was our first capital starting during the Revolution, and on and off until the capital moved to Washington in 1800, at which time it was called Washington City.

Other cities that have briefly served as the capital are Baltimore, Maryland; Lancaster, Pennsylvania; York, Pennsylvania; Princeton, New Jersey; Annapolis, Maryland; Trenton, New Jersey; and New York City, New York. It returned to Philadelphia in between all of these up to Princeton. It went from Princeton to Annapolis to Trenton to New York City without returning to Philadelphia. Therefore, the Declaration of Independence and Constitution were written and signed in Philadelphia, but the Bill of Rights was written and signed in New York City.

The final and interim locations of our capital were partially determined by practical concerns such as travel time, and partially by political concerns including slave states versus free states and industrial states versus agricultural. A complete list of Constitutional Signatories is included in Appendix II.

S MIS

CELLANEOUS PROVISIONS

RESOURCES

1. General Benedict Arnold
www.usnews.com/news/national/articles/2008/06/27/benedict-arnold-a-traitor-but-once-a-patriot

2. Crimes and Criminal Procedure: Extradition
www.state.gov/documents/organization/71600.pdf

3. Maine and the Missouri Compromise
www.massmoments.org/moment.cfm?mid=81
www.loc.gov/rr/program/bib/ourdocs/Missouri.html

4. Kentucky (becoming a state)
www.history.com/topics/us-states/kentucky

5. Tennessee (becoming a state)
www.tnhistoryforkids.org/places/state_of_franklin

6. West Virginia (becoming a state)
www.wvencyclopedia.org/articles/2034

7. Vermont (becoming a state)
vermonthistory.org/explorer/vermont-stories/becoming-a-state/the-14th-state
www.sec.state.vt.us/kids/history.html

8. Texas (becoming a state)
www.tsl.texas.gov/treasures/republic/index.html

9. Hawaii (becoming a state)
www.nytimes.com/2012/03/11/books/review/lost-kingdom-a-history-of-hawaii.html?_r=0

10. Manifest Destiny
www.ushistory.org/us/29.asp

11. Philippine Independence
www.history.com/this-day-in-history/philippine-independence-declared

12. Return of the Panama Canal Zone
history1900s.about.com/od/1910s/fl/The-Panama-Canal.htm

CHAPTER 12

13. Puerto Rico
welcome.topuertorico.org/history6.shtml

14. Guam
guam-online.com/wp1/guam-history/us-territory/

15. Northern Marianas Islands
www.abc.net.au/ra/pacific/places/country/northern_marianas.htm

16. US Virgin Islands
www.vinow.com/general_usvi/history/

17. Louisiana Purchase
www.loc.gov/rr/program/bib/ourdocs/Louisiana.html

18. Seward's Folly
www.loc.gov/rr/news/topics/folly.html

CHAPTER 13
THE PREAMBLE TO THE BILL OF RIGHTS

Congress of the United States begun and held at the City of New-York, on Wednesday the fourth of March, one thousand seven hundred and eighty nine.

THE Conventions of a number of the States, having at the time of their adopting the Constitution, expressed a desire, in order to prevent misconstruction or abuse of its powers, that further declaratory and restrictive clauses should be added: And as extending the ground of public confidence in the Government, will best ensure the beneficent ends of its institution.

The colonists had already experienced a lot of persecution and undeserved punishments both here and, for immigrants, in their home countries. Because of this, many states already had a Bill of Rights included with their state Constitution. It is not surprising, then, that the Constitution could not be ratified until the Founders agreed that a Bill of Rights protecting individual freedoms and rights would be added during the very first Congress.[1] It was relatively easy to deliver on this promise since there were so few members of the first Congress. (Fewer members meant fewer opinions and fewer arguments about what to include and how to phrase things.) The Bill of Rights secured certain rights beyond the possibility of being encroached upon by Congress and the government, since federal law over-rules state law, per the US Constitution.

RESOLVED by the Senate and House of Representatives of the United States of America, in Congress assembled, two thirds of both Houses concurring, that the following Articles be proposed to the Legislatures of the several States, as amendments to the Constitution of the United States, all, or any of which Articles, when ratified by three fourths of the said Legislatures, to be valid to all intents and purposes, as part of the said Constitution; viz.

ARTICLES in addition to, and Amendment of the Constitution of the United States of America, proposed by Congress, and ratified by the Legislatures of the several States, pursuant to the fifth Article of the original Constitution.

No document in the world furnishes greater security for personal liberty than the Unites States Constitution and its Amendments. Things that are forbidden in them have often been done in other countries, and still are even today. When our Constitution was written, the countries the colonists came violated their liberty in many ways. Our forefathers, knowing that human nature is the same in all ages, were determined that they should not lawfully take place in our country.

The rights they gave us are not, however, absolute. You have freedom of speech, but you may not use it to harass or endanger others. You have the right to bear arms, but building and business owners may choose not serve you if you do and certain weapons are restricted to the Armed Services and/or police. We have freedom of the press, but not if it endangers national security. You have the right to own property of all kinds, not just real estate. Those can also be enforced and protected, or limited, by laws and contracts.

Can you think of any other checks on the absolute use of these rights? Are they justified or not? Should any (or all) of our rights be absolute? Why? Should any rights be more limited than they are? What and why? What weapons does it make sense to restrict to the Armed Services/Law Enforcement Officers? Pepper Spray? Tanks? Nuclear bombs? Tear Gas? Revolvers? All weapons? No restrictions?

Some of the Amendments in the Bill of Rights are designed to prevent dictators and despots, people who control everything about a country and its citizens, from taking control because the first citizens our country had just had a Revolution to escape the dictatorial King George.[2] They knew first-hand how dangerous dictators could be and how rare and precious liberty and freedom truly are. Many immigrants to our country even today are escaping similar situations. For more than a few, the ability to simply walk around the block without fear or turn on a tap and have safe, clean drinking water is an amazing freedom.

During the meetings of the committee that framed the Constitution, Benjamin Franklin proposed praying one day.[3] He said, "I have lived a long time, and the longer I live, the more convincing proofs I see of this truth, that God governs in the affairs of men. And if a sparrow cannot fall without His notice, is it probable that an empire can rise without his aid?"

Do you think that Franklin was right, and that God aided the Founders in writing our Constitution, even the parts about not having a state religion? How do you think his saying this would be viewed today?

The first ten Amendments and the 27th Amendment were all written at almost the same time as the Constitution itself. (The 27th was proposed in 1789 but not ratified by enough states until 1992.) The 11th and 12th Amendments were written less than fifteen years after the Constitution was ratified. In the following two hundred plus years, there have been a mere fourteen additional changes to this Constitution. Prohibition and its Repeal cancel each other out, leaving only twelve changes in all this time. Of these, three were related to the

Civil War and abolishing slavery, which some of the Founding Fathers wanted to do when the nation was founded but were unable to accomplish, like the 27th Amendment, leaving nine changes. In 1947, the 22nd Amendment made George Washington's policy of voluntary Presidential term limits official. Again, not a real change from what the Founders wanted, leaving **eight changes in over two hundred years**.

The remaining changes include three extending voting rights to more citizens (the 19th, 24th, and 26th), two related to the newly created office of the President and its line of succession (the 20th and 25th); one related to the new concept of an independent Capital City (the 23rd); and two changes (the 16th and 17th) that went against what the Founders wanted by instituting the income tax and having direct elections for Senators instead of state legislatures selecting them.

For a new form of government to be created, unlike any other in use on earth, and to be so well written that after two hundred years it has required so few real changes, is amazing.

RESOURCES

1. The Bill of Rights: It's History and Significance
law2.umkc.edu/faculty/projects/ftrials/conlaw/billofrightsintro.html

2. Dictators and Despots
www.infoplease.com/spot/topdespots1.html
parade.com/110573/davidwallechinsky/the-worlds-10-worst-dictators/

3. Benjamin Franklin's Constitutional Convention Address on Prayer
www.americanrhetoric.com/speeches/benfranklin.htm

CHAPTER 14
THE BILL OF RIGHTS:
AMENDMENT I

AMENDMENT I (DISCUSSION PART 1)

Congress shall make no law respecting an establishment of religion, or prohibiting the free exercise thereof; or abridging the freedom of speech, or of the press; or the right of the people peaceably to assemble, and to petition the Government for a redress of grievances.

Please re-read this Amendment carefully. The portion up to the first semi-colon is called the Establishment Clause. The words "separation of church and state" do not appear here, or anywhere else in the Constitution, or in any of its Amendments, or in any of the *Congressional Records* of the Constitutional debates. These words come from a letter that Thomas Jefferson wrote in 1802, during his first term as President. The text of the letter said "thus building a wall of separation between Church & State."

This phrase from this letter is widely used in interpreting and discussing the 1ˢᵗ Amendment, despite the fact that Jefferson was the US Ambassador in Paris during the Constitutional Convention so he could not attend it. Also despite the fact that it was apparently written for political reasons (per an article from the Library of Congress, as noted in Appendix VII) and not to explain or justify any part of the Constitution, certainly not in the way *The Federalist* papers were.[1] The words seem to encapsulate what is meant by this amendment, but summaries always miss details and nuances.

Jefferson's letter, called the Danbury Letter (Appendix VII), was sent to a group of New England Baptists, a religious minority in Danbury, Connecticut. They were concerned with the way their state was treating them. Jefferson conferred with several New England politicians in his Cabinet while writing it and political concerns clearly seemed to influence this letter.

The Library of Congress and FBI worked together to uncover the original, unaltered draft, or preliminary, text of this letter. In his draft, Jefferson included the phrase "your religious rights shall never be infringed by any act of mine" and other text related to then-current political issues, in addition to the line commonly shortened to "separation of church and state."

The specific language "a wall of separation between church and state" specifically reflected Baptist beliefs at that time. The words may have been chosen more to make them agreeable to what the group he was writing to rather than as a literal explanation of his exact beliefs on the 1st Amendment. Or not. We cannot know how he intended it, especially since this letter was largely unnoticed for fifty years after he wrote it and wasn't widely used legally until 1947. Its application was controversial at that time.

That was nearly 150 years later. Common knowledge changed a lot in this time. For instance, at the time Jefferson wrote this letter, many people would have known that Baptists in Connecticut were a minority who worried about how their state government was treating them. They would have also known that Jefferson was unhappy that the press was portraying him as an Atheist for not declaring days of Feast and Thanksgiving as Washington and Adams had.[2] George Washington's Thanksgiving Proclamation of 1789 is worth reading.[3]

By the late 1940s, state-level politics and political mud-slinging circa 1800 were no longer exactly common knowledge. Context matters, and that is part of the context in which this letter was written.

> *Context includes the events, beliefs, and other relevant data surrounding a fact, event, or document, which are generally understood at the time it is written and not described in it.*

We know that *The Federalist* papers were written for the sole purpose of explaining the new Constitution and convincing people to support it. There is no reason to think this letter was written for a similar reason, particularly since it was written years after ratification. We can't know the exact reasons Jefferson chose to write the Danbury letter or to make the edits he made. We do know that he was not present either when the Constitution was written or when the Bill of Rights was written. (Jefferson served as Secretary of State under President Washington; he was not in Congress.) He was undoubtedly in close contact with at least some of those who were and would have known their values and beliefs in general, but he simply wasn't there for the discussions and debates.

Religion and God were included in public life when this letter was written. The Founding Fathers prayed during the Constitutional Convention, while drafting the Declaration of Independence, throughout the Continental Congress, at Valley Forge, and many, many other times. They often had religious officiants, pastors and such, come to say prayers for them.

There are definitely records of both Washington and Adams, our first two presidents and members of the Constitutional Convention, establishing days of fasting and thanksgiving for the nation to give thanks to God.[4] Jefferson objected to these on political grounds but not on 1st Amendment grounds. There are even records of Thomas Jefferson allowing religious groups to hold services, including four hour communion services, in executive office buildings of the US government.[5] That is more of the context of this letter.

While it is true that not all of the Founders were church-going Christians, we also know that many of them, including Jefferson, were De-ists. Deists believe in a god but not necessarily in a specific religion (including Christianity), which is very different from being an Atheist. An Atheist believes there is no God or other Supreme Being(s).

Relying too much on one document, particularly one written by a politician in office, to interpret this or any other clause or portion of the Constitution, no matter what their intentions, runs the risk of ig-noring the varied early history of our country and the actual experi-ences of the Founders and other early immigrants with state religions, among other things.

For example, Virginia (one of the first colonies) was founded during the (Protestant) reign of Queen Elizabeth I. She became Queen when her Roman Catholic sister Mary died. Mary was called Bloody Mary because she killed people for practicing the new Anglican (Protestant) religion founded by their father.[6] Killing people for not practicing the monarch's religion was common, and a change of monarch often led to a change of the state (required) religion. Having been a Protestant during a Catholic reign herself, Elizabeth was fairly tolerant (for her time) of Roman Catholics, but she did still punish them.[7]

Many early colonists fled their home country to escape religious per-secution. Sadly, many set up their new colonial charters so they in turn persecuted people from other religions. Many people died rather than betray their faith. Many more continued to practice in secret and in the face of great danger if they were discovered.

This was still true when the US Constitution was written. A few col-onies maintained state religions even after they adopted the US Con-stitution, which only prohibits the federal government from estab-lishing a religion, not state governments. It clearly states "Congress shall make no law respecting an establishment of religion." This was binding for the national, but not state, government.

Once again, to be clear: in the first years under the US Constitution, some states still had state religions and this was not considered a vio-lation of the 1ˢᵗ Amendment or of the US Constitution.[8] The Bill of

Rights to the US Constitution was binding for the federal government, but not the states. States had their own Constitutions and many also had their own Bill of Rights. The 14th Amendment changed this by beginning to apply the Bill of Rights and other amendments to the states as well as the federal government.

When our Founding Fathers wrote this Amendment, it is a virtual certainty that they were not thinking that putting the Ten Commandments in a Courthouse or saying a prayer at the start of public events might somehow offend someone or cause a miscarriage of justice. In fact, the Northwest Ordinance passed by the Continental Congress while the Constitutional Convention was in session includes this, "*Article the Third.* Religion, morality and knowledge, being necessary to good government and the happiness of mankind, schools and the means of education shall forever be encouraged." [9]

While the Continental Congress and Constitutional Convention were two separate bodies, this law was one of many that remained in effect under the new Constitution. If the Founders had felt this statement violated their new Bill of Rights, then they would have replaced or amended the Northwest Ordinance. They did not.

Current events, the Founders' families, and immigrants all have stories of people being killed and suffering because they refused to change their religion when their monarch did. The Founders knew, or knew of, people who were killed for saying the rosary in their own homes, for owning books the government didn't approve of, or for something similar. At least some of them undoubtedly knew about the New England Quaker (a Christian denomination) colonists who were kicked out of New England for being Quakers and not following the state religion.[10] When the Quakers returned and were caught practicing their religion a second time, they were killed. The horrors of the Salem Witch Trials weren't very long before, either.[11]

In the specific case of Founding Father John Jay, his grandfather moved to New York when the French King revoked, or took back, the Edict of Nantes in 1685 and he lost everything he owned.[12] The 1598 Edict treated Protestants like his grandfather with unusual tolerance for Europe at the time, including their civil and property rights.[13] The Revocation of the Edict stripped these rights from Protestants so that many, probably including Jay's grandfather, lost both their rights and their property.[14]

> How would you feel about a law that cost your grandparents and great-grandparents everything they had worked hard for their whole life, even the home they lived in? What if that same law took away some of their freedoms and rights as well? How hard would you work to prevent something like that from ever happening to your family and friends again? What kinds of things do you think you might do to prevent it?

The National Archives has lists of Executive Orders from our Presidents, starting with FDR; many have been amended, revoked, or superseded by a later President.[15] (All Presidents have written them, the rest simply aren't online at this time.) Since Executive Orders aren't written or passed by Congress, Congress isn't involved in revoking or changing them, either.

Similarly, the Edict of Nantes was written by the King of France and a later King simply revoked it. Europeans who did not follow the state religion were safe from persecution if, and only for as long as, their King so desired. The Founders were determined to make this safety a permanent feature of our nation, one which could not be removed by the whim of one or even a few men.

> A state religion is one where the state, or government, uses some of the taxes it collects from all its citizens to help pay the expenses of one religion, including buying land, building churches, paying clergy, and anything else the church needs.
>
> In countries with a state religion, those who are not part of it can be denied rights including the right to vote and the right to hold office. If the government is not paying a religion's expenses and does not require people to join it, then it is not a state religion.

Throughout our history, since before our Revolution, many waves of religious refugees have moved here.[16] Like Jay's grandfather, many of these refugees lost their land, their possessions, and sometimes even their freedom and loved ones for not following the state religion.[17]

In addition to believing that not having a state religion was the right choice, the cold hard fact that the US and her member states were flat broke had to have made this appealing. It was a practical as well as an ideological choice. Not paying the operating expenses for a religion saved money, and not trying to enforce one state religion across the varied state governments simplified the unification process. The Virginia Statute for Religious Freedom (Appendix VI) had shown a way forward on this topic.

The Founding Fathers could see the good that might be done when people were free to put forth new ideas and speak their minds. They saw how much better things were when people were allowed to practice whatever religion they chose. To reiterate, they didn't try to remove religion from public life. When you look at their day-to-day actions, they routinely infused God through prayer and by acknowledging God in other ways, including official days of fasting and thanksgiving.

Ignoring context in anything risks completely misunderstanding it. Did Jefferson really mean that nothing related to God should be permitted into any aspect of our government? Would he and the other Founders have thought saying "one nation under God" in the Pledge of Allegiance was a violation of this?

Based on just the words in the Danbury letter, what do you think? Considering not just this one letter, but also their other words and deeds, what do you think? Does it change things to consider more sources, including the original draft version of the Danbury letter?

Would the Founders want our country to include God the same ways they did but limited to the Protestant Christian God with whom they were most familiar? Would they want to include God, but in a different way? Would they want to remove God entirely? In our modern society, made up of far more cultures and religions than Colonial society, what do you think?

Separation of church and state is a complex issue that comes up frequently in both the news and daily life, which is why so much space is being devoted to it in this book. While separation of church and state is a good and necessary part of our government, determining when and if something crosses that line of separation can be extremely tricky, and can be highly dependent on circumstances that an observer may, or may not, know.

Imagine a teacher sitting quietly at her desk with her hands folded in her lap, eyes closed, silently praying the rosary, mostly hidden from passersby, in a planning period when she has no classes. A student enters the empty classroom and asks what she is doing. Do you think it is a violation of church and state to explain that she is praying the rosary because her mother is ill and she is praying for her to get well? For that matter, is it a violation for her to be praying or even holding the rosary on school grounds? Is it ok for her to say that she is praying because her mother is ill and she's afraid she'll go to hell because she never accepted Jesus? Does it matter if the school is Catholic, Jewish, Muslim, or public?

Should she ignore the student's question, make a remark like "you can figure it out," or lie? (How do you think each of these responses would make the student feel?) Does it make a difference if she knows that the student is Protestant, Atheist, Buddhist, or some other faith? What if the teacher is seen with a symbol of a different religion, such as a prayer rug, instead of a Catholic rosary? Does it make a difference if the student is in first grade, seventh grade, eleventh grade, or even college? How is the situation different if the conversation is during class? What do you think she can say, if anything, without violating the intention of the Founders? Is that how this clause is applied today? If not, how has it changed? Is this an improvement? Is it fair to punish her for fol-lowing her own beliefs?

Is it fair to punish her based on a third party person's interpreta-tion of events, or their reaction, if they hear about it later or as they pass in the hallway? How likely are they to hear the whole story?

What if the conversation was adults in an office lunch room? Would that make it any different? Would it matter if she did not have the rosary or another clear religious symbol in her hands?

It is easy to say there needs to be a complete separation of church and state, removing all religious references from public life, but the reality is far less clear-cut than that makes it sound. People cannot remove and ignore their faith simply because they are in a school, a courtroom, or an office any more than they could agree to change religion simply to please their monarch. Religion is an extremely per-sonal matter and it is very easy to offend someone else.

Context, including location, matters as well. Something that is ac-ceptable in your home or a break room is not necessarily accepta-ble in the classroom or an office. If a school, office, or other facility is run by or part of a specific faith, would you expect to see that in their buildings? How about symbols of another faith?

For example, would you expect a Muslim daycare to have pictures of Jesus or prayer rugs set up facing Mecca? Is it reasonable to re-quire them to have facilities for other faiths?

In 1776, the reality is that virtually everyone in the United States was either a Protestant Christian or was extremely familiar with the Protestant Christian faith. This included Deists and others who did not belong to the Christian church, and Catholics, who were a small minority in Colonial America. Even in the Christian faith, there are far more differences today than there were two hundred years ago.

Within the country as a whole, the comparative differences among the religions are staggering. In addition to Christians, Jews, and Muslims, there are Mormons (a faith that didn't exist in 1776), Buddhists, Hindus, Atheists, and a seemingly endless list of other religions.

How do you think this affects interpreting, implementing and enforcing the Establishment Clause today?

Dictators often kill anyone who is a different ethnic group or doesn't follow their preferred religion, which is another reason to prevent state religions. They will often set one ethnic group against another, even if they have lived together in harmony for centuries or the "differences" are essentially made up, as happened with the Hutus and Tutsis in Rwanda.[18] Dictators even set things up so that either they personally or their government are worshipped as if they are God.

Sometimes people with very strong faith can resist doing things they believe very strongly are wrong. This is a problem for Bad Guys. Some of the most persistent Resistance groups in Nazi Germany contained large numbers of Christians.[19] In early Communist Russia, they were Russian Orthodox (Christians).[20] In modern Tibet, they're Buddhist.[21]

Sometimes dictators forbid all religions, as Communist China and the Soviet Union both did.[22] Other times they will force everyone to follow their state religion or only permit leaders they approve of, like the monarchs our Founding Fathers were familiar with.

AMENDMENT I (DISCUSSION PART 2)

Congress shall make no law respecting an establishment of religion, or prohibiting the free exercise thereof; **or abridging the freedom of speech, or of the press; or the right of the people peaceably to assemble, and to petition the Government for a redress of grievances**.

Fleeing religious persecution was only one of the reasons people chose to come here. The Founding Fathers would also have known, or known about, people who were killed because they spoke out or wrote against abuses by their government. Even gathering together in a group was prohibited if the government thought people were unhappy with them, especially if they were bold enough to try to tell the Monarch ways to improve "their" government. Monarchs were believed to have been chosen by God and the idea that anyone else could know more than they did was not even considered a possibility, particularly if that person was a mere commoner, not a nobleman.

In 1733/1734, a New York printer named Peter Zenger printed a series of articles critical of the colonial Governor.[23] There are always at least two sides to every story, and they all usually have at least some truth to them. Part of the truth of this is that Zenger and his paper were funded by a political opponent of the Governor, and the attacks were at least partially motivated by that. As a result, the colonial government accused Zenger of seditious libel for printing articles critical of them, regardless of whether he wrote them. Libel is damaging someone else's good reputation by spreading lies or false information in a written, not spoken, form. Sedition is trying to get people to revolt against, or be very unhappy with, their government.

At the time, it didn't matter that what he printed was true. It was still illegal to print it because there was no freedom of the press. Zenger's defense lawyer appealed directly to the jury at his trial.[24] The jury returned a verdict of "not guilty" even though they were only supposed to consider whether he had actually printed those articles. His case did not change the law so that demonstrating the truth of a statement was a defense in libel cases, but it did show that Americans felt very strongly that citizens should be allowed to criticize their government. The Founders undoubtedly knew of this and similar cases, which are clearly reflected in this section on freedom of speech and the press.

Freedom of speech is not, however, absolute. Time, manner, and place are also taken into account. If you go to a Scouting event, and start shouting "fire!" when the evening bonfire starts, everyone will probably start running over to enjoy the bonfire. If you do the same thing in a crowded movie theater, people will probably panic and try to escape the building, thereby causing a lot of damage to people and property. (Justice Oliver Wendell Holmes used the theater example in *Schenk v. United States* in 1919.)[25] Freedom of Speech also does not force one person to let another person talk about anything they want to on private property. It refers to public areas.

Freedom of assembly is not absolute either. There are many times and places when you need to get a permit to have a large assembly so that you do not interfere with the activities of other citizens or become a nuisance or public safety hazard. And again, it refers to public areas, not private property.

The final item, freedom to petition the government for a redress of grievances (to fix problems) is often overlooked. And yet, it was the King's refusal to listen to colonial petitions that led to our Revolution. This is hardly an afterthought or a minor point!

Today, the White House website has an area specifically for petitions from citizen.[26] Options include create a petition and open petitions, with tabs for "Popular" and "Recent Petitions." The most popular petition today has over 150,000 signatures. While many of them are destined to fail or be ignored (remove the head of a political party from their post, end cancer), they remain a powerful way for people to send a message about what matters to them.

There are petitions to award a Medal of Freedom to a WWII vet and to pardon another person. With an upcoming election, there are quite a few about "improving" the political process. There are also petitions related to public health and safety.

Petitions are a way for even the poorest, most disenfranchised citizens to show the government what they really believe needs fixed. In the colonial era, it was taxation without representation, newly levied (higher) taxes, and trade restrictions. Today, it's voting rights, government corruption, entitlements, and the economy (including the outsourcing of jobs overseas)

.

CHAPTER 14

RESOURCES

1. *The Federalist* papers
www.foundingfathers.info/federalistpapers/

2. Jefferson's Religious Beliefs
www.monticello.org/site/research-and-collections/jeffersons-religious-beliefs

3. Washington's Thanksgiving Proclamation of 1789
www.heritage.org/initiatives/first-principles/primary-sources/washingtons-thanksgiving-proclamation

4. Adams' Proclamation of Humiliation Fasting and Prayer
www.wallbuilders.com/libissuesarticles.asp?id=44

5. Religion and the Founding of the American Republic
www.loc.gov/exhibits/religion/rel06-2.html

6. Queen "Bloody" Mary
departments.kings.edu/womens_history/marytudor.html

7. Elizabeth I and the Catholic Church
www.historylearningsite.co.uk/tudor-england/elizabeth-i-and-the-catholic-church/

8. Religion and the State Governments
www.loc.gov/exhibits/religion/rel05.html

9. The Northwest Ordinance
www.loc.gov/rr/program/bib/ourdocs/northwest.html

10. How Quakers First Came to New England
digital.library.upenn.edu/women/marshall/country/country-III-27.html

11. Timeline of the Salem Witch Trials
historyofmassachusetts.org/timeline-of-the-salem-witch-trials/

12. The Papers of John Jay
dlc.library.columbia.edu/jay

13. Edict of Nantes
www.britannica.com/event/Edict-of-Nantes

14. Revocation of the Edict of Nantes
history.hanover.edu/texts/nonantes.html

15. Presidential Records: List of Executive Orders
www.whitehouse.gov/the-press-office/presidential-records

16. Remaking of America 1678-1690
www.loc.gov/today/cyberlc/feature_wdesc.php?rec=4290

17. Refugee Admissions
www.state.gov/j/prm/ra/index.htm

18. Rwanda: How the Genocide Happened
www.bbc.com/news/world-africa-13431486

19. Opposition and Resistance in Nazi Germany
education.cambridge.org/media/653316/opposition_and_resistance_in_nazi_germany.pdf

20. Communist Russia and the Russian Orthodox Church
ir.library.oregonstate.edu/xmlui/bitstream/handle/1957/21678/Husband
WilliamHistory.SovietAtheismRussian.pdf?sequence=1
www.countrystudies.us/russia/38.htm

21. Tibetan Buddhism in Communist China
politicsandreligionjournal.com/images/pdf_files/engleski/volume6_no2/topgyal.pdf

22. The Soviet Union: Anti-Religious Campaigns
www.loc.gov/exhibits/archives/anti.html

23. Peter Zenger
law2.umkc.edu/faculty/projects/ftrials/zenger/zenger.html

24. Introduction to the Free Speech Clause
law2.umkc.edu/faculty/projects/ftrials/zenger/freespeech.htm

25. Schenk v. United States
www.americanbar.org/groups/public_education/initiatives_awards/students_in_action/schenck.html

26. Petitions to the White House
petitions.whitehouse.gov/petitions

CHAPTER 15
THE BILL OF RIGHTS:
AMENDMENTS II–V

AMENDMENT II

A well regulated Militia, being necessary to the security of a free State, the right of the people to keep and bear Arms, shall not be infringed.

T he General Court of the Massachusetts Bay Colony organized the first militia regiments in 1636.[1] From the Pequot War in 1637 through today, the Army National Guard has participated in every war or conflict fought by the US. General Washington formed the Continental Army (parent of the modern Active Duty Army) at Valley Forge from state militia volunteers.[2]

State militias have a special place dealing with local disasters, including floods, hurricanes, and tornadoes, following the orders of the state Governor. It is the state's responsibility, not the federal government's, to handle natural and other local disasters. The federal government only steps in to help *after* a state requests aid. This dual role makes the militias a special asset to the states.

Militias also guaranteed that every state had a defense force available when the active duty military force was tiny, we had hostile neighboring nations, and the federal Armed Services were days away. Trips that only take a few hours or at most days for modern Americans took days or months before planes, trains, and automobiles were invented. Communication that is immediate with today's phone system, including requests for help, also took days using written letters sent on horseback or boats.

The Founders believed strongly that a large standing army, which we now have, is *always* a threat to liberty. They understood that the military can be used to overthrow any government, and that it is also hugely expensive. They used state militias both to reduce the size of the national armed forces and to counter the threat a large national military can pose if (when) the government becomes corrupt or dishonest.

This concern is also a reason that the oath every commissioned officer takes, like politicians' oaths, is to uphold and protect the *Constitution* of the United States of America and *not* to any individual person or office, including the President or the Congress.

As Chairman Mao Zedong, leader of Communist China, philosopher of communist theory, and student of revolution, said in more recent years, "Political power grows from the muzzle of a gun." The Founders lived long before him, but they understood this idea and wanted to make sure that political power in the US remained with *the people*, so they protected our right to own and carry firearms (guns).

When the Constitution was written, the most advanced firearms used black powder. Reloading was slow and cumbersome. "Rapid fire" was anything but, compared to even the slowest weapon today.

Do you think the Founders would alter or limit "the right of people to keep and bear arms" in any way if modern weapons like automatic rifles or small easily hidden handguns had existed then? How and why?

A government must protect its people through national policy or, if that fails, through military force. Large weapons like canons, tanks, and bomber aircraft are reserved for the government in every country. The ownership of private weapons of a more manageable size varies directly with the nature of the government. The less free the government, the less likely citizens are to have weapons to defend themselves. (Re-read the Mao Zedong quote above.) Our Founders have ensured that American citizens cannot easily be disarmed.

In Russia, both Tsarist and Communist, only the rich and the military were ever really allowed to have weapons. This meant that the people couldn't fight back against the dictators (tsars, Communist Party leaders, and others) who ran their country. Dictatorships often have similar rules. When the National Socialist (Nazi) Party came to power in Germany in the 1930s, one of their first actions was to confiscate weapons from the Germans and the citizens of each country as they took over.[3] The Italian Fascists in the 1930s and Chinese Communists in the 1940s did the same.[4] When dictators come to power, they quickly confiscate people's weapons so they can't fight back.[5]

What do you think about gun control? What rules and limits do you think are reasonable and/or necessary? What do you think goes too far? What groups, if any, do you think should be prevented from buying or using firearms (guns)? What age limits, if any, do you think there should be on owning or using firearms?

Should there be different limits for different weapons? Are there any types of firearms you think should be banned from sale to private citizens? Why?

As noted above, this and all our other freedoms are not without restrictions. You cannot own tanks, nuclear bombs, or certain other weapons reserved for the military, and states can regulate firearms, including open (the weapon is visible) and concealed (the weapon is hidden by clothing, a purse, or something else) carry rules, within their boundaries. Most also have rules preventing those who are mentally ill or criminal from legally owning firearms.

What happens when a criminal, including one working for a corrupt or dishonest government, comes to a home and threatens the family? What do you think will happen if the criminal has weapons and they don't? Do you think Bad Guys prefer attacking people who are armed or unarmed?

If the homeowners are armed, and trained in proper and safe usage of those weapons, how does that change the probable outcome? (If you own a firearm or have one in your home, it is extremely important to be trained in its use and take safety precautions, including storing it safely and securely when the owner is not carrying it.)

How do you think restrictive gun laws impact criminals? How concerned are they with following the law? Do you think they would be willing to break the law and buy a gun illegally? How do you think their criminal actions impact law abiding citizens who want to buy a gun for self-defense, hunting, or other legal uses?

If you lived in an area with restrictive gun laws that kept you, as a law abiding citizen, from owning a gun, but that had a lot of gun violence from criminals, how would this make you feel? How would it make you feel about guns and gun control if people were shot and killed in your neighborhood or school? Would it make a difference to you if those guns were legally registered and owned or illegal?

Google "Kristallnacht" (a Nazi action), "Italian fascists", and "Chinese Communists." Does reading about the impact of anti-gun laws in those countries change or reinforce your opinions on gun control laws at all? Do you think it could happen here? Why?

Hunting is one reason people have firearms. Many people in the United States own rifles for hunting, some of which are very high powered. Some need to hunt to have enough food to feed their family. Others feed their family with what they hunt, even though they could afford to feed them without hunting, so they have money for other things. Still other hunters donate what they kill to feed needy families in their community. Many of the animals killed by hunters are not readily available in the grocery store. Have you ever seen venison (deer) at your grocery store?

Each state sets rules, including hunting season, weapons, and how much each hunter can kill. Hunting season is the dates it is legal to hunt for each type of prey and varies for different weapons, and it is never during mating or birthing season. Bow hunting, black powder, and rifles each have their own seasons for deer hunting, for example.

For some animals, most specifically deer, hunting is the only form of population control and states use hunting season/limits for population control. If the population gets too high, they extend the season or increase the limits. If it starts getting low, they shorten the season or decrease the limits. If people stopped hunting deer, they would quickly be overpopulated and starve to death. They also pose a safety hazard because they spread Lyme Disease and cause traffic accidents, both of which get worse as their overpopulation gets worse.

Does knowing that affect how you think of hunting and firearms? How? What makes the biggest difference in your opinion? How do you feel about the 2nd Amendment? What do you think the primary purpose is?

Why do you think the Founders felt so strongly about the right to bear arms? Do you think hunting was the only, or primary, reason for the 2nd Amendment? What experiences in their lifetimes might have made them feel so passionately about this? For what reason and for what purpose do you think they wanted to be so certain American citizens would always be able to "bear arms"?

Going back and thinking about the absolute monarchies of 17th and 18th centuries and their similarity to 20th century nations such as the Soviet Union (Communist Russia), Communist China, Fascist Italy, and Nazi Germany, what other concerns do you think they might have had?

In drafts of the Virginia Constitution, but not the final version, Thomas Jefferson wrote, "No freeman shall ever be debarred the use of arms."[6]

In Federalist #46 James Madison wrote, "Notwithstanding the military establishments in the several kingdoms of Europe, which are carried as far as the public resources will bear, the governments are afraid to trust the people with arms."[7]

Patrick Henry said, "Are we at last brought to such humiliating and debasing degradation, that we cannot be trusted with arms for our defense? Where is the difference between having our arms in possession and under our direction, and having them under the management of Congress? If our defense be the real object of having those arms, in whose hands can they be trusted with more propriety, or equal safety to us, as in our own hands?"[8]

George Washington told Congress in his first annual address to them in 1790, "A free people ought not only to be armed but disciplined; to which end, a uniform and well digested plan is requisite: and their safety and interest require that they should promote such manufactories, as tend to render them independent on others for essential, particularly for military supplies."[9]

There are many other, similar quotes from our Founding Fathers. Most are real, but some are false, such as one popular quote where Washington supposed compared firearms to liberty's teeth. There are also misquotes online—quotes that are largely but not entirely correct.

One misquote is the one above being changed to "a free people ought not only to be armed and disciplined but they should have sufficient arms and ammunition to maintain a status of independence from any who might attempt to abuse them, which would include their own government."

Where do you think the false and altered ones may come from? How do you think a false quote becomes widely accepted and oft-repeated? Do you think the internet has made it easier for that to happen, harder, or had no effect?

AMENDMENT III

No Soldier shall, in time of peace be quartered in any house, without the consent of the Owner, nor in time of war, but in a manner to be prescribed by law.

King George did not pay the rank and file soldiers enough to pay for all their own clothing, food, and housing expenses. As a result, American colonists were forced to house and feed his troops without being paid for the expense.[10] In 1774, the second Quartering Act was considered one of the Intolerable Acts, which contributed to the start of the Revolutionary War.[11]

If you were a soldier risking your life, how would you feel if the government did not pay you enough to cover your basic living expenses of food, clothing, and shelter (somewhere to live)? How would you feel if the people you were supposed to protect weren't willing to provide you with these basics while you risked your life to keep them safe? Do you think this might make soldiers a bit cranky? How else might it make them feel? Do you think they would feel inspired to do their best job?

How would you feel if the government forced you to house a bunch of soldiers in your home, without your permission and without paying you for the expense of it?

What if a bunch of soldiers came into your house, tossed you and all your stuff into the hallway, and wouldn't let you use your own room? Then they went to the kitchen and ate all your food, leaving nothing for your family, and demanded that your family clean up after them? What if they beat you for not having enough food they liked and didn't get in trouble for any of it?

Throughout history, many armies from many countries and many cultures have done, and some continue to do, these things and worse.

American soldiers don't do these things, here or anywhere in the world, because the Founding Fathers made it very clear that it's not OK for them to do. All our soldiers receive military housing or a housing allowance to ensure they are never in the position that British soldiers were during the Revolutionary War period. We were the first nation in modern history to specifically forbid, or prohibit, this and to enforce that prohibition, which is just as important. Once again, other countries have followed our example. And, once again, this still happens in some places.

AMENDMENT IV

The right of the people to be secure in their persons, houses, papers, and effects, against unreasonable searches and seizures, shall not be violated, and no Warrants shall issue, but upon probable cause, supported by Oath or affirmation, and particularly describing the place to be searched, and the persons or things to be seized.

This clearly states that there may be no *unreasonable* searches and seizures. It does not say that there may not be *any*. If there is reason to believe that you are a criminal, a traitor, or a terrorist, the government can and will search and possibly seize your property, but it must get a warrant first.

When the government gets a warrant, it clearly states the place to be searched so they can't get a warrant and then start searching all the neighbors' homes, or searching the person's office even though there was no evidence of wrong-doing at work. It also states what can be seized so that our citizens can be sure the government won't come in and just steal their property. If they get a warrant to search your computer and files because you were stealing money from work, they can take your computer as evidence, but they cannot take your wife's new diamond earrings unless they were on the warrant, and they are supposed to clearly record exactly what was taken.

Once again, the Founding Fathers did a great job in preventing abuses that were widespread in other areas from ever becoming part of our culture.

How would you feel if your friend got mad at you and told his fam-
ily that you stole his expensive new birthday present, even though
he knew he had lost it?

What if they then stormed over to your house with a police officer,
pushed past your family and ransacked your room looking for it–
without giving you any explanation or telling you what they were
looking for or why? And during the process they took your unworn
designer sneakers, a new game, and some cash–all of which are
totally unrelated to the lost gadget?

Living here, that sounds unbelievable since that family and the po-
lice officer would be in jail for violating the 4th Amendment, but it
still happens other places. It was also common in the past.

One commonly cited example of our government violating this is when Japanese Americans (including many children) were rounded up, taken from their homes and businesses, and put in internment camps during World War II.[12] Many were American citizens from the day they were born, and our government–*their own government*–took everything from them, including their civil rights, their freedom, and their dignity.

Many families lost previously successful businesses; a few had friends and neighbors who took over and cared for their businesses until they returned, but most simply lost everything they could not carry with them to the camp, and had little to no time to pack. Much smaller numbers of German and Italian immigrants were interned as well on fears that they might be sympathetic to the Axis powers we were fighting in Europe.[13] Some had lived here for decades.[14] But it wasn't on the same scale as the Japanese internment.

No matter what their citizenship status, immigrant or citizen, this was wrong. Even at the time, even those who implemented the policy may have known it was wrong. Why? This action was not taken by Congress but rather by FDR signing Executive Order 9066 in Febru-ary 1942, two months after the attack on Pearl Harbor.[15] No act of Congress and no part of our legal code sanctioned this. It was done by Executive Order, and carried out by the military.

Do you think Congress would have authorized this, if they had voted on it and had their names officially listed as voting for or against it? Do you think they were confident they were doing the right thing and that American citizens would agree that it was the right thing? Why?

Do you think the Founders would have approved of using an Executive Order or the military in this way? Do you? Congress had to know that people were being interned, including American citizens, because it was not secret at all. However, they may have chosen to ignore it since they were not directly responsible and they may even have convinced themselves that the camps were something different (and more acceptable) than they really were. Why do you think they permitted it to happen? What part do you think racism may have played?

In comparison to the treatment of Japanese, in 1939 FDR appointed naturalized citizen Felix Frankfurter to the US Supreme Court.[16] Frankfurter was born in Austria, a country that voluntarily became part of Nazi Germany.

At the same time, Asians were subject to strict immigration restrictions.[17] (Google "Chinese Exclusion Act.") These restrictions prevented many Japanese and other Asians from becoming US citizen while their children were US citizens by birth. However, they were a smaller, more recent, group of immigrants who looked "different" with a "different" culture. The Austrian's appearance and culture were closer to the "average" American appearance and culture.

Do you think this impacted how Japanese were treated versus Italians, Germans and other European immigrants? How? Why do you think the Chinese Exclusion Act remained in effect? How else do you think it affected their treatment?

Contrary to government publicity photos, internment camps were nothing like the comfortable homes and businesses the Japanese were forced to abandon, and they were not free to leave.[18] The people put in these internment camps were here legally and their loyalty was to the US. They had done nothing wrong and they had hurt no one. The government officially investigated them and found nothing suspicious, but it still interred them.[19]

> *Why do you think the government felt it necessary to do this? Do you think they wanted to believe these images themselves, rather than admit the truth of these camps, or was it strictly about appearances?*

This is very rare in our country, and it is not accepted here. The Japanese camps were ultimately closed before World War II ended, partially as a result of multiple cases that made it to the US Supreme Court, and it is even less acceptable now.[20]

Think about how differently things went after the 9/11 attacks. There have been no internment camps or similar actions taken toward Arab-Americans or Muslims. They have generally been free to continue their lives unless there is evidence that they, personally, have committed or are planning to commit a crime. As with any situation or law, there are examples of injustices, but they are nothing like the widespread Japanese internment of World War II in terms of either scale or public acceptance.

> *What do you think of this change? Why do you think things are different now? How do you think media coverage affected how either group was treated?*

AMENDMENT V

No person shall be held to answer for a capital, or otherwise infamous crime, unless on a presentment or indictment of a Grand Jury, except in cases arising in the land or naval forces, or in the Militia, when in actual service in time of War or public danger; nor shall any person be subject for the same offence to

be twice put in jeopardy of life or limb; nor shall be compelled in any criminal case to be a witness against himself, nor be deprived of life, liberty, or property, without due process of law; nor shall private property be taken for public use, without just compensation.

Historically, monarchs grabbed people and jailed them without warning or telling them what they had done, and with no way to get their freedom back. Imprisonment might result in lost property, permanent physical injury, even death. This guarantees a jury of US citizens shall hear evidence and decide if there is enough evidence to go to trial. If not, the case is dismissed. This amendment makes it harder to put someone through all the disruptions and unpleasantness associated with a trial unless there is a real reason for it.

However, military cases, especially in time of war, are not *necessarily* subject to the same rules. There are things the military are expected to do when they are serving in a war that only another person who has served in a war can understand well enough to judge. Other offenses (speeding, shoplifting) are subject to civilian rules.

Clearly, soldiers and sailors can do things for which civilians might be put in jail (killing, for instance, within very strict guidelines), so the military has its own system of military justice for these cases. Military courts are separate from regular civilian courts because having civilians judge them would actually deny military defendants a fair trial. Civilians almost certainly cannot understand the circumstances well enough to judge them fairly. This protects their rights.

The 5th Amendment also makes it illegal for the government to try citizens more than once for the same crime, which is called double jeopardy. However, criminal and civil courts are separate and there can be one trial in each, as there was with OJ Simpson.[21] He was found not guilty in the criminal court, which could have sent him to jail, but guilty in the civil court, where he was slapped with a large fine.

In a criminal case, the defendant has broken a law and if they are found guilty, then they will go to jail or pay a large fine to the government, although they may also be sentenced to serve community service. In a civil case, they cannot be sent to jail and any fines are paid to their victim.

There can be no doubt that a person is guilty ("guilty beyond a shadow of a doubt") to get a guilty verdict in a criminal trial. In a civil trial the jury just has to be pretty sure ("preponderance of evidence"), reflecting the more severe punishments in a criminal case compared to a civil case. In the worst criminal cases, someone who is found guilty can be sentenced to capital punishment, which is a nicer sounding way of saying they will be killed for their crime(s).

In a civil case, the defendant either has to pay the plaintiff a certain amount or stop/start doing something. When someone doesn't do what they have promised under a contract, called breach of contract, a civil lawsuit can be brought against them. An example of a civil case would be a person who is being evicted from their apartment or having their home foreclosed. They are in breach of contract because they stopped paying money they agreed to pay in exchange for their home or apartment.

Civil suits can help individual consumers protect themselves if a business they are dealing with does something wrong. No one is sent to jail or executed in civil cases. Because they "only" require "a preponderance of evidence," which is easier to prove than "beyond a reasonable doubt," a defendant can be found "not guilty" in a criminal trial and "guilty" in a civil trial. For example, if you pay for your car to be repaired and the mechanic damages it, you can bring a civil suit to recover the money it cost you.

Sometimes in movies, TV, or even life, you'll hear someone say, "I plead the fifth" when they're asked if they've done something wrong. This is what they're talking about—the 5th Amendment. It says that no one has to answer a question if the answer will prove they did something wrong and their testimony could be used against them in court. They also don't have to testify against their husband or wife, but they do have to testify against their own parent or child if asked.

Private property cannot legally be seized by the federal government just because they want it, especially without payment. The government must go through a whole process that ends with payment. The owners must be paid a fair rate for it, although they don't have to be happy it. This is called *eminent domain*.[22] (This was discussed briefly under Article 1, Section 8.) The most common reasons for this in the US are to enable building public utilities and transportation projects, including highways and railroad right of way. Smaller amounts can also be seized for simpler projects like sidewalks or street lighting, as long as the owners are paid fairly for it and the proper legal steps are taken to demonstrate the public need for it.

This amendment is the reason criminals must be read their "Miranda Rights" when they are arrested. Ernesto Miranda was arrested in 1963 in *Miranda v. Arizona* the police did not tell him that he had the right to have an attorney present.[23] He admitted to criminal actions, which he might not have done if he had a lawyer there. The Supreme Court eventually ruled that this made his admission inadmissible in court—it had to be ignored as if it had never been made. He was still found guilty because of other evidence when he was retried.

The following is a basic Miranda Rights warning and it is probably very familiar to you from television and movies.

"You have the right to remain silent. Anything you say can and will be used against you in a court of law. You have the right to speak to an attorney, and to have an attorney present during any questioning. If you cannot afford a lawyer, one will be provided for you at government expense."

A re-trial can happen if there is a problem with the original trial. A re-trial throws out the original trial and starts the process over again, including jury selection. Neither a retrial nor an appeal is considered double jeopardy. An appeal asks a higher court to consider whether the previous trial was done correctly and does not have a jury.

The 5th Amendment safeguards many rights for US citizens but it will not stop anyone's family from grilling them over who left the big mess in the kitchen–and it won't stop both of a kid's parents from punishing the kid separately, even if it is double jeopardy. It only protects you from actions by the government.

THE BILL OF RIGHTS: AMENDMENT II-V

RESOURCES

1. Massachusetts Bay Colony/Militia Roots
www.history.army.mil/reference/mamil/MAMIL.HTM

2. Pequot War (1637)
colonialwarsct.org/1637.htm

3. German National Socialists (Nazis) and Gun Confiscation
www.stephenhalbrook.com/registration_article/registration.html

4. Italian Fascists and Italian Gun Control Laws
www.davekopel.com/2A/Mags/Italy.htm

5. Chinese Gun Culture
www.atimes.com/atimes/China/LF24Ad02.html

6. Thomas Jefferson Quotes
www.monticello.org/site/jefferson/no-freeman-shall-be-debarred-use-arms-quotation

7. Federalist No. 46: The Influence of the State and Federal Governments
www.constitution.org/fed/federa46.htm

8. Patrick Henry Quotes
www.madisonbrigade.com/p_henry.htm

9. George Washington Quotes
www.madisonbrigade.com/g_washington.htm#QUOTES

10. The Second Quartering Act
worldhistoryproject.org/1774/6/2/second-quartering-act

11. The Intolerable Acts
www.socialstudiesforkids.com/wwww/us/intolerableactsdef.htm

12. Japanese Internment Camps
history.howstuffworks.com/history-vs-myth/japanese-internment-camp3.htm

13. German and Latin American Internees
gaic.info/index.php

14. Italian American Internment
www.italianhistorical.org/page19a.html

15. Executive Order 9066
www.archives.gov/education/lessons/japanese-relocation/

16. Justice Felix Frankfurter
www.oyez.org/justices/felix_frankfurter

17. Chinese Exclusion Act
www.hoover.archives.gov/exhibits/China/Chinese_Americans/index.html

18. Japanese Internment Photo Archives
www.calisphere.universityofcalifornia.edu/jarda/browse/daily-life.html

19. Japanese Internment
www.freeinfosociety.com/article.php?id=10

20. Japanese Interment and the US Supreme Court
www.historylink.org/index.cfm?DisplayPage=output.cfm&file_id=2070

21. The Difference Between Civil and Criminal Court
www.rbs2.com/cc.htm

22. Eminent Domain
www.expertlaw.com/library/real_estate/eminent_domain.html

23. Miranda Rights
www.usconstitution.net/miranda.html?ModPagespeed=noscript
supreme.justia.com/cases/federal/us/384/436/case.html

CHAPTER 16
THE BILL OF RIGHTS:
AMENDMENTS VI–X

AMENDMENT VI

In all criminal prosecutions, the accused shall enjoy the right to a speedy and public trial, by an impartial jury of the State and district wherein the crime shall have been committed, which district shall have been previously ascertained by law, and to be informed of the nature and cause of the accusation; to be confronted with the witnesses against him; to have compulsory process for obtaining witnesses in his favor, and to have the Assistance of Counsel for his defense.

The 5th Amendment affirms that American Citizens must be told why they are being charged and the 6th Amendment guarantees that they will be judged quickly by a petit or trial jury.[1] A jury is a group, six to twelve for a civil trial and twelve for a criminal trial, who listen to all the evidence and arguments related to a case and decide if they think that evidence shows the person is guilty or not guilty.

If they believe the person is guilty but the evidence does not show it, they must still find them not guilty. In this country, people are assumed innocent until proven guilty beyond a reasonable doubt in criminal court, which is the opposite of what is true in many other countries. It is a part of our Common Law heritage from Great Britain and is not written anywhere in the Constitution or its amendments. It is harder to prove someone is guilty beyond a reasonable doubt than that they are innocent.

Let's go back to the example of your friend saying you stole his things. If their family tried to steal it back and got caught, they would be tried to see if they're guilty. What do you think would happen if it took five years to go to trial? For the defendant (the one defending themselves and trying to prove their innocence), it could be hard to get any work and earn money with a criminal complaint against them. People might avoid them and their friends might not hang out with them because of it. For the plaintiff (the one with a complaint), it will be a long time until justice is delivered for what happened.

What do you think the verdict will be if all the jurors are friends and family of the people who went through your room? Do you think there is any chance they will be found guilty? Of course not. What if they are all your friends? Do you think they will listen to anything the defendant says? Perhaps there was a reason you don't know about for their actions.

For both sides, the longer you wait, the less likely it is that witnesses will remember things accurately, which makes it harder for justice to prevail. How much can you remember about an important day five years ago? Think of one and try to remember as much detail as you can. Now try it with a similar day from six months ago. Now try this morning.

Details can be very important in understanding how or why something happened. Which day can you remember in more detail, and is it by a lot or a little? That is why having an impartial jury and prompt trial are so important.

An impartial jury is one that hasn't already decided if the person is guilty or not guilty.

Jurors' names are selected from a list of registered voters, drivers' license holders, or a combination of the two.² When potential jurors receive a summons telling them to come to the courthouse to be in a jury pool (the group from which jurors are picked for each case), they are legally required to show up and do it. The judge and attorneys ask potential jurors questions and select the ones they think best for the case.³ The others are sent back to the jury pool where they may be selected for another case or sent home. Their regular jobs are required to give them time off, although that doesn't mean they have to pay them their regular pay.

Requiring trials be public keeps the entire process more honest.

This clause means people cannot refuse to appear in court as witnesses if they are called, and that people have to be told exactly what they are being charged with. This amendment also commits the government to providing a lawyer for anyone accused of a crime, even if they can't afford to pay for one, no matter what the circumstances. (This was definitively established by *Gideon v. Wainwright* in 1963.)[4]

AMENDMENT VII

In Suits at common law, where the value in controversy shall exceed twenty dollars, the right of trial by jury shall be preserved, and no fact tried by a jury, shall be otherwise reexamined in any Court of the United States, than according to the rules of the common law.

Civil cases over a certain value are also tried by jury. The dollar mentioned here is the Spanish milled dollar, the international currency of the day.[5] It was a silver coin also called "pieces of eight" because it was worth eight reales (bits–the number of pieces it could be broken into to pay smaller amounts), and it was minted in Mexico and other Spanish colonies. England forbade her Colonies from minting coins, so using Spanish coins was common practice.

Twenty dollars was a lot of money at the time.

AMENDMENT VIII

<u>Excessive bail shall not be required, nor excessive fines imposed, nor cruel and unusual punishments inflicted.</u>

Once again, this is an attempt to prevent problems that were widespread before our country was founded. The states would not have insisted on the Bill of Rights if these were not fairly common problems.

Bail is when one person pays money to get someone out of jail and as proof that they will return when they are required to. If they do not return for court dates, the person who posted bail loses that money. Excessive bail left people who were not rich stuck in jail for a very long time.

While they were there, they couldn't work to grow food on their farm, take care of their children, or run their business/do their job. It also made preparing their defense more difficult. Many people were in jail because they owed money. Because they couldn't work, they couldn't earn the money to pay the fines, so they couldn't get out of jail, which meant they couldn't work, so…. You can see where this is going. It was a vicious circle. Excessive fines could leave people with no money to feed or care for their family, and could ultimately cause them to lose everything.

In the past, torturing people was part the justice system. Many criminal punishments were things we would consider torture today. Torture was used in spying to get information about other countries. Medieval castles sometimes even had torture chambers. Our Founding Fathers clearly thought this was A Bad Thing and made actual torture illegal here. This does not mean you never have to do anything unpleasant, and no matter how big the stack of work you have to do at home is, it does not count as cruel and unusual punishment, but actual torture is forbidden.

AMENDMENT IX

<u>The enumeration in the Constitution, of certain rights, shall not be construed to deny or disparage others retained by the people.</u>

Just because a right is not listed in the Constitution does not mean you do not have that right. The right to privacy is an example of a right covered by the 9th Amendment but not specifically listed in the Constitution. This means that the federal government may not come in and take your diary; it does not mean your parents, grandparents, or anyone else will be jailed if they enter your room and read your diary.

Privacy rights go beyond just your diary, the bathroom, and your conversations. You have certain privacy rights for your computer and other electronic data as well. These rights can vary, depending on who owns the hardware you are using, written agreements related to computer use (e.g., an agreement that anything you create during work hours/at the office belongs to your employer) and where you are (a library computer versus one at home). How strong those privacy rights are depends in part on you. Many programs, including word processors and spreadsheets, allow you to password-protect individual files when you save them. If you keep those passwords secret, so no one else knows them, then those files are normally reasonably secure.

When you use the internet, you can choose to not accept cookies from each website and to limit how much personal data you put online, including social networking sites. For example, I never put my real birthday on social websites, so I never have to worry someone can use information from there to steal my identity. If you are not vigilant about personal security on your computer, you can lose it. If you never protect your work and post it online where other people can easily read and download it, then they can copy and use it. If you allow every website you visit to put all the cookies it wants on your computer and leave them there indefinitely, then you have given up a little bit more of your privacy.

> *Cookies save and transmit data about what you do online, and while you do need to accept some of them for some websites to work, you do not need to accept all of them from every website, nor do you need to allow them to stay on your computer once you stop using that website.*

Our individual rights under the Constitution are like privacy settings. If we do not care about and watch over them, then we may lose them. If we continually accept giving up little bits of them, we will eventually find they are gone entirely, just like a big cookie disappears one bite at a time.

Our rights are protected by the Constitution, but it can be changed via amendments, and even Constitutional protection does not matter if the Courts and the country ignore that protection in practice.[5] Segregation and poll taxes are the most infamous examples.[6]

AMENDMENT X

The powers not delegated to the United States by the Constitution, nor prohibited by it to the States, are reserved to the States respectively, or to the people.

State sovereignty versus federal (central) government power has been fought over within our country since its founding. All of Chapter 19 in this book is devoted to the topic. This clause strengthens state sovereignty by clearly stating that if a right was not specifically given to the federal government, such as coining money and declaring war, then that right belongs to the states.

RESOURCES

1.   What is a Jury Trial?
www.wisegeek.com/what-is-a-jury-trial.htm

2.   Jury Pool
research.lawyers.com/jury-pool.html

3.   Jury Selection in Criminal Cases
criminaldefense.homestead.com/juryselection.html

4.   Gideon v. Wainwright
www.oyez.org/cases/1962/155

5.   Spanish Milled Dollar
www.columbiagazette.com/smd.html

6.   A Challenge to Jim Crow in the Nation's Capital
americanhistory.si.edu/brown/history/4-five/washington-dc-1.html

7.   Poll Taxes
www.u-s-history.com/pages/h425.html

CHAPTER 17
CONSTITUTIONAL AMENDMENTS
XI–XVI

AMENDMENT XI

PASSED BY CONGRESS MARCH 4, 1794. RATIFIED FEBRUARY 7, 1795.

NOTE: ARTICLE III, SECTION 2, OF THE CONSTITUTION WAS MODIFIED BY THE 11TH AMENDMENT.

The Judicial power of the United States shall not be construed to extend to any suit in law or equity, commenced or prosecuted against one of the United States by Citizens of another State, or by Citizens or Subjects of any Foreign State.

This protects states from being sued in Federal Court by other states or by citizens of other states. States can only be sued in their own state courts.

In the 1792 case *Chisholm v. Georgia*, Mr. Chisholm sued the state of Georgia to force it to pay money owed for goods purchased during the Revolutionary War.[1] This led directly to passage of the 11th Amendment because the Founders wanted it to be clear that states were sovereign entities, their own government, not just a lesser level of the federal government.

AMENDMENT XII

PASSED BY CONGRESS DECEMBER 9, 1803. RATIFIED JUNE 15, 1804.

NOTE: A PORTION OF ARTICLE II, SECTION 1, OF THE CONSTITUTION WAS SUPERSEDED BY THE 12TH AMENDMENT.

The Electors shall meet in their respective states and vote by ballot for President and Vice-President, one of whom, at least, shall not be an inhabitant of the same state with themselves; they shall name in their ballots the person voted for as President, and in distinct ballots the person voted for as Vice-President, and they shall make distinct lists of all persons voted for as President, and of all persons voted for as Vice-President, and of the number of votes for each, which lists they shall sign and certify, and transmit sealed to the seat of the government of the United States, directed to the President of the Senate; -- the President of the Senate shall, in the presence of the Senate and House of Representatives, open all the certificates and the votes shall then be counted; -- The person having the greatest number of votes for President, shall be the President, if such number be a majority of the whole number of Electors appointed; and if no person have such majority, then from the persons having the highest numbers not exceeding three on the list of those voted for as President, the House of Representatives shall choose immediately, by ballot, the President. But in choosing the President, the votes shall be taken by states, the representation from each state having one vote; a quorum for this purpose shall consist of a member or members from two-thirds of the states, and a majority of all the states shall be necessary to a choice. [And if the House of Representatives shall not choose a President whenever the right of choice shall devolve upon them, before the fourth day of March next following, then the Vice-President shall act as President, as in case of the death or other constitutional disability of the President. --]* The person having the greatest number of votes as Vice-President, shall be the Vice-President, if such number be a majority of the whole number of Electors appointed, and if no person have a majority, then from the two highest numbers on the list, the Senate shall

choose the Vice-President; a quorum for the purpose shall consist of two-thirds of the whole number of Senators, and a majority of the whole number shall be necessary to a choice. But no person constitutionally ineligible to the office of President shall be eligible to that of Vice-President of the United States.

SUPERSEDED BY SECTION 3 OF THE 20TH AMENDMENT.

This section changed how the President and Vice President are elected. Previously, Electors voted for all the candidates at the same time in Presidential elections. The one with the most votes was President, and the next-most was Vice-President. Today, we vote for a "ticket" that specifies one person who will be President and another who will be Vice-President.

Our first President under the Constitution, George Washington, was elected unanimously. Our second, John Adams, received the most votes in 1796 and his archrival Thomas Jefferson the second most, making him Vice President. In addition to being rivals in the race for President, they were from different political parties and held different views about what the government should do. This was technically the only time we ever had a President and Vice President from different political parties.

In 1800, Jefferson and Aaron Burr both ran for President but agreed that Jefferson was to be President and Burr to be Vice President. Unfortunately, they tied. When Burr did not cede the position to Jefferson and eventually came in second after 36 rounds of voting, it left bad feelings. Jefferson chose a different man as his second Vice President, which is proof enough of the damage done.

How would you feel in Jefferson's position, either as Vice President or President? How would you feel in Adams' position? Why do you think Burr refused to follow his original agreement with Jefferson?

Two of our first three Presidents were handicapped by having a Vice-President they disliked, distrusted, and found difficult to work with. This Amendment was passed in 1803, following the Jefferson/Burr debacle, and ratified in less than eight months, before another Presidential election was held.

> *How much do you think Adams and Jefferson listened to their Vice-Presidents? How much would you listen to your Vice-President in a situation like this? Was this a good solution?*

In some ways, having two strong people with different views as President and Vice President seems like it might be an improvement over the current system, where the President tends to have a much stronger personality, stronger views, stronger everything, than the Vice President, a person who could end up as President someday. After all, nine of them have.

> *Imagine President Krabs and Vice President Plankton. Do you think they could manage to agree with each other enough to govern? Do you think they could get past the bitter rivalry that started when Mr. Krabs opened the Krusty Krab and Plankton started trying to steal the Krabby Patty Secret Formula?*
>
> *Now imagine President Sandy and Vice President SpongeBob. How do you think they would do compared to Krabs and Plankton? Do you think Sandy's problem solving skills and SpongeBob's ability to get along with anyone will help them perform better?*

This amendment also requires that at least one of the two candidates, Presidential and Vice Presidential, be from a different state than the Electors who vote for them. It doesn't technically *require* the two candidates to be from different states, but no candidates would voluntarily give up all the votes from their home state, which they would probably (but not definitely) win. Therefore, this requirement effectively requires a Presidential candidate to choose a Vice Presidential candidate from another state, although they are technically free to choose any natural born citizen they want to.

This requirement was added to keep one state from having too much political power at the national level. Their size means that larger states tend to be more influential even without the VP and President both being from there. This created a more powerful disincentive, or discouragement, for politicians from larger states with more electoral votes. Losing all the California votes is far costlier in a Presidential election than losing all the Rhode Island votes.

Why do you think this requirement was included? Why do you think it was written to discourage and not outright forbid it? Or do you think they intended it to actually forbid it?

What concerns did small and large states have about other parts of our government? Was there any specific state or states the others might have been concerned would get too much power? Which one(s) and why? What states do you think others may worry about getting too much power today?

AMENDMENT XIII
PASSED BY CONGRESS JANUARY 31, 1865. RATIFIED DECEMBER 6, 1865.

NOTE: A PORTION OF ARTICLE IV, SECTION 2, OF THE CONSTITUTION WAS SUPERSEDED BY THE 13ᵀᴴ AMENDMENT.

SECTION 1

Neither slavery nor involuntary servitude, except as a punishment for crime whereof the party shall have been duly convicted, shall exist within the United States, or any place subject to their jurisdiction.

SECTION 2

Congress shall have power to enforce this article by appropriate legislation.

Slavery ended as a result of the Civil War, even though ending slavery per se was not the reason it was started. President Lincoln issued something called the Emancipation Proclamation during the Civil War. This was US Navy Order No. 4 issued by the Commander in

Chief (President) on 14 January 1863, not a law from Congress or a Presidential Executive Order.[2] It freed, or emancipated, all the slaves in states that were in rebellion (the Confederate States), but did not free slaves in states that remained in the Union, such as Maryland.

Issuing a Naval Order instead of either an Executive Order or a law was not random. Because it was a Navy Order from the Commander in Chief, it only applied to states in rebellion and under eventual military rule. An Executive Order from the President or a law from Congress would have applied to all the states, and that would not have been popular with the slave states fighting for the Union. In addition, emancipation wasn't hugely popular and many Congressmen would not have wanted to face their constituents if they voted for it. The Naval Order helped keep their jobs safe.

What do you think of the way this was handled? How differently might the Emancipation Proclamation have been received if it was a law or an Executive Order that applied to all the states? How could that have affected the war efforts?

Do you think Congress would or could have passed it? How might that law, requiring many men to agree on the wording and provisions, have been different?

The President and Commander in Chief are the same person, but those are slightly different roles. We all have different roles in life. One person might be a choir member at church but the chorus director at school. Even though you are the same person, you would behave differently and have different responsibilities in these two positions. It is the same idea here.

In addition, because it was issued by the President and not a law that started in Congress, a future President could simply have revoked the Emancipation Proclamation, as the French Edict of Nantes was revoked nearly two centuries earlier. The reality of revoking it would, of course, have been extremely complex and difficult to accomplish because freed slaves would not have gone back easily or voluntarily to their former "masters." That does not change the fact that a presidential action, such as an Executive or Naval Order, can be revoked much more easily than a law passed by Congress, and of course that it is extraordinarily difficult to revoke a Constitutional amendment. Therefore, Congress amended the Constitution to sanction this action and to free *all* the slaves in *all* the states in a manner that cannot be changed quickly or easily.

This amendment barely passed, but it did pass.

This is one of three Amendments passed right after the Civil War that helped blacks a great deal, but they certainly did not end discrimination. Many forms of discrimination continued to be widely practiced, particularly in the South. These included forcing blacks to sit at the back of the bus and to use "separate but equal" facilities, as legalized by *Plessy v. Ferguson*.[3] Others included poll taxes, literacy tests for voting, and prohibitions on inter-racial marriages, although there were many more.[4]

One unintended side-effect of making things less unequal for blacks, which is not even remotely the same as saying they were made equal, was an increase in racism against Asians. Asians were not here in large numbers the way Africans were. The reasoning was that at least the former slaves had been here for about as long as Europeans had been. Asians were simply foreigners. Legalized discrimination against Asians, such as the Chinese Exclusion Act and Japanese internment during WWII, continued until the 1960s.[5] When the Civil Rights Movement ended separate-but-equal and other discriminatory practices illegal against all races that included Asians.

AMENDMENT XIV
PASSED BY CONGRESS JUNE 13, 1866. RATIFIED JULY 9, 1868.

NOTE: ARTICLE I, SECTION 2, OF THE CONSTITUTION WAS MODIFIED BY SECTION 2 OF THE 14TH AMENDMENT.

SECTION 1

All persons born or naturalized in the United States, and subject to the jurisdiction thereof, are citizens of the United States and of the State wherein they reside. No State shall make or en-

force any law which shall abridge the privileges or immunities of citizens of the United States; nor shall any State deprive any person of life, liberty, or property, without due process of law; nor deny to any person within its jurisdiction the equal protection of the laws.

The Dred Scott Decision in the 1857 case *Dred Scott v. Sanderson* said that African Americans who had been slaves, or whose ancestors had been slaves, were not and could not become American citizens, and that they were not protected by the Constitution.[6] The same decision declared the Missouri Compromise unconstitutional because Congress did not have the authority to ban slavery in territories, in the opinion of the Supreme Court. The 13th, 14th and 15th Amendments combined to fully overturn *Dred Scott.*

What do you think of the original Dred Scott Decision? Was it fair? What do you think the Founders would have thought of it?

Dred Scott is proof that even the Supreme Court makes mistakes. It is not their only decision that was later found to be faulty. It is one of the worst examples, along with *Plessy v. Ferguson,* which legalized Separate but Equal. Separate but Equal not only permitted but actually encouraged state laws to be applied differently to different groups of citizens.

Plessy was over-turned when Oliver Brown, a Kansas welder, sued his local school district.[7] The school district was forcing his little girl to take a long bus ride, bypassing at least one closer school, to attend a not-so-good school because of her skin color. He wasn't a rich man, and he wasn't a powerful man. He was a determined father, and he had a bigger positive impact on more American lives than most rich and powerful men.

Brown was working class father trying to get the best for his little girl when he started *Brown v. Board of Education,* the case that overturned the Plessy decision.[8] *Plessy* was made by nine men who were considered to be some of the wisest and best educated lawyers of their time. Much like the story of the Emperor's New Clothes, sometimes it takes someone who is not rich or educated to point out to those who are just how wrong they are. The hard part, of course, is getting them to listen. It's almost as hard as believing in yourself and your cause enough to take a fight for justice all the way to the Supreme Court.

Would your parents take on a fight like this for you? Who or what would you take on a fight like this for? Do you think you could do it, if you felt really strongly? What would you do to protect your family and the ones you love from injustice?

This first section of this amendment was written specifically to protect the rights of former slaves, some of whose ancestors had been here for generations. It is also the reason that if someone comes into our country and has a baby here, that child is a US citizen even if their parents are not. Before 1952, this had an odd impact on Asians.[9] They were barred from becoming US citizens by the "Act of February 18, 1875" but their children were born here and so were citizens. An immigrant is someone who immigrates or moves here, including even children and babies; immigrant's children are the first generation of citizens born here, or first generation.

The clause "and subject to the jurisdiction thereof" is the reason that diplomat's children are not US citizens even if they are born here. It is also the reason Indians were denied US citizenship until 1924: their tribes were considered foreign governments. They are also often called Native American, but the government agency remains Bureau of Indian Affairs. In both cases, they were subject to the jurisdiction of that other government, not the US government.

How fair was it to prevent immigrants from becoming citizens based solely on the country they immigrated from? Do you think it is right that anyone born here is a citizen, whether their parents are or not, or do you think it should be changed? Why, and how? Should Indians have full US citizenship? What do you think of the original choice to not give them citizenship?

This amendment makes it clear that US citizenship is conferred under jus soli (right of the soil) and not jus sanguinis (right of blood). Jus soli means that you are a citizen because of where you were born (the land, or soil). For most of our history, the US has had more land than people and it still has very few people for the amount of land compared to other areas, including much of Europe, Asia, and Africa. When we had a lot of land and not a lot of people or money, jus soli helped increase how many citizens we had.

Jus sanguinis says that a newborn is a citizen of a country if their parents are, no matter where they are born. Today, the majority of countries that give citizenship based just on being born there (jus soli) are in North or South America, although some European countries are becoming less strict about that. However, not all jus soli nations grant citizenship to someone whose parents are in the country illegally.

This clearly states that the parents of a new-born citizen must be "subject to the jurisdiction" of this country. Anyone who is here illegally isn't truly subject to many of the laws of this land, its "jurisdiction," because those only apply to citizens. Examples include social security, employment laws, and many more.

When a woman comes here (legally or not) and has a baby, that baby has US citizenship, even if neither parent does. If the mother is here illegally, that baby is called an "anchor baby" because it is the "anchor" that keeps the rest of the family in this country. The US tries not to split up families.

Do you think the Founders would believe "anchor babies" should have US citizenship or citizenship in the same nation as their parents? (Remember: This amendment came a century after the original Constitution and was addressing the issue citizenship as it relates to former slaves.) What do you think their solution would have been?

The last part of this section is called the Equal Protection Clause.[10] The Equal Protection Clause was designed to prevent states from applying laws differently to different groups of citizens. It does not guarantee equal results. It guarantees equal *protection* under the law.

Individual people are not always treated the same, but that does not mean they are being treated unfairly. Doctors and nurses are allowed to go into operating rooms when a patient's family members are not because the medical staff has to be there and has training to keep everyone safe. Police officers and ambulance drivers can speed if they need to for their job. This is not discrimination or a violation of anyone's rights because everyone in each group is treated the same and the groups are not determined by something outside of people's control. People can get training and become doctors or police officers. They cannot become a different skin color or gender.

Both before and after passage of the US Constitution, some state legislatures were set up so that each county, regardless of population, had one representative in the state Senate, just as each state has two representatives in the US Senate. The Founding Fathers would have been aware of these examples when they wrote the Constitution, particularly since many of them served in colonial representative bodies. On the basis of the Equal Protection Clause of Section 1 of this amendment, the Supreme Court required states to change this after the 1961 case of *Reynolds v. Sims* so that both houses in state legislatures base their representation on population.[11]

Do you think states were violating the Equal Protection Clause? Why, and how? Do you think the Supreme Court should have been involved in how state governments are set up? Why?

SECTION 2

Representatives shall be apportioned among the several States according to their respective numbers, counting the whole number of persons in each State, excluding Indians not taxed. But when the right to vote at any election for the choice of electors for President and Vice-President of the United States, Representatives in Congress, the Executive and Judicial officers of a State, or the members of the Legislature thereof, is denied to any of the male inhabitants of such State, being twenty-one years of age,* and citizens of the United States, or in any way

abridged, except for participation in rebellion, or other crime, the basis of representation therein shall be reduced in the proportion which the number of such male citizens shall bear to the whole number of male citizens twenty-one years of age in such State.

This was written to protect the right of freedmen, those men who were once slaves but were now free. It clarified that all men, including freedmen, count as a whole person for purposes of determining the number of Representatives. This is the first time the Constitution specifically brings up gender. It only protects the *male* right to vote. It very specifically did not give women the right to vote. Needless to say, many women were not pleased about this.

The statement "Indians not taxed" makes it seem that if residents did not pay taxes, then they did not have the right to vote. Why do you think this was? Do you take better care of things when you pay for them, or when they are free? If you go to a restaurant, are you more careful of how much you have for dinner if you pay for each item, if you choose a set meal for a set price (like a fast-food meal that includes a burger, fries and drink for one price), or if it's an all-you-can-eat buffet someone else is paying for?

Does thinking about that change your thoughts on why they might have not counted those who do not pay taxes toward the figures for representatives? Do those who do not pay taxes count toward representation today? Is this change and improvement?

This also deprived those who were active in the Confederacy of their right to vote in national or state elections for the legislature, judges, or executive officers (e.g., President, Governor). The number of Representatives was reduced for states that seceded because men who were active in the Confederacy were no longer counted toward representation. The age of 21 was specified because no one under age 21 was eligible to vote until the 26th Amendment was passed in 1971.

SECTION 3

No person shall be a Senator or Representative in Congress, or electer of President and Vice-President, or hold any office, civil or military, under the United States, or under any State, who, having previously taken an oath, as a member of Congress, or as an officer of the United States, or as a member of any State legislature, or as an executive or judicial officer of any State, to support the Constitution of the United States, shall have engaged in insurrection or rebellion against the same, or given aid or comfort to the enemies thereof. But Congress may by a vote of two-thirds of each House, remove such disability.

It was thought best to punish men who had served in Congress, other elected office or the US Armed Services but who later joined the Confederacy in rebellion. The last sentence in this clause shows that even in the immediate years after a traumatic event like the Civil War, Americans might be willing to overlook the faults and mistakes of another if they are sorry for what they have done—at least in theory. In individual cases, some former Confederate officers and enlisted people took the Oath of Allegiance to the United States and served in the military during the Spanish American War in 1898.

SECTION 4

The validity of the public debt of the United States, authorized by law, including debts incurred for payment of pensions and bounties for services in suppressing insurrection or rebellion, shall not be questioned. But neither the United States nor any State shall assume or pay any debt or obligation incurred in aid of insurrection or rebellion against the United States, or any claim for the loss or emancipation of any slave; but all such debts, obligations and claims shall be held illegal and void.

SECTION 5

The Congress shall have the power to enforce, by appropriate legislation, the provisions of this article.

CHANGED BY SECTION 1 OF THE 26TH AMENDMENT.

Congress wanted to make sure that there would never be any question as to the payment of any loss to those who fought *for* the Union, including pensions (retirement) for anyone who fought for it in the military. This made it equally clear that while they would repay debt the Union had incurred, they were not going to repay any debts from the Confederacy in their fight *against* the Union. After all, the US government did not incur those debts, the Confederate government did.

This also ensured that former slaveholders could not sue the government to be repaid for the value of their newly-freed slaves. However, if those same slave-owners were still paying off slaves they had bought before the amendment was passed, they were required to continue paying off their debt because it was a valid debt.

AMENDMENT XV.
PASSED BY CONGRESS FEBRUARY 26, 1869. RATIFIED FEBRUARY 3, 1870.

SECTION 1

The right of citizens of the United States to vote shall not be denied or abridged by the United States or by any State on account of race, color, or previous condition of servitude--

SECTION 2

The Congress shall have the power to enforce this article by appropriate legislation.

This guarantees that all Americans have all the same rights, no matter what color or race they are. This amendment combined with the 13th and 14th Amendments to nullify the *Dred Scott* Decision by the Supreme Court, so it was as if it had never existed.

Once again, the Constitution does not actually guarantee *anyone* the right to vote. It does specify things that cannot be used to deny the right to vote, particularly race and gender. For example, if a state chose to re-institute a requirement that all voters must be property owners, that would be perfectly constitutional. It just wouldn't be very popular.

AMENDMENT XVI
PASSED BY CONGRESS JULY 2, 1909. RATIFIED FEBRUARY 3, 1913.

NOTE: ARTICLE I, SECTION 9, OF THE CONSTITUTION WAS MODIFIED BY THE 16TH AMENDMENT.

The Congress shall have power to lay and collect taxes on incomes, from whatever source derived, without apportionment among the several States, and without regard to any census or enumeration.

This established the income tax, which is a tax that takes a portion of everyone's income, the money each person earns. Under the current system, the tax rate (how large a percentage must be paid) changes based on how large that income is. It is called a progressive tax because it gets progressively bigger as you earn more money, going from 10% up to 35%. People who earn more don't just pay more because X% of 100 is more than X% of 10. People with larger incomes pay more because they have to pay a higher percentage of their income.

As of 2010, nearly half of all Americans do not pay *any* federal income tax at all.[12] That's a rate of 0% compared to a top rate of 35%. Many people pay additional taxes such as Social Security on top of that, making the effective top rate higher than 35% although there are still people who pay 0%. Different types of income are also taxed at different rates. Income from a job, property, stocks, etc. are all taxed at different rates.

We did have an income tax one time before this amendment. It was established by the Revenue Act of 1861 to help pay Civil War expenses but was repealed when the war was paid for ten years later.[13] The constitutionality of an income tax was uncertain because the US Constitution clearly states that direct taxes are to be levied based on states' populations. (Proportional taxation was another reason the census was important.)

That does not happen under the income tax. As a result, the Supreme Court ruled the income tax unconstitutional in *Pollack v. Farmers' Loan and Trust Co* in 1895, but the decision was not popular with many citizens.[14] The Industrial Revolution and all the excesses of the Gilded Age were in full swing when this amendment passed and many citizens believed that the new class of super-wealthy entrepreneurs (Rockefeller, Vanderbilt, Carnegie Mellon, and their peers) and very large businesses (railroads, mills, factories, etc.) should pay more to support our government.[15]

Because of this, people were initially convinced to support the income tax by being told it was only intended to "soak the rich."[16] They used that exact term. Since it was taking money from other people, it was quite popular. Not much has really changed. Newspapers and politicians are still calling for higher taxes for "the rich" and people's support of it depends directly on how close they are to the income level for "the rich."

The first income tax in the 1910s was 1% on the equivalent of over $300,000 in late 1990s money ($20,000 in 1913) and 7% on the equivalent of over $7.5 million ($500,000). The complete form was four (4) pages.[17] Very few people were anywhere near those income levels, leading to wide support. Even after several decades, only 5% of the population had to file income tax returns in 1939. Today, 80% of the population, including anyone with over $5,700 in earned income, must file a return.

What do you notice about those numbers? Does it sound like the income tax still just "soaks the rich"? What do you think the people who supported this tax on "the rich" would think if they saw it today?

Since this was sold as a way to "soak the rich," how much support do you think it would have gotten if everyone who earned $5,700 *or more had been forced to file? What if everyone who earned $360 per year, the 1913 equivalent, was forced to file?*

Do you think the income tax is good, bad, or neutral? How and why?

The Founding Fathers strongly opposed taxes like this. They feared letting the federal government have that much money.

In the 1790s, taxing whiskey producers caused an event called the Whisky Rebellion that was one of the first true tests of our new Constitution.[18] The tax on whiskey producers was actually accepted relatively well by larger producers. It was the small-scale manufacturers who were the most angered by the tax because it hurt them the most financially. Taxation, with or without representation, provokes strong reactions from Americans.

Do you think it still happens that taxes are written with the intention of taxing big businesses ("soaking the rich") but that hurt small businesses? What difference, if any, do you see in having an income tax on citizens and businesses? Many small businesses are taxed as individual income rather than as businesses. Does that fact affect your opinion?

Who do you think has more resources to figure out how to avoid paying taxes, rich people/large businesses, average income people/small businesses, or poor people/tiny businesses? Which group do you think is most affected by tax increases?

Do you think the Founders' fears were justified? Has the federal government shown that it can handle large amounts of money responsibly? Why and how?

There is a very old saying, far older than our country, "nothing is certain but death and taxes." If you doubt the power and reach of the IRS (Internal Revenue Service), consider this: Al Capone was a mob leader in the 1920s and early 1930s. The police, the FBI, every possible law enforcement agency tried to get a case that would stick and end his gangland reign. The agency that finally managed to put Al Capone in prison was the IRS, for tax evasion.[19]

Much like stopping at a red traffic light even when there are no other cars around, people comply with the rules established by the IRS because the consequences of not complying are far too severe to risk. If the IRS determines that you owe them money, they can simply seize it from your bank account, or seize your assets (including your house and car). Those assets will be sold to pay the money they think is due them.

"For example. If the system be established on basis of Income, and his just proportion on that scale has been already drawn from every one, to step into the field of Consumption, and tax special articles in that, as broadcloth or homespun, wine or whiskey, a coach or a wagon, is doubly taxing the same article. For that portion of Income with which these articles are purchased, having already paid its tax as Income, to pay another tax on the thing it purchased, is paying twice for the same thing; it is an aggrievance on the citizens who use these articles in exoneration of those who do not, contrary to the most sacred of the duties of a government, to do equal and impartial justice to all its citizens."–Thomas Jefferson, letter to Joseph Milligan, April 6, 1816

"An unlimited power to tax involves, necessarily, a power to destroy; because there is a limit beyond which no institution and no property can bear taxation."–John Marshall, McCullough v. Maryland, 1819

CHAPTER 17

RESOURCES

1. Chisholm v. Georgia
www.georgiaencyclopedia.org/articles/government-politics/chisholm-v-georgia-1793

2. US Navy Order No. 4: Emancipation Proclamation
www.history.navy.mil (search: Emancipation Proclamation)

3. Separate but Equal
http://americanhistory.si.edu/brown/history/1-segregated/separate-but-equal.html
www.watson.org/~lisa/blackhistory/post-civilwar/plessy.html

4. Sample Literacy Tests (they aren't really about literacy)
www.crmvet.org/info/lithome.htm

5. The Chinese Exclusion Act (1882)
www.ourdocuments.gov/doc.php?flash=true&doc=47

6. The Dred Scott Decision
americancivilwar.com/colored/dred_scott.html?ModPagespeed=noscript

7. Separate is Not Equal
americanhistory.si.edu/brown/history/index.html

8. Brown v. Board of Education
www.watson.org/~lisa/blackhistory/early-civilrights/brown.html

9. Letters from the Japanese Internment
www.smithsonianeducation.org/educators/lesson_plans/japanese_internment/slow_return.html

10. The Equal Protection Clause
www.law.cornell.edu/wex/Equal_protection

11. Reynolds v. Sims
www.casebriefs.com/blog/law/constitutional-law/constitutional-law-keyed-to-chemerinsky/fundamental-fights-under-due-process-and-equal-protection/reynolds-v-sims/

12. Is it true that only 53% of Americans pay income tax?
money.howstuffworks.com/only-53-percent-pay-income-tax.htm

13. History of the US Income Tax
www.loc.gov/rr/business/hottopic/irs_history.html

14. Pollack v. Farmers' Loan and Trust Co.
www.britannica.com/event/Pollock-v-Farmers-Loan-and-Trust-Company

15. Promotion and Passage of the 16th Amendment
www.taxhistory.org/www/website.nsf/Web/THM1901

16. "Soaking the Rich" and the 16th Amendment
mises.org/library/soak-poor
www.bloombergview.com/articles/2012-09-20/soak-the-rich-tax-policies-never-even-got-them-damp

17. 1913 Tax Form
www.irs.gov/pub/irs-utl/1913.pdf

18. The Whiskey Rebellion
www.earlyamerica.com/milestone-events/whiskey-rebellion/

19. How the IRS took down Al Capone
voices.washingtonpost.com/local-breaking-news/how-the-irs-took-down-al-capon.html

CHAPTER 18
CONSTITUTIONAL AMENDMENTS
XVII–XXVII

AMENDMENT XVII
PASSED BY CONGRESS MAY 13, 1912. RATIFIED APRIL 8, 1913.

NOTE: ARTICLE I, SECTION 3, OF THE CONSTITUTION WAS MODIFIED BY THE 17ᵀᴴ AMENDMENT.

The Senate of the United States shall be composed of two Senators from each State, elected by the people thereof, for six years; and each Senator shall have one vote. The electors in each State shall have the qualifications requisite for electors of the most numerous branch of the State legislatures.

When vacancies happen in the representation of any State in the Senate, the executive authority of such State shall issue writs of election to fill such vacancies: Provided, That the legislature of any State may empower the executive thereof to make temporary appointments until the people fill the vacancies by election as the legislature may direct.

This amendment shall not be so construed as to affect the election or term of any Senator chosen before it becomes valid as part of the Constitution.

THE BILL OF RIGHTS AMENDMENT XVII-XXVII

This changes the way Senators are elected. Instead of being elected by state legislatures, they are now directly elected by the people of their state. When this amendment was passed, the legislative electoral process had stopped working. Corruption and legislative deadlocks resulted in Senatorial vacancies and other problems. Sometimes state legislatures were completely unable to reach a decision and their seats remained vacant, sometimes for literally years at a time.[1]

What other ways can you think of to solve these problems without completely changing the electoral process?

When Senators were elected by State Legislatures, they were really representing the states' interests. The House of Representatives represented citizens and the Senate represented the states. As representatives of the states, Senators would have been slow to agree to laws that passed large costs, or large regulations, on to the states. As representatives of citizens, they have different concerns.

As originally envisioned, Senators represented the interests of states. The House of Representatives represented the interest of individuals. To understand how these are different, consider how the needs of a group such as a school district or business can differ from those of individual students or employees. Although they are often the same, such as when a business gets a new client and makes more money or a county builds a new pool for everyone to use, they aren't always the same. A business might make more money in the short term building a new plant overseas, but that almost certainly won't be what the employees want, unless the plant creates a lot of pollution in the community. A school district might cut free time and recess for students to help improve test scores, but that won't make the kids (or teachers) happy. It is similar with the interests of states and citizens: they are often the similar but not the same.

This also clarifies how a replacement is chosen if a Senator cannot complete their term of office, and clearly states that it doesn't affect

CHAPTER 18

anyone who was elected before this amendment was ratified. Any incumbent Senators were allowed to finish their term and run for re-election when their term expired.

If you were a state Legislator, would you vote to keep a Senator who voted for laws that were costing the state a lot of money to follow? Why is that the responsible choice? Which way do you think is better, citizen-elected or legislature elected?

AMENDMENT XVIII
PASSED BY CONGRESS DECEMBER 18, 1917. RATIFIED JANUARY 16, 1919. REPEALED BY 21ST AMENDMENT.

SECTION 1

After one year from the ratification of this article the manufacture, sale, or transportation of intoxicating liquors within, the importation thereof into, or the exportation thereof from the United States and all territory subject to the jurisdiction thereof for beverage purposes is hereby prohibited.

SECTION 2

The Congress and the several States shall have concurrent power to enforce this article by appropriate legislation.

SECTION 3

This article shall be inoperative unless it shall have been ratified as an amendment to the Constitution by the legislatures of the several States, as provided in the Constitution, within seven years from the date of the submission hereof to the States by the Congress.

Until the 16th Amendment authorized the income tax, revenues from taxing alcohol were essential to fund the federal government. Quite simply, they were one of the biggest sources of revenue for the government.[2] In just a few short years, the income tax brought in enough

250

money to make prohibition possible.

This was called Prohibition because it prohibited, or forbade, manu-facturing, selling, or transporting alcohol. Prohibition is an example of a "vice" law and quickly proved both unpopular and ineffective. Vice laws are intended to uphold the morals and values of a commu-nity by making immoral acts illegal. It was repealed by the 21st Amendment and is no longer in effect.

> *What modern laws can you think of that are probably vice laws? How effective are they? Is that the best way to combat vice, or can you think of a better way?*

AMENDMENT XIX
PASSED BY CONGRESS JUNE 4, 1919. RATIFIED AUGUST 18, 1920.

The right of citizens of the United States to vote shall not be denied or abridged by the United States or by any State on account of sex.

Congress shall have power to enforce this article by appropriate legislation.

In 1776, Abigail Adams wrote and asked her husband John to "re-member the ladies" while they were writing the Declaration of Inde-pendence.[3] The completed Declaration specifically says "all men are created equal." Over 130 years later, Women's Suffrage, or right to vote, finally passed and guaranteed that women could not be denied the right to vote because of their gender. Because federal law over-rides state laws, even if a state had not given women the right to vote, this gave them the right to vote in state and local elections.

> *Woman began working outside the home during World War I (1914-1918). How do you think this might have affected passage of this amendment? Do you think it made it easier or harder to get it passed?*

CHAPTER 18

AMENDMENT XX

PASSED BY CONGRESS MARCH 2, 1932. RATIFIED JANUARY 23, 1933.

NOTE: ARTICLE I, SECTION 4, OF THE CONSTITUTION WAS MODIFIED BY SECTION 2 OF THE 20TH AMENDMENT. IN ADDITION, A PORTION OF THE 12TH AMENDMENT WAS SUPERSEDED BY SECTION 3.

SECTION 1

The terms of the President and the Vice President shall end at noon on the 20th day of January, and the terms of Senators and Representatives at noon on the 3d day of January, of the years in which such terms would have ended if this article had not been ratified; and the terms of their successors shall then begin.

The Constitution specifies how long the President, Vice President, and Congressmen's terms are to last. Changing the date new people take office affects how long the outgoing person is in office, even if it is only by days or hours, so changing the start date matters.

If the Electoral College cannot choose a President or Vice President, then the House of Representatives or Senate, respectively, votes and chooses the new one. Before this change, there was a chance that representatives who had just been voted out might still be in office and so be able to choose the new President.

What dangers or problems can you see if that happened?

SECTION 2

The Congress shall assemble at least once in every year, and such meeting shall begin at noon on the 3d day of January, unless they shall by law appoint a different day.

This changed Article 1 Section 4 of the Constitution, which specifies that Congress meets on the first Monday in December. It allows for the date to be changed with a law so a Constitutional amendment is not necessary for future changes.

SECTION 3

If, at the time fixed for the beginning of the term of the President, the President elect shall have died, the Vice President elect shall become President. If a President shall not have been chosen before the time fixed for the beginning of his term, or if the President elect shall have failed to qualify, then the Vice President elect shall act as President until a President shall have qualified; and the Congress may by law provide for the case wherein neither a President elect nor a Vice President shall have qualified, declaring who shall then act as President, or the manner in which one who is to act shall be selected, and such person shall act accordingly until a President or Vice President shall have qualified.

This Amendment clarifies how the President is elected and part of the line of succession, and describes how to proceed if the President-Elect dies before taking office. It also clarifies how to proceed if a President-Elect and/or Vice-President-Elect do not qualify for the office. It does not, however, state in what way these officers should "qualify" for the office. The fact that they are already the President-Elect and Vice-President-Elect implies that this is separate from winning the election.

What do you think they mean by "qualifying"?

SECTION 4

The Congress may by law provide for the case of the death of any of the persons from whom the House of Representatives may choose a President whenever the right of choice shall have devolved upon them, and for the case of the death of any of the persons from whom the Senate may choose a Vice President whenever the right of choice shall have devolved upon them.

This gives Congress the right to determine how to proceed if one or more Presidential/Vice-Presidential candidates dies when the House of Representatives or Senate is responsible for deciding the election.

SECTION 5

Sections 1 and 2 shall take effect on the 15th day of October following the ratification of this article.

If Section 5 was not here and the states had ratified this in December, then Congress would have been forced to rush to accommodate the change. This ensured there was adequate time to make the change.

SECTION 6

This article shall be inoperative unless it shall have been ratified as an amendment to the Constitution by the legislatures of three-fourths of the several States within seven years from the date of its submission.

The earliest amendments had no deadline for ratification, so they could theoretically still be ratified and made part of our Constitution. In fact, an amendment originally proposed with the Bill of Rights was ratified nearly sixty years after this amendment, nearly 200 years after being sent to the states. This section gave states a deadline to keep this amendment from floating around indefinitely.

AMENDMENT XXI
PASSED BY CONGRESS FEBRUARY 20, 1933. RATIFIED DECEMBER 5, 1933.

SECTION 1

The eighteenth article of amendment to the Constitution of the United States is hereby repealed.

The Great Depression started in 1929. By 1933, the federal government desperately needed more money. As mentioned in the discussion of the 18th Amendment, alcohol taxes were historically a huge source of revenue. Re-legalizing and taxing alcohol was a logical (and effective) choice, particularly given how extremely unpopular and ineffective prohibition was.

SECTION 2

The transportation or importation into any State, Territory, or Possession of the United States for delivery or use therein of intoxicating liquors, in violation of the laws thereof, is hereby prohibited.

SECTION 3

This article shall be inoperative unless it shall have been ratified as an amendment to the Constitution by conventions in the several States, as provided in the Constitution, within seven years from the date of the submission hereof to the States by the Congress.

This article repeals, or takes back, the 18th Amendment, Prohibition, and made alcohol legal again.[4] This is the only time a Constitutional amendment was repealed by another amendment. As discussed, the financial strain of the Great Depression on the federal government was the main reason it was repealed.[5]

AMENDMENT XXII
PASSED BY CONGRESS MARCH 21, 1947. RATIFIED FEBRUARY 27, 1951.

SECTION 1

No person shall be elected to the office of the President more than twice, and no person who has held the office of President, or acted as President, for more than two years of a term to which some other person was elected President shall be elected to the office of President more than once. But this Article shall not apply to any person holding the office of President when this Article was proposed by Congress, and shall not prevent any person who may be holding the office of President, or acting as President, during the term within which this Article becomes operative from holding the office of President or acting as President during the remainder of such term.

This creates term limits for the President, which means any American can only be elected to the position of President two times (for two terms, eight years total), or for a maximum of not more than ten years if they replace a previous President mid-term. George Washington refused to serve more than two terms and all the presidents after him followed in this tradition, even though it wasn't a legal requirement, until Franklin Delano Roosevelt (FDR) served four terms. When he died during his fourth term, Congress passed this Amendment quickly (for Congress).

Harry Truman was President when this Amendment was proposed and it specifically did not apply to him. However, like all Presidents before him except FDR, he chose not to run for more than two terms.

SECTION 2

This article shall be inoperative unless it shall have been ratified as an amendment to the Constitution by the legislatures of three-fourths of the several States within seven years from the date of its submission to the States by the Congress.

What problems can you think of with term limits? If there are term limits, what incentive beyond their own conscience does a person have to do their best and most honest job?

What problems can you think of with not having term limits? Why do you think Congress and the states passed this so quickly? Why do you think it was proposed in 1947, not earlier in our history?

AMENDMENT XXIII
PASSED BY CONGRESS JUNE 16, 1960. RATIFIED MARCH 29, 1961.

SECTION 1

The District constituting the seat of Government of the United States shall appoint in such manner as Congress may direct:

A number of electors of President and Vice President equal to the whole number of Senators and Representatives in Congress to which the District would be entitled if it were a State, but in no event more than the least populous State; they shall be in addition to those appointed by the States, but they shall be considered, for the purposes of the election of President and Vice President, to be electors appointed by a State; and they shall meet in the District and perform such duties as provided by the twelfth article of amendment.

SECTION 2

The Congress shall have power to enforce this article by appropriate legislation.

When the Founding Fathers called for the creation of a Federal City (now called Washington, D.C.) to serve as our capital, they hoped that city could be kept out of national politics. Part of that was not giving it representation and voting rights that states received. They didn't expect many people to live there. It also originally contained land from two states, so having citizens vote for representatives from either the Maryland or Virginia delegation would have been difficult. As discussed earlier, the Virginia land was later retroceded so modern D.C. only has land from Maryland.

Our Capital City ended up being forced to accept taxation without representation, as their license plates say. To be fair, at least some of people who live there work for Congress or the military and keep a permanent address someplace else. This means they can and do vote (absentee) someplace else. Many others are diplomats from other countries. However, there are still a large group of citizens living in D.C. who do not have Congressional representation. This amendment ensures they can vote for the President.

D.C. has been trying to get voting Congressional representation as well for many years but it would take another amendment for this to happen, and would make them the only city in the country with its own Congressional delegation.

In 2010, D.C.'s population was just over 600,000. In comparison New York City's was over 8.2 million and Chicago's over 2.8 million. Even the population of nearby Baltimore (far from one of the largest US cities) was 30,000 more than D.C. All of these other cities are ably represented by their state Congressmen.

In case you were wondering, the population of Montana was 989,000, North Dakota 672,000, and Alaska 710,000.

D.C. has non-voting representatives in Congress to argue for what they want because Congress has controls the city government. D.C. has a Mayor and City Council, but Congress reviews all their laws before they go into effect and retains control of the budget.

Do you think it would be fair for D.C. to have its own Congressional delegation of two Senators and at least one Representative? Is it fair for them to have no voting representation, as it currently stands? Is there another Congressional delegation they could reasonably be made part of? Is there another solution

Could they vote for Senators and Representatives who would be part of the delegation from another state, such as Virginia or Delaware or Alaska? Which state's delegation, and why?

What do you think is the fairest way for citizens living in D.C., a single medium size city, to be represented in Congress?

Registering to vote, which is required before you can vote, and actually voting are two important responsibilities of citizenship. So is participating in political campaigns. How do you think exercising these rights are helped or hindered (hurt) by living in D.C.? Do you think D.C. residents are more or less likely than people in other areas to communicate with elected officials or know about current events? What other responsibilities or duties can you think of that come with citizenship? How much do you think politics is a part of daily life for everyone in DC, even those not directly in politics? Do you think this is good, bad, or irrelevant for the nation?

AMENDMENT XXIV
PASSED BY CONGRESS AUGUST 27, 1962. RATIFIED JANUARY 23, 1964.

SECTION 1

The right of citizens of the United States to vote in any primary or other election for President or Vice President, for electors for President or Vice President, or for Senator or Representative in Congress, shall not be denied or abridged by the United States or any State by reason of failure to pay poll tax or other tax.

SECTION 2

The Congress shall have power to enforce this article by appropriate legislation.

Saying you may not be denied something is not the same thing as guaranteeing you will get it. Because states set voting qualifications, they have sometimes written them so they can deny specific groups the right the vote. Poll taxes are a primary example. Southern blacks were largely poor and could not afford to pay poll taxes. Whites generally could. Therefore, they passed poll taxes to prevent blacks from voting. Poll taxes existed in the Colonies since at least the early 1600s, but they were not necessarily linked to voting.[6] This changed after the Civil War. Since poll taxes were not preventing anyone from voting based on their color or gender, but rather on not paying a tax, they weren't illegal until the 24th Amendment passed in 1964, even though they clearly violated the intention of the other amendments.

Recently, states have passed laws requiring voters prove legal residency. What do you think of this? Is it the same as a poll tax? How else can voter fraud be prevented? (Among other things, voter fraud is when someone who isn't eligible votes, or someone who is eligible votes more than once in the same election.)

If you object to the form of proof required, what do you think would be better and why? Why do you think the required form is unfair? Most commonly, it is a legal document with a photograph such as a state issued ID or Driver's License. How many adult citizens do you know who do not have one of these? What else do you need an ID for? (If you don't have one yet, ask an adult.)

Without a requirement such as this, people can use easily obtained documents such as a utility bill to prove residence. People could use a utility bill from an old address, or a friend or family members home. How could that contribute to voter fraud, or do you think it couldn't? What other problems can you see?

States setting voter qualifications has led to three amendments being ratified to prevent them from denying specific groups their voting rights. Those amendments prevent excluding voters based on gender (19th Amendment), race (15th) and age, if they are at least 18 (26th).

Because some states had a significant history of using any means possible to prevent certain groups, mostly blacks and other minorities, from voting, the Voting Rights Act was passed in 1965, one year after the 24th Amendment itself.[7] It was clearly intended to keep those areas from simply implementing new, slightly different, rules to disenfranchise those they didn't want to let vote. A special provision in Section 5 requires areas with a history of voting restrictions to get federal approval ("pre-clearance") before implementing new voting practices or procedures, including redistricting, to ensure that they do not deny any citizen of their right to vote and gave federal officials the ability to register voters.[8] Because "pre-clearance" isn't limited in duration, these areas are still subject to extra federal oversight more than 50 years later.

AMENDMENT XXV
PASSED BY CONGRESS JULY 6, 1965. RATIFIED FEBRUARY 10, 1967.

NOTE: ARTICLE II, SECTION 1, OF THE CONSTITUTION WAS AFFECTED BY THE 25TH AMENDMENT.

THE BILL OF RIGHTS AMENDMENT XVII-XXVII

SECTION 1

In case of the removal of the President from office or of his death or resignation, the Vice President shall become President.

This is the primary reason we have a Vice-President. It is also the reason that the Vice-President, like the President, must be a natural-born citizen. If the Vice-President was not a natural born citizen, then they could not assume the Presidency if the need arises, and that is one of only two tasks the Constitution specifically gives the Vice President.

SECTION 2

Whenever there is a vacancy in the office of the Vice President, the President shall nominate a Vice President who shall take office upon confirmation by a majority vote of both Houses of Congress.

There is a line of succession for the Presidency that starts with the Vice President, goes to the Speaker of the House, and continues from there. The President is not bound to follow that line in choosing a new Vice President because it might end up in a situation similar to the Adams/Jefferson and Jefferson/Burr Presidencies when the two did not work well together. The complete line of succession is for the catastrophic possibility of having the President, Vice President and potentially others in the government all die at virtually the same time, before a new Vice President can be selected and sworn in, not for simply filling a vacant office. (It's also great material for apocalypse movies.)

Like the President, the Vice-President is mortal and the office may become vacant. Also like the President, it could be bad for the country to leave the position vacant, although it has often been left empty in the past. In fact, every single time the Vice Presidency was vacant from the founding of our nation until after this amendment was ratified, the position remained vacant until the next election. The general belief was that the position should be filled by someone the people elected, thus the choice to wait for the next election to fill the post.

Do you agree that it should only be filled by someone the people voted for? If so, how should this amendment be changed?

What is truly amazing is that it did not matter on any of those occasions, but only a few years after this amendment passed, it did. If this clause had not been in effect, Richard Nixon probably would have left the Vice Presidency vacant when Spiro Agnew resigned, since that was the tradition. As you will see below, that could have created a problem, except that this amendment had just been passed and the Vice Presidency was not vacant.

When Spiro Agnew resigned and Gerald Ford became Vice President, and again when Richard Nixon resigned and Vice President Ford became President, this clause was used to choose a new Vice President.[9] Ford was the House Minority Leader from 1965, the year Congress passed this amendment, until he became Vice President in 1973 and President in 1974.

When Ford became President, he nominated New York Governor Nelson Rockefeller to fill the empty job of Vice President. From August 1974–January 1977, neither the President nor the Vice-President of the United States were men who had been elected to those positions. Instead, they were selected using the provisions of this amendment.

If the President had followed the Presidential line of succession and the Speaker of the House had become the new Vice President, then Republican President Nixon would have been stuck with a Democratic Vice President. How well do you think that would have worked? When Nixon resigned, the new Speaker would, in turn, have become Vice President. Control of the White House would have moved from a Republican President and Vice President to a Democratic President and Vice-President without an election. What do you think US citizens would have thought of that? Would that have been right?

SECTION 3

Whenever the President transmits to the President pro tempore of the Senate and the Speaker of the House of Representatives his written declaration that he is unable to discharge the powers and duties of his office, and until he transmits to them a written declaration to the contrary, such powers and duties shall be discharged by the Vice President as Acting President.

The most common reason for invoking this is a Presidential illness or surgery. If the current President is struck by appendicitis, he should immediately notify Congress; the Vice President will become Acting President while he undergoes surgery and recovery; and then the office will be returned to the President. This ensures that we always have a chief executive in place, even if they are struck by a sudden illness or injury that prevents them from performing their duties.

In 1985, Ronald Reagan had surgery for colon cancer and transferred power to Vice President Bush for just under eight hours.[10] He followed these procedures but specifically did not invoke this amendment, possibly to avoid setting a precedent future presidents would have to follow for routine procedures. When George W. Bush had colonoscopies (a quick, routine medical procedure) in 2002 and 2007, he chose to invoke this amendment. As of this writing, these are the only times this clause has been invoked and all three ended when the President sent a letter saying he was resuming his duties.

Why do you think Congress felt this was needed now when it had not been for so much of our history? There have been times the President was incapacitated for weeks without handing over power to anyone else. How do you think that would play out today? What kinds of effects might it have? Do you think it is really necessary to do this when the procedure will last only a few hours?

SECTION 4

Whenever the Vice President and a majority of either the prin-

cipal officers of the executive departments or of such other body as Congress may by law provide, transmit to the President pro tempore of the Senate and the Speaker of the House of Representatives their written declaration that the President is unable to discharge the powers and duties of his office, the Vice President shall immediately assume the powers and duties of the office as Acting President.

If the President is shot or has a stroke, he probably cannot notify Congress that he cannot perform his duties until his recovery is complete. This provides a remedy for that situation.

Reagan was shot in 1981 and this clause was not invoked, although it is not clear why.[11] He was the first President to survive an assassination attempt while serving as President. Why do you think it was not invoked? Do you think it should have been?

Thereafter, when the President transmits to the President pro tempore of the Senate and the Speaker of the House of Representatives his written declaration that no inability exists, he shall resume the powers and duties of his office unless the Vice President and a majority of either the principal officers of the executive department or of such other body as Congress may by law provide, transmit within four days to the President pro tempore of the Senate and the Speaker of the House of Representatives their written declaration that the President is unable to discharge the powers and duties of his office. Thereupon Congress shall decide the issue, assembling within forty-eight hours for that purpose if not in session. If the Congress, within twenty-one days after receipt of the latter written declaration, or, if Congress is not in session, within twenty-one days after Congress is required to assemble, determines by two-thirds vote of both Houses that the President is unable to discharge the powers and duties of his office, the Vice President shall continue to discharge the same as Acting President; otherwise, the President shall resume the powers and duties of his office.

In 1881, President Garfield was shot and it took eleven weeks for him to die, including 8 days in a coma and periods of hallucinations. His only official action was signing an extradition act. If the President is badly injured and no longer able to do his job, even if he believes he is, as Garfield may have, this provides a way for Congress to remove him from office. This is yet another, admittedly new, part of our system of checks and balances.

Woodrow Wilson was an invalid after he suffered a stroke and spent several days in a coma while in office. FDR had serious health problems that are well-known now, although the Press Corps cooperated with the White House to cover his disability at the time. Following the death of President John Kennedy in 1963, Lyndon Johnson, who had suffered a heart attack, became President and like others before him, he left the Vice Presidency empty until his next election in 1965.

Having a President with serious known health problem and no Vice President finally convinced Congress to clarify the line of succession for the Presidency and the procedures to follow if the President dies, becomes critically ill, or is otherwise unable to carry out the job of President.[12] The nomination and confirmation process can still take several months, so there is still a time when there is no Vice President, but it is an improvement over leaving the office vacant until the next election.

> Do you think that having a President incapacitated or the office vacant for a few hours or even weeks would have made much difference one or two hundred years ago?
>
> Consider how quickly (or slowly) news, people, weapons, and everything else moved. How does that compare to how fast they move today? Could we leave the office vacant or occupied by someone who is incapacitated for weeks, or even hours, today?

AMENDMENT XXVI
PASSED BY CONGRESS MARCH 23, 1971. RATIFIED JULY 1, 1971.

NOTE: AMENDMENT 14, SECTION 2, OF THE CONSTITUTION WAS MODIFIED BY SECTION 1 OF THE 26TH AMENDMENT.

CHAPTER 18

<u>SECTION 1</u>

The right of citizens of the United States, who are eighteen years of age or older, to vote shall not be denied or abridged by the United States or by any State on account of age.

<u>SECTION 2</u>

The Congress shall have power to enforce this article by appropriate legislation.

This lowered the voting age from 21 to 18. Prior to passage of this Amendment, 18 was old enough to die for this country, including in Vietnam, but not to vote for it. The American public demanded this Amendment to correct that, and the fact that it was ratified at warp speed, faster than any other amendment, proves that even Congress is capable of responding quickly to what citizens want.

AMENDMENT XXVII
ORIGINALLY PROPOSED SEPT. 25, 1789. RATIFIED MAY 7, 1992.

No law, varying the compensation for the services of the Senators and Representatives, shall take effect, until an election of representatives shall have intervened.

Our representatives can't give themselves a pay raise. Well, they can, and do, but now they don't take effect until after the next national election, so it isn't technically "for them" since they might not be there when it comes into effect. This gives the citizens a chance to vote a bunch of them out if they don't approve. This does not in any way limit the size or frequency of their pay or benefit increases. The reality is that the majority of Congressmen are re-elected for quite a few terms, so they still get the raises when they come into effect.

This amendment took longer than any other to be ratified, and it very nearly didn't. By 1792, only seven of the eleven needed states (¾ of the states) ratified it. Eighty-one years later, in 1873, Ohio ratified it to show their anger when Congress gave itself a very large pay raise.

In 1978, Wyoming approved it to protest another Congressional pay raise, but by this time ¾ of the states was thirty eight states. It might have sat there with a mere nine states ratifying it, but a twenty year old student in Texas named Gregory Watson decided to write a college paper on it in 1982, and part of that paper was a call to action to get states to finally ratify it.

Many people write things in a place or two, or talk to a few friends about things that need done. Watson actually continued contacting states after his class was finished. Maine and Colorado passed it in 1983 and 1984. By 1989, a majority of states had ratified it. In 1992, the 27th Amendment was ratified. This was something James Madison, the Father of the Constitution, had tried and failed to do two hundred years earlier, but Watson did it in ten years. As with Mr. Brown and his Supreme Court case for his daughter, one regular person made a real difference in our nation.

CHAPTER 18

RESOURCES

1. Vacant Senate Seats and Passage of the 17th Amendment
www.senate.gov/artandhistory/history/common/generic/SeventeenthAme
ndment.htm

2. How Taxes Enabled Prohibition and Led to its Repeal
taxfoundation.org/blog/how-taxes-enabled-alcohol-prohibition-and-also-
led-its-repeal

3. Reproduction of Abigail Adams' "Remember the Ladies" Letter
history.hanover.edu/courses/excerpts/165adams-rtl.html

4. How Prohibition Worked
history.howstuffworks.com/historical-events/prohibition.htm

5. Did Prohibition Really Work? Prohibition as Public Health Innovation
www.ncbi.nlm.nih.gov/pmc/articles/PMC1470475/

6. The History of Poll Taxes
www.encyclopediavirginia.org/Poll_Tax#start_entry

7. Voting Rights Act (1965)
www.ourdocuments.gov/doc.php?flash=true&doc=100

8. The 1965 Voting Rights Act Enactment
www.justice.gov/crt/history-federal-voting-rights-laws

9. Letter from House Minority Leader Ford to President Nixon
www.archives.gov/education/lessons/ford-nixon-letter/

10. What is the 25th Amendment and when has it been invoked?
historynewsnetwork.org/article/812

11. The Reagan Shooting in 1981
www.newsmax.com/RonaldKessler/president-ronaldreagan-JamesV-
HickeyJrThomasJ-Baker/2011/03/16/id/389604/

12. Presidential Disability
www.usconstitution.net/consttop_pdis.html?ModPagespeed=noscript

CHAPTER 19
STATE SOVEREIGNTY VERSUS FEDERAL POWER

When the US Constitution was written, epic debates raged over how to divide power between state and federal governments, and over how much power to allow government in general. Although everyone finally agreed and ratified the Constitution, part of that agreement was to essentially avoid a few topics they couldn't agree on. Because the Founders worded things vaguely on the toughest issues and left them to be resolved later, they still had to be resolved later.

Of all these issues, slavery was the most obvious, but taxation and spending issues were important too. Arguments over slavery were so heated that the Constitution actually forbade revisiting the topic for 20 years, until 1808. Over the years, this state/federal power struggle has erupted in many different ways ranging from states simply ignoring federal laws, to states leaving the Union during the Civil War, to state and federal governments suing each other.

It is honestly quite surprising that there more topics did not lead to heated debates, given the diversity of the states that joined to become these United States of America. Slaveholding and free, and industrial and agrarian were just the tip of the iceberg of differences. New and established. Small and large. Voting requirements varied by state.[1] A few states initially gave "property owners" (including women) the right to vote. By 1787, only New Jersey still allowed it.[2]

Some states still had state religions when the US Constitution was adopted and were very intolerant of other faiths, although the specific religion varied. Some states already practiced tolerance and did not have a state religion.

In many states, only a tiny area within 100 miles of the Atlantic Ocean was settled. The rest was frontier. No part of Rhode Island, Connecticut, or New Jersey reaches as far as 100 miles from the ocean. Climate, products (crops, industrial goods) and natural resources–all varied a lot among and even within the colonies.

The states were incredibly diverse, just like the states still are today. Because they did not want to live under a strong central government like a monarchy again, and because there were such huge differences among the colonies, they were quite insistent on ensuring that state's rights were protected as surely and strongly as individual rights.

This fear of central power resulted in the Articles of Confederation (Appendix III). As discussed earlier, the Articles did not give the federal government enough power to guarantee our country would survive. Shay's Rebellion in Massachusetts was a key turning point in making a more powerful central government less unacceptable to the states.[3] It demonstrated that the federal government was too weak to protect the states from a true rebellion, invasion, or other danger.

Because they still weren't exactly excited about having a stronger central government and were very concerned about protecting states' rights, the states sent representatives to a Constitutional Convention to amend the Articles, not intending to replace them.

The delegates tasked with fixing the Articles quickly concluded that they could not be repaired, only replaced. They replaced the Articles with the Constitution we know in complete defiance of the instructions from their state governments. The "they" in this instance means the delegates, not the states.

The states themselves were not entirely ready for that, even after Shay's Rebellion, so in order to complete it and get it ratified, the Founders had to ensure that state's rights were protected fairly strongly and to complete the new Constitution very quickly.

You may sometimes hear people discuss having another Constitutional Convention, sometimes shortened to "Con Con" and more recently referred to as an Article V Convention, as discussed in Chapter 12. Some people fear that an Article V Convention could lead to a runaway convention that totally changes our structure of government, just as the Constitution replaced the Articles of Confederation.[4]

What do you think about this possibility? Do you think an Article V Convention might really result in a complete restructuring of our government, just like the Constitution restructured the government of its time? How easy or hard do you think that would be to accomplish today? Do you think it's a good idea? What scares you about an Article V Convention? What changes would you like to see if there is one?

Does it surprise you to know states have called for an Article V Convention?[5] Why do you think it hasn't happened yet? (Hint: A Constitutional Convention must be held if the legislatures of two thirds of the states call for one.) Do you think it's harder to be the first state to make the call, to make it after a few others have, or to be the one who makes the final call that triggers the Convention? Why?

Because they were authorized to amend the Articles of Confederation, not to create a new Constitution, the Framers worked in total secrecy. The Founders were so committed to secrecy that they even kept the windows shut in July in Philadelphia, long before air conditioning was invented.

As a result, we have very little information regarding the actual debates. Most of what we have is from *The Federalist* papers.[6] Alexander Hamilton, John Jay, and James Madison wrote and published this series of articles anonymously under the pen name Publius to convince the public to adopt the new Constitution. The author's names became public knowledge after Alexander Hamilton's death years later.

Of course, these were not the only speeches and letters for or against the new Constitution. Those against are called the Anti-Federalist Papers, although they didn't use that name at the time.[7]

What other reasons can you think of for the Founders working in total secrecy? Can we know what arguments they put forth for or against any section? Can we know exactly which men were in favor of or opposed to any specific part? Do you think knowing all of this would affect the way the Constitution is read and understood, or interpreted?

Think about the impact Jefferson's Danbury letter has had on the 1st Amendment. If we knew that George Washington argued strongly against one point of view or interpretation, but that David Brearley of New Jersey argued strongly for it, which view do you think most Americans would favor? What if Ben Franklin and James Madison were at loggerheads over a point?

Do you think the views of largely forgotten Founders like Brearley would be viewed as being as important as those of more famous ones? Would that be fair or right? Do you think their choice to keep the proceedings secret–there were very few records kept of the discussions–was a wise one? Why or why not?

The arguments over slavery were largely put to the side for a brief period after the Constitution was ratified because the Constitution specified that slavery couldn't be ended until after 1808, when importation of more slaves was set to end, but that doesn't mean the issue was in any way lessened or forgotten. These concerns grew with our nation grew and as new states were added, particularly when slaveholding states became concerned that non-slaveholding states might outnumber them. If that happened, laws or even an amendment forbidding slavery could be passed by Congress, regardless of what individual states wanted.

When the 1820 Missouri Compromise[8] and the Compromise of 1850[9] each passed, the balance between slave-holding and non-slave-holding states was restored and tensions lessened for a time. When Abraham Lincoln was elected in 1860, tensions rose to new heights. Eleven Southern states seceded, or left the Union, to become the Confederate States of America, which led to war. Quite a few names were used for that war including "The War Between the States," "War of the Rebellion," and the "War of Northern Aggression" before "the Civil War" became the generally accepted term.

Why do you think each of these names came into use? How do they show the political views of the people using the name? What do you think of each name? How do you think each name influences readers' perception of events? What part did state's rights play in the outbreak of the Civil War?

The very way we referred to our country reflected our origin as thirteen separate and totally independent states that were not necessarily happy to become part of one nation. It was "these" United States and used plural verbs, not "the" United States using singular verbs (e.g., "these United States have 15 states" compared to "the United States has 50 states") before the Civil War. Between the Civil War and 1900, it gradually changed to the modern singular usage.

Using the plural implied the US was made up of many smaller parts. Using the singular implied it had grown into one cohesive unit. The trauma of the Civil War and its aftermath, including the addition of new territories and states, finally bound us together as *The*, not *these*, United States. As this name change implies, before the Civil War people identified more strongly with their individual states than with the nation as a whole. For example, Robert E. Lee believed slavery was evil, but when Virginia seceded, so he reluctantly went too. He became a general in the Confederate, not the Union, Army because he was a Virginian first and an American second.

After the Civil War, citizens of the United States started identifying as a nation instead of a collection of states.

> *What do you think of this name change? Do you think it shows any real difference? How do you think of yourself? Do you think of yourself as a US citizen (or American) first, or do you feel more strongly about your state or city?*
>
> *Without this change in sentiment, do you think the 17th Amendment would have been ratified? (After the 17th, citizens elected Senators instead of Legislatures selecting them.)*

At the same time, the federal government began taking more and more powers upon itself, including many things that had been the states' responsibility. There is one specific clause called the Interstate Commerce Clause (Article I, Section 8, Clause 3) that the Federal Government has used to become much more powerful compared to the states. It says that Congress shall have the power "to regulate Commerce with foreign Nations, and among the several States, and with the Indian Tribes." This is interpreted to mean any transaction that goes, or could go, across state lines. It is used to justify a lot of what the federal government regulates, and states have decided to not enforce some of these federal regulations within their boundaries.

When a state ignores, or decides not to enforce, federal laws they believe are unconstitutional within their state boundaries, it is called nullification. This was first suggested by Thomas Jefferson and James Madison in response to the Alien and Sedition Acts of 1798, but the theory wasn't acted upon for thirty years.[10] When he and Madison proposed nullification, he was the Vice President under John Adams, the President who signed these acts into law. They *really* didn't agree politically.

In 1828 and 1832, Tariff Acts (taxes) that heavily favored industrial (Northern) interests over agricultural (Southern) interests were passed.[11] South Carolina believed these Acts were unconstitutional and acted to nullify them. (In short, they refused to enforce the laws.) This triggered the Nullification Crisis of 1832 and South Carolina very nearly seceded from the Union before a compromise was reached with the Tariff of 1833.[12] Slavery and the money and power attached to it weren't the only reason South Carolina and the other Confederate states seceded, but they were clearly important in the Civil War. In these earlier nullification cases, the argument was more purely economic.

More than 200 years after Jefferson proposed the idea, nullification is still happening, although taxation issues are no longer the focus. This time, there is no national movement, no states have threatened secession, and the federal response is generally muted to non-existent. For example, Montana and several other states passed laws to nullify federal firearms laws. The 2009 Montana Firearms Freedom Act states that federal gun regulations do not apply to guns manufactured within the state that remain within the state because they are not part of interstate commerce, and therefore are not subject to the Interstate Commerce Clause[13].

States have also passed laws allowing sale and use of medical marijuana within the state, despite federal laws that it is illegal. Most, but not all, of these laws only make it legal for people with specific medical problems, just like many other addictive drugs such as morphine are only legal for people under a doctor's care. Part of the reasoning is that nothing in the Constitution gives the government the right to regulate the plants people choose to grow on their private property.

How do you think the 10th Amendment, which reserves any rights not specifically given to the federal government for the states, relates to these different cases? How do you think the 2nd Amendment relates the Firearms Freedom Act? Do you think people should be able to grow any plant, including marijuana?

How do you think things have changed in how our government operates and the expectations people have of what the federal government may and may not do between 1832 and today?

> *How do the states' actions and the federal government's respons-*
> *es differ? Can you think of other examples of nullification in the*
> *news? What do you think about states doing this? Why do you*
> *think they are doing it?*

Slavery ended after the Civil War, but the effects of it clearly did not.
The federal government passed many laws, and three amendments, in
an attempt to force states to treat blacks the same as whites. Some
were declared unconstitutional by the Supreme Court (1875 Civil
Rights Act) and states simply found ways around others (poll taxes).
Racism persisted, and persists still.

> *How have these traditional divisions changed or stayed the same?*
> *What examples can you give? How does moving power between*
> *the state and federal levels affect program funding, regulation,*
> *and function? How do you think changing who has power in dif-*
> *ferent areas has affected state and federal government interac-*
> *tion? How could this relate to issues like nullification?*

"Separate but equal" ensured "colored" people did not have access to
the nicer facilities "whites" used. They were jailed, lynched (killed,
often by hanging), and otherwise brutalized for simple, everyday
things whites could do freely and without fear. Legal slavery ended
about 150 years ago, but it has been barely 50 years since citizen de-
mands during the 1960s Civil Rights Era finally gave non-whites
(Asians as well as blacks) equal rights. Many women were also denied
opportunities and education until after the Civil Rights Era.

> *How do you think you would feel if you knew your parents or*
> *grandparents were denied the right to vote because of their skin*
> *color? How would it feel to know that they were beaten or jailed*
> *trying to do things we take for granted today, like voting or even*
> *helping someone of a different race cross the street? What if you*
> *knew they had been unable to pursue their dream job or get a*
> *good education because of their skin color, gender, or "foreign"*
> *name?*

Do you think the federal government was justified? Realistically, was there another way to fight for justice? Would states have done the right thing?

The federal government forced states to start providing integrated schools in the 1960s, which meant that they couldn't decide which school a child would attend based on that child's skin color. This was part of an overall ban on the "separate but equal" policy that permitted states and businesses to provide different facilities (including schools, water fountains, train cars, and restaurant seating) for "colored" (black) and white people. In reality, the facilities were never really equal because the whites were treated better. Do you think a train car with luggage in half the car and no separate dining area is as nice as one with seating, bathrooms, and access to a dining car? You can probably guess, but the whites are the ones who had access to food in the dining car. "Coloreds" weren't even permitted to pass through cars for whites to get to the dining car.

As discussed above, *Brown v. Board of Education* helped overturned *Plessy v. Ferguson* to end separate but equal, but it didn't happen by itself. It was part of a far larger effort.

Under separate but equal, black people were not allowed to eat in many Southern diners. This changed in 1960 when four young black men returned to college from a vacation in North Carolina and refused to accept segregation.[14] They entered a Woolworths Department Store in Greensboro, NC and sat at a whites-only lunch counter.

When these young men sat down, there was an older white lady sitting at the counter watching them. They assumed she was upset by their actions in refusing to leave the counter. When she left, she did indeed tell them that she was upset—but not that they were refusing to leave. She told them that she wished they had done it ten years earlier! They had judged her by her color, and her age, as surely as others judged them.

Tens of thousands of others eventually joined them in protesting whites-only service in many towns and cities. The efforts of these regular people pushed both businesses and the government to do the right thing and finally end the era of "separate but equal" that the Supreme Court had started with their ruling in *Plessy v. Ferguson*. This is an example of why we need both a federal government and citizens who work hard to correct wrongs that they see. Without federal power, this might still be a work in progress. But without citizen's efforts, the federal government might have continued to ignore it.

How else can states fight a law they believe is unconstitutional?

The post-Revolutionary and Civil War/Reconstruction eras were not the only times the federal government's power grew a great deal in a few years.[15] The Great Depression and FDR's New Deal in the 1930s are another clear example.[16] Many new social programs started then. Within a few years, the Supreme Court overturned many parts of the New Deal because it felt the federal government was taking powers the Constitution reserved for the states.[17] Once again, in the mid to late 1960s with Lyndon Johnson's Great Society, the federal government became involved in areas that had strictly been the responsibility of states and started a lot of new social programs.[18]

Specifically, the federal government has generally been responsible for regulating activities among the states (but not within any state) and extending beyond our borders. These include commerce (business), foreign policy, and defense. This is similar to the way a computer network regulates access among the work stations inside and outside of the network, but not on individual desktops. State governments have been responsible for internal concerns such as public health, safety, and welfare. (Welfare here means making sure everyone is doing well, not the government program that provides people with money to pay for living expenses.)

About the same time, the federal government also changed its policy of staying out of education, which states were responsible for. The first steps toward federal control of education started after the Soviets (Russians from 1917 to 1991) launched Sputnik in 1957.[19] President Eisenhower and the federal government decided to offer states additional money for a variety of reasons, including helping to improve math and science education.[20] A few years later, they offered more money to improve teacher pay. If these issues sound familiar, that's because they are still issues. The federal government's involvement has not fixed these problems, although that doesn't mean it hasn't made a difference. It has definitely added more paperwork, rules, and standards teachers and schools have to follow.

> *How can federal involvement in education be a good thing? How about more standards and rules for teachers and schools to follow? How can each of those be a bad thing? Do you think they are good, bad, or mixed, overall? How and why?*

Today, the federal government controls massive amounts of money and can use that power indirectly to force states to do what it wants in education, transportation, and many other areas. This is how both 55 mph speed limit and a 21 year old minimum drinking age laws were forced through.[21] The funds can reach the states either directly or indirectly.

One of the biggest indirect sources of federal funds is military bases, and the federal government can close military bases, even large ones. This may mean a lot of unemployed civilians, people who do not work in the active duty for the armed services, near the bases and a lot of lost income for local businesses. Military bases often employ civilians in a wide variety of jobs including accounting, computer work, and other support positions. They also support the local economy by everyday activities like buying groceries and going to the movies. Even when the base clearly needs closed because it isn't used, completely closing it can be a long and difficult process, but even reducing how many people are stationed there can be very painful for towns, counties, and states that rely on those funds.

More directly, the federal government can cut funding for schools, roads, infrastructure projects, and many other things if states do not follow the rules it sets. Of course, if they are happy with a state government, the federal government can also build locate new bases there, pay companies to do large projects, and many other things that can bring in a lot of money.

In 1974, the federal government used this power to force all the states to adopt a 55 mph speed limit by threatening to stop federal funding for road construction and maintenance for states that did not. This was justified under the Interstate Commerce Clause discussed above. The 55 mph speed limit, repealed in 1995, was designed to force Americans to save fuel during the 1970s fuel crisis.

Congress used this power again in the 1980s. This time, they forced states to increase the drinking age to 21. In *South Dakota v. Dole* in 1987, the Supreme Court ruled that this was constitutional in part because the states could keep a lower drinking age–if they chose to accept losing 5-10% of their federal highway funding.[22] That's a very large amount of money to give up.

What do you think of that ruling? Do you agree that the states had a real choice? Do you think they could really afford to give up that much money? If they did give it up, how do you think the citizens of that state would feel about it?

Do you think the federal government has the right to withhold funding from states if they don't obey federal dictates? Not all are laws; some are regulations from federal agencies Does you think it makes a difference if it's a law or a regulation? Why? How are they different?

They also use this economic power to force states to follow federal guidelines and meet federal standards in many (many) areas. Trying to make sure everyone meets certain minimum standards sounds like a good idea and can be a very good thing, as with ending "separate but equal", but different people and places are, well, different. Just like "one size fits all" clothing, "one size fits all" federal laws don't always work out as well as the bureaucrats writing them think they will.

Do you think an energy conservation law limiting air conditioning to the hottest four hours of the day plus 15 minutes an hour the rest of the day is a good idea? It would save a lot of electricity and you could still get some cooling.

How do you think this would be received in Alaska or Hawaii? People might not really care too much. They don't need it very much and their electric bill would be lower. If you tried the same

bill in in Arizona or Florida, how do you think people would respond? Not everyone can afford an efficient modern air conditioning system and good insulation for their home, so it would almost certainly cause health problems such as heat exhaustion, at a minimum, for some people.

Does this help you understand how the size of our nation makes it harder to have one-size-fits-all rules?

Clearly, balancing the need for a central government with the Founders' desire to limit its size, strength, and expense is a difficult balancing act. There are things that need to be maintained and regulated at the national level, such as our transportation systems (highways, airways, waterways, and railways), national parklands (another American innovation), and defense. There are others that have clearly been reserved to the states. Among these responsibilities are maintaining a militia (the National Guard), education, voter qualification, and determining qualifications for most offices.

The federal government ensures that states are not doing things that reflect the state's beliefs or needs but that are bad for the country as a whole. For example, if one state has a river that flows through it and into a nearby state, the second state could use that water to irrigate farmland. If the first state decides to dam the river so no one else has access to it, then everyone might have less food because that farmland can no longer produce as much. The federal government usually works with the states involved to reach an agreement that benefits as many people as possible, just as they have with the Virginia/Maryland dispute over the Potomac River.

CHAPTER 19

After you install your computer OS and the basic productivity and utility programs such as a word processor and firewall, you probably installed a lot of other programs. The different regulatory agencies and departments within the government are like those extra programs. Some need to go across all the states to work well, just like a massively multiplayer online game needs to access the internet and have lots of people logged in and playing to be fun. Others work better when they are controlled locally, just like it's more fun to play your own music on your iPod™ instead of listening to someone else's selection.

The different departments of the federal government are like computer programs. Some, like the Bureau of Indian Affairs, have been around since our country was founded and really don't use a lot of resources, like Minesweeper™. Some, like the National Park Service, provide a clear service that you can walk up to, see, and enjoy, like your photo gallery. Some, like Agriculture, work behind the scenes to achieve their goals, just like your desktop. We all know we need agriculture and farmers, but most of us never really see what Ag does or what kinds of resources it uses, which is also like a computer desktop program (screensavers, backgrounds, printer drivers, etc.).

Others, like the Environmental Protection Agency (EPA), are very public about their activities and goals. You may like them or hate them, but there is no mistaking their existence or what they are working toward. Some, like the military, are resource-hogs that use a lot of money, time, and resources. That is not a judgment–it simply is. Armies and navies have always been the biggest expenses of any government throughout history.

The most important questions to ask of each program–government or computer–is not what resources it uses or how much, but whether it truly needs to do everything it is doing, how well it is using those resources, and if someone else could do it better/more efficiently.

Adding programs, and cool new updated features for existing programs, can be fun on a computer or in the government, but it can also lead to bloatware.[23] That is software that has been bloated, or swollen, with features that are unnecessary or use too many resources compared to the benefit received. For instance, if you add a new calculator program, a very simple task, and it uses as much memory as photo editing software, a much more complicated task, then you have probably just installed bloatware. Bloat prevents a program from using its resources efficiently and can cause it to do unnecessary work.

There are programs and bureaucracies in the government that are bloatware. They start out small, with one clear task, but things keep getting added until their original purpose may be hard to find. Sometimes the bloat is written into the original code creating the program to get it passed (in government, this is commonly called pork or pork barrel politics) and sometimes it is added a little bit at a time over many years.[24]

It is also important to look at what the hardware can handle. Each program takes a certain amount of resources, primarily memory including "free" memory, and so does each data file you save. Free memory is space that does not have anything saved on it, so it is free for programs to use for processing while they are running. The less free memory you have, the slower and less efficiently programs run.

It is the same with the government. Each program takes a certain amount of resources, including money, staff, and space. Once those resources are used up, it gets harder and harder to install and successfully run new programs. You can add some resources by raising taxes and/or hiring more people, just as you can add extra memory to let your computer run more software, but that "fix" doesn't change the basic problem in the government or on your computer, and you can't keep doing it forever. Needs and wants have to be balanced in the government, just like they do in your life and on your computer.

As things have changed and become more complicated in our world, the federal government has taken on more and more responsibilities, and more and more powers, but some things never seem to change. In 2012, over half the states were suing the federal government because they believed the new Patient Protection and Affordable Care

Act, sometimes called Obamacare, to be unconstitutional, and the federal government was suing the state of Arizona over their immigration law for the same reason. Federal versus state power remains an issue even after over 222 years.

> What do you think of the rulings on these cases? What do you think of the fact that they went all the way to the Supreme Court?
>
> *Which case do you think was more difficult for the Court to rule on? How do you think the timing on these rulings—the summer before a Presidential election—could have impacted the election?*

RESOURCES

1. Voting in Early America
www.history.org/Foundation/journal/Spring07/elections.cfm

2. Letters Between Abigail and John Adams
www.thelizlibrary.org/suffrage/abigail.htm

3. Shay's Rebellion
www.massmoments.org/moment.cfm?mid=30

4. Article V Convention FAQs
www.conventionofstates.com/faq

5. States with a Standing Call for an Article V Convention
www.sweetliberty.org/standing_calls.htm

6. The Federalist Papers
www.constitution.org/fed/federa00.htm

7. The Anti-Federalist Papers
www.thefederalistpapers.org/anti-federalist-papers

8. The Missouri Compromise
www.loc.gov/rr/program/bib/ourdocs/Missouri.html

9. Compromise of 1850
www.loc.gov/rr/program/bib/ourdocs/Compromise1850.html

10. Alien and Sedition Acts of 1798
www.ourdocuments.gov/doc.php?flash=true&doc=16

11. Favored Northern Interests
www.cyberlearning-world.com/lessons/ushistory/19thcentury/nullify6.htm

12. Nullification Crisis of 1832/Nullification Proclamation
www.loc.gov/rr/program/bib/ourdocs/Nullification.html

13. Firearms Freedom Act
www.firearmsfreedomact.com

14. Ending Segregation
www.npr.org/templates/story/story.php?storyId=18615556

15. Reconstruction
www.history.com/topics/american-civil-war/reconstruction

16. New Deal
www.encyclopedia.com/topic/New_Deal.aspx

17. New Deal Overturned
publicpolicy.pepperdine.edu/academics/research/faculty-research/new-deal/supreme-court-cases/

18. Great Society
www.encyclopedia.com/topic/The_Great_Society.aspx

19. Sputnik
www.eisenhower.archives.gov/research/online_documents/sputnik.html

20. The US Response to Sputnik and Federal Involvement in Schools
www.whyfiles.org/047sputnik/main2.html

21. National 55 MPH Speed Limit
www.history.com/this-day-in-history/nixon-signs-national-speed-limit-into-law

22. *South Dakota v. Dole*
www.supreme.justia.com/cases/federal/us/483/203/case.html

23. Bloatware
www.webopedia.com/TERM/B/bloatware.html

24. Pork Barrel Politics
www.investopedia.com/terms/p/pork_barrel_politics.asp

CHAPTER 20
DIFFERENT KINDS OF GOVERNMENT

J ust as computers have different OSs, there are different forms of government. Some are as similar as the modern Windows and Apple desktops. Some are as different as MS-DOS[1] and WebOS.[2] Some look really nice and are user-friendly, like a Graphical User Interface (GUI, pronounced goo-ee).[3] This basically means the OS uses graphics, or pictures, to represent things, like using a trash can as the place to put things to dispose of, instead of making the user learn code. Others can really only be understood by computer programmers.

There are a lot of choices, depending on what you are doing and when. MS-DOS is rarely used anymore and WebOS wasn't invented yet in the 1970s. It is the same way with governments, although change is much slower. We have our Constitution for our OS, but other countries have other OS that work for them. Style of government fall out of use eventually as surely as new ones come into favor. Some are more user-friendly and allow people more freedom; others make sure that only a few select individuals ever have any power.

When our forefathers rebelled against Great Britain, they had to form a new government, and they had to decide the form it would take. Until the twentieth century, only three basic kinds of government, or a variation on them, were really used. These were monarchies, republics, and democracies, and most of them were some form of monarchy or principality, a smaller version of a monarchy. When our new government formed after the Revolution, more than a few people wanted George Washington to take the title of King since it was what they had always known, but he adamantly refused.

MONARCHY

A monarchy is a government headed by a single person who usually inherited the position from a relative. Normally this was their father, the King, but it might also be the Queen, uncle, or other relative if the last King or Queen died childless. Most monarchs have done nothing to earn their power or to prove they should be trusted with it. They are simply the eldest son of the previous monarch, or the eldest daughter if there is no son.

The line of succession for monarchies usually goes from the monarch to their eldest son, their next eldest son, etc.; then to their eldest daughter, next eldest daughter, etc.; then through the monarch's brothers and then sisters. Any male in the line inherits before any female in the same generation. This is called primogeniture.[4] A modern example is Great Britain, where the line of succession in 2010 started with Prince Charles and continued to Prince William and then Prince Harry. Once William and Katherine had children, the succession became Prince Charles, Prince William, Prince George, Princess Charlotte, and then Prince Harry. Primogeniture meant that if William had an older sister, he and Harry would still be ahead of her in the line of succession. However, Britain is modernizing their system so that starting with William's children, succession will be based strictly on birth order and gender won't be considered.[5] He just happened to have a son first.

The monarch has different titles in different countries. In empires, the traditional titles are Emperor/Empress, Tsar/Tsarina, or Sultan/Sultana. In a kingdom, it is traditionally King/Queen. If it is a principality, then the title is Prince/Princess, as in the Principality of Monaco. These are only guidelines and not absolutes because sometimes a kingdom grows into an empire, or an empire shrinks and becomes a kingdom, but the traditional titles are kept. Even when Great Britain was an Empire, they used King/Queen.

Historically, there were two kinds of monarchies, absolute and limited. An absolute monarch had total power over everyone and everything in their country. They could do anything they wanted, to–kill or torture their subjects (people), take their possessions, steal their land, anything at all. They could even force people to leave their family, to live and work so far away that they could not see them again. If the ruler is a good person who can be trusted, this works well. But if they are not a good person or cannot be trusted, then it can be terrible.

THEOCRACY

Theocracies are very similar to monarchies but the ruler is a religious ruler, like the Pope in Vatican City. Like monarchies, they can be absolute or limited.

ABSOLUTE MONARCHY

Absolute monarchies have effectively been replaced by dictatorships, such as in North Korea. Most of these are theoretically parliamentary republics ruled by a person who was chosen by the people, or Communist nations theoretically run by the people, but the reality is that the dictator has unlimited power. Any "elections" are for show and do not affect power in the nation.

LIMITED MONARCHY

A limited monarchy is one where the monarch shares their power with a parliament. The constitution and laws of the country place specific limits on the monarch's power. Many absolute monarchies became limited monarchies over the course of centuries. This happened in the United Kingdom, Norway, Sweden, and Denmark. Other monarchies changed to parliamentary democracies, theocracies), or dictatorships.

British Kings and Queens now share their power with the House of Lords and the House of Commons. The monarchs are little more than figureheads. The Magna Carta, signed in 1215, began the process of limiting the monarch's power in England and increasing the nobles' (aristocrats') power relative to the Crown.[6] It did nothing for the common people, but the Magna Carta did help inspire the US Constitution and started Britain down the path toward the Rule of Law and away from an absolute monarchy. The Rule of Law means that the government has to obey the law too, not just the citizens.

The transition away from a monarchy was more abrupt and violent in some countries, such as France and Russia. The French Revolution was inspired by the recent American Revolution and they established a republican government, for as long as they could keep it.[7] The French monarchs, much of the aristocracy, and tens of thousands of others were beheaded using the guillotine during their Revolution.

Russia was in the progress of becoming a limited monarchy before the Russian Revolution ended their monarchy during World War I.[8] It soon became a Communist nation, and murdered everyone in Tsar Nicholas Romanov II's family and anyone who might have a claim to the throne because they were related to him. This guaranteed that their royal family can never be restored to the throne. The Russian Romanov dynasty is far from the only dynasty to end this way.

A dynasty is a monarch and all the rulers descended from them, from the first person in that family to rule to the last. Military conquerors have often founded dynasties. The Ptolemaic Dynasty in Ancient Egypt started when Alexander the Great conquered Egypt and his General, Ptolemy, became Emperor. It lasted until Rome took power when Queen Cleopatra died.[9]

REPUBLIC

A republic, also called a democratic republic, is a government where the supreme power is vested in the people, or delegated to representatives elected by the people. A republic can bind people together by strong ties of fellowship, as in a bond of affection and friendship, and by shared beliefs. Ancient Rome started as a republic, although it became an empire in later years.

DIFFERENT KINDS OF GOVERNMENT

DEMOCRACY

A democracy, also called direct democracy, is when every eligible voter does in fact vote on every item. In practice, democracy only works on a very small scale such as a home or classroom, or perhaps a town. On a larger scale, even finding a room for everyone to meet becomes too difficult. Three hundred years ago, the colony of Plymouth was a direct democracy. There were very few people living there so they could all meet to make laws.

The USA is a representative democracy. Because we are so much larger now than Plymouth circa 1600, the people send representatives to act for them. They are called representatives because their job is to represent the people. As you know, these representatives meet in the city of Washington, D.C. to make our laws. It is also considered a limited government because it is not all-powerful, like a dictatorship. It is only allowed to do the things the people say it may do, although its powers have clearly increased over the years.

No government operates in isolation any more than any computer does. Just as you probably use your computer to do research, play games, and socialize (social networks, email, blogs) on the World Wide Web (internet), our government is part of international organizations including the United Nations, the International Monetary Fund, and NATO. We interact with many countries with many different kinds of governments in these and other organizations. We also have treaties and trade agreements with all kinds of governments, so we must work together no matter how different our national OSs (or governments) may be.

CHAPTER 20

Resources

1. MS-DOS
www.webopedia.com/TERM/D/DOS.html

2. WebOS
www.webopedia.com/TERM/W/webos.html

3. GUI (Graphical User Interface)
www.webopedia.com/TERM/G/GUI.html

4. Primogeniture
www.encyclopedia.com/topic/primogeniture.aspx

5. British Monarchy Ending Primogeniture
www.telegraph.co.uk/news/uknews/theroyalfamily/8854981/Centuries-
old-rule-of-succession-in-British-Royal-family-scrapped-by-
Commonwealth.html

6. The Magna Carta (complete text)
archives.gov/exhibits/featured_documents/magna_carta/translation.html

7. French Revolution
www.encyclopedia.com/topic/French_Revolution.aspx

8. Russian Revolution
www.encyclopedia.com/topic/Russian_Revolution.aspx

9. Ptolemaic Dynasty
www.livius.org/articles/dynasty/ptolemies/

Chapter 21
Inspirations for our Government

The United States is far from the only modern country with a democratic or republican government, but it does have the oldest written national constitution. The only older written constitution in the world still in use is the constitution for the state of Massachusetts, adopted in 1780.

Our Constitution is different from those of many other countries because it is based on British jurisprudence, normally called common law, and other countries based theirs on civil law, which is in turn based on Roman law. (Jurisprudence is the way judges and courts decide cases.) Most of the original thirteen colonies were founded or taken over very early on by the British, regardless of where individual colonists came from.

THE MAGNA CARTA

The Magna Carta was issued in England in 1215 and says, in short, that English Kings and Queens have to obey the law.[1] The Magna Carta was written to increase nobles' power relative to the Crown–commoners concerns were irrelevant–and it started the long slow process of reducing the monarch's absolute power. In practice, monarchs still mostly did what they wanted, but not entirely what they wanted. While not much of it remains in our modern legal code, British Common Law was still an important part of the legal code in colonial America. It helped inspire our Constitution, in part because so many state charters were based on it but also because it was the first charter to limit the power of a monarchy at all. And of course, that was an institution we were in the process of discarding entirely. In addition, the Magna Carta was normally studied in law school and a majority (35 out of 55) of the Constitutional Convention delegates had studied law either here or in Britain, so the Founders were quite familiar with it.[2] Technically, any British common law decisions from before our Revolution are still part of our legal tradition and can be cited by US lawyers.

COMMON LAW

Common law, the basis of British and American jurisprudence, is when judges base their decisions on previous cases (precedents) and rulings, not strictly on the wording in laws that have been passed. Common law started with community traditions, or what was commonly considered legal.[3] Because of this, even without a law that says "murder is illegal," common law courts (and common sense) can find a person guilty because of the precedents. While we clearly now have lots—and lots and lots—of laws and precedents (previous decisions by other judges) for judges to review when they make their rulings, common law is still an important part of how our government and judicial system work. This emphasis on past rulings makes legal proceedings more predictable.

CIVIL LAW

Some American colonies that later became part of the US had colonial charters from the civil law countries of Spain, Portugal, and France.[4] These territories eventually became part of the US through purchase (the Louisiana Purchase) or military conquest (Florida, California, and much of the West). As a result, even though every state except Louisiana now bases their jurisprudence on common law, many state legal codes have elements of civil law. Community property in marriage is the most common.

In contrast to common law, the civil law used by Spain, France, and most of Europe is based on the Roman legal system and relies on written laws, not past judicial decisions. Precedent, or prior judgments, is far less important. This leaves civil law far more dependent on how judges interpret laws and makes it somewhat less predictable. This type of law is common in areas that were heavily colonized by Spain, such as Latin America. The theoretical benefit of civil law it that people can read and understand the laws themselves. Realistically, no one can read and be familiar with all the laws in any country, even a small one.

The distinction between civil law and common law jurisprudence is most obvious in Louisiana. Their jurisprudence is strongly influenced by the Napoleonic Code in place at the time of the Louisiana Purchase from France.[5] The Napoleonic Code was one of the first modern attempts to codify, or write down, the rules of law (legal code) in a clear format. It is one specific civil code, not a generalized idea or theory, just as the United States Code is a specific legal code. The Napoleonic Code was written when Napoleon was the head of state in France. It was an attempt to modernize French laws and provide one national set of laws instead of many local sets. This Code included radical innovations such as allowing religious freedom and requiring government jobs to be given to the most qualified, not best-connected, candidate. Previously, the hiring official often gave the job to a friend or relative. The Napoleonic Code was written after our Constitution guaranteed many freedoms to Americans, including these, but it was still radical in Europe.

MORE BRITISH IDEAS

Unsurprisingly, common law is only one of the ideas and practices we took from Great Britain. The Bank of England was the basis for the new Central Bank proposed by Alexander Hamilton and started in 1791.[6] It lasted for twenty years. Other ideas include a bicameral legislature, Bill of Rights, Supreme Court, and State of Union Address.

CHAPTER 21

A bicameral legislature has two houses, as opposed to a unicameral legislature which has only one. The British government the colonists knew so well has a bicameral legislature. The smaller upper house is the House of Lords and members are appointed, not elected. Members of our smaller upper house, the Senate, were originally selected (appointed) by state legislatures, not elected by the citizens.

The larger British lower house is the House of Commons and is elected by popular vote, as is our House of Representatives. Unlike the British system, our representatives must live in the state they represent, so the Founders did not merely copy what they were familiar with. They copied what they thought worked well and changed what they thought needed improvement. The system evolved when it crossed the Atlantic.

Some state constitutions already included a Bill of Rights, which is one reason states were so adamant that the national constitution must include one. The national Bill of Rights was inspired by the English Bill of Rights[7] and the Virginia Declaration of Rights[8] from 1776 (Appendix V). The Virginia Declaration of Rights was also partially based on the English Bill of Rights, but it introduced the idea that power comes from the people, not the monarch, thereby justifying our right to revolt against the British government. The Virginia Declaration clearly said that people have freedom of religion. Reading it shows its relationship to the US Bill of Rights.

Our Supreme Court was based on the judicial committee of the Privy Council of England, which was, and is, the supreme, or highest, court in certain colonial conflicts.[9] They could over-turn laws passed by the legislature and signed into law if they conflicted with a colony's charter, British law, or common law. The Privy Council was also the final appeal in conflicts. It is easy to see these elements in our Supreme Court, which was written as "supreme Court" with a small s in the Constitution, implying it was a description not necessarily a name.

The Founders did not specifically give the Supreme Court the power to declare laws unconstitutional but they also did not deny it to them. The first time the Supreme Court declared an act of Congress unconstitutional was in 1794, under President Washington.[10] The first important case to establish this Supreme Court power ("judicial review") was *Marbury v. Madison* in 1803 under President Jefferson with Chief Justice John Marshall leading the Supreme Court.[11] Given that they exercised this power under two of our most prominent Founders and while many of them were still alive and active, it seems safe to conclude that the Founders accepted it.

In any event, this power was rarely used until after the Civil War. The post-war era when federal lands west of the Appalachians started becoming territories and states led to some of this increase. The upheavals and changes caused by the Civil War, most particularly the changes involved in Reconstruction and ending slavery, led to more. As our federal government has grown and laws multiplied (both in numbers and length), the Court has considered more Constitutional cases, so that this now takes most of the Court's time.

As you can see, while our government was new in many respects, particularly as a large representative democracy with an elected chief executive instead of a monarch, it also relied heavily on what colonists already knew and were familiar with. As revolutionary as it was in many things (conduct expected of soldiers, forbidding a state religion, no ex post facto laws), it was in many other ways an evolution of the British system (Supreme Court, bicameral legislature), rather than the creation of an entirely new system. In terms of government structure, in many ways it was more like the American *Evolution* than the American *Revolution*.

Very few things are truly totally new in the world with nothing at all similar preceding them, even things that are huge changes. This is as true of government as it is with anything else.

CHAPTER 21

RESOURCES

1. Magna Carta
www.britannica.com/topic/Magna-Carta

2. Overview of the Founding Fathers
www.archives.gov/exhibits/charters/constitution_founding_fathers_overvi
ew.html

3. Common Law
legal-dictionary.thefreedictionary.com/Common+law

4. Civil Law
legal-dictionary.thefreedictionary.com/Civil+Law

5. Napoleonic Code
www.britannica.com/topic/Napoleonic-Code

6. Bank of England
www.bankofengland.co.uk/about/Pages/history/default.aspx

7. English Bill of Rights
avalon.law.yale.edu/17th_century/england.asp

8. Virginia Declaration of Rights
www.archives.gov/exhibits/charters/virginia_declaration_of_rights.html

9. Judicial Committee of the Privy Council of England
www.jcpc.uk

10. First Act to be Declared Unconstitutional by SCOTUS
constitutionality.us/SupremeCourt.html

11. Marbury v. Madison
www.ourdocuments.gov/doc.php?flash=true&doc=19

Chapter 22
What Do You Think?

These questions are just that, questions to make you really think. They are not intended to justify or promote one particular viewpoint, or any actions that have been or may be taken, and do not have right or wrong answers.

1. There are different kinds of success, and different definitions of failure. Which of the Founders did you think were successful? All of them? Of those who were successful, were they all successful in the same areas? Which areas do you think they were successful in? Do you think you could accomplish as much in another field? What do you base that on?

2. Which of the Founding Fathers, if any, do you think would be fun or interesting to talk to, take a trip with, have as a teacher, or be related to?

3. In what ways were the Founders failures? What mistakes do you think they made in the Constitution? The Constitution has 27 amendments. Do you think there have been a lot of real changes or not? What do you think of the amendments? Were they good

additions/changes or not? Why? Which of these, if any, do you think could or should have been included when it was originally written? (Abigail Adams would have liked the 19th included!) Which couldn't have been? Why? How have changes in our country since 1787 made those Amendments possible, or necessary?

4. In 1794, in *Notes on the State of Virginia,* Thomas Jefferson wrote, *"And can the liberties of a nation be thought secure if we have lost the only firm basis, a conviction in the minds of the people that these liberties are the gift of God? That they are not to be violated but with His wrath?"* Do you think the 1st Amendment would be viewed differently if this quote was viewed alongside, or instead of, the "wall of separation" quote from the Danbury letter?[1]

5. Do you think the "wall of separation" letter would be viewed differently if Jefferson had not removed the line 'confining myself therefore to the duties of my station, which are merely temporal, be assured that your religious rights shall never be infringed by any act of mine"? Why is it a good idea to check more than one source, or more than one version of a document if there are multiple drafts, to understand something?

6. John Dickinson wrote extensively against the British treatment of the American colonies, but he did not support the Declaration of Independence. And yet, after we declared our Independence, he supported the Articles of Confederation and helped create our Constitution. In particular, he helped hammer out the Great Compromise so that everyone (individual citizens and states of all sizes) was represented fairly in our Legislature.

Why do you think he made those choices? Do you think you could make a choice as unpopular as his decision not to sign the

Declaration of Independence, based solely on what you believe?

7. Do you think our government is still doing what the Founders wanted? Do you think it has stopped doing what the Founders wanted? (It could be following in some areas and not in other areas.) Can you give any examples either way, including amendments or current legislation? What changes and what continuities do you think they would be surprised to see?

8. What do you think about the Great Compromise for the Legislature where one house has equal representation for all the states and one has more representation for states with more citizens? Was it a good idea? What about it works well and what problems are there that the Founding Fathers didn't foresee?

9. Why do you think that having equal representation for all states in the Senate is the only part of the Constitution that cannot be changed without unanimous approval by all the states? Why do you think they felt it necessary to safeguard this one particular point so very strongly? Do you think changing Senatorial elections so citizens elect Senators instead of state legislatures was good, bad, or neutral? What do you think the Founding Fathers would have thought?

10. Except for FDR, every President from Washington through Truman chose to only serve two terms. Do you think this was the right thing for them to do? Do you think two terms is the right amount, or should Presidents serve more or only one? If you think it should be different, what would be improved by having the same President for that number of terms? Do you think the length of the term should be different? Do you think the 22nd Amendment, term limits for the President, was a good idea? Was it necessary? Why do you think it was passed when it

was, shortly after FDR died?

11. Why do you think the Founders agreed to set aside the topic of slavery in both the Declaration of Independence and the Constitution? Do you think they should have made a different choice, based on what they knew at the time? Do you believe that they expected slavery to continue and grow stronger or become weaker and fade away? Why, and what impact might that belief have had on the way they wrote the Constitution? If you could go back in time, do you think there is anything you could tell them about the future that might change their decision?

12. Did you notice that one state and its contributions are discussed more than the others? The state Declaration of Rights is even included in the Appendixes. That state is Virginia. Why do you think so many prominent Founders (George Washington, Thomas Jefferson, Patrick Henry, George Mason) and ideas came out of Virginia? George Mason brought many of the ideas for the Constitution with him to the Constitutional Convention. Thomas Jefferson wrote the Declaration of Independence, although it was altered before signing. The Virginia Statute for Religious Freedom and Virginia Declaration of Rights both influenced the Bill of Rights.

Consider how the following might have been related to Virginia's influence: state size, state affluence (how many people had the money to afford education and books), state age (older states tended to have larger towns and populations and better education), coastal length (settlement generally started at the coast and moved inland later, often along rivers), and distance from Philadelphia, our early capital.

The 4th Amendment includes the following statement, "the right of the people to be secure in their persons, houses, papers, and effects, against unreasonable searches and seizures, shall not be violated." Even the most basic version of the Income Tax Form established by the 16th Amendment requires Americans to submit proof of their income from all sources including bank accounts and inheritance; how many people (including children and elderly relatives) live in their home; much money they have saved for retirement and their children's college; how much their home is worth, and how much they paid in taxes and mortgages, if they own it; what vehicles they own, taxes paid for them, and their value (in many, but not all, areas); and much more. Americans must detail their entire financial life and all their major assets (valuable things they own), including all the account numbers and balances, for the government to peruse.

Do you think the act of merely filing taxes is a burden on American citizens or not really? How much time do you think is required to simply compile this information? How do you feel about citizens being required to provide all of this personal information to the government, who then keeps copies of it for years? Do you think it is a possible violation of the 4th Amendment or do you think that would be a distorted reading of that amendment? Do you think it is reasonable for the government to require such detailed personal financial information? If not, what alternatives can you think of?

13. The income tax enabled our government to do more for the citizens, but doing more for others isn't always for the best, despite good intentions. There is a saying, "give a man a fish, he eats for a day; teach a man to fish and you feed him for a lifetime."

How do you think this applies to the idea that the government doing things for citizens isn't always for the best? What examples can you think of where the government doing things for citizens is good, and where it is too much? What kinds of things should the government do for the citizens? What minimum standards do you think the government should follow for caring for our citizens? What requirements and limits do you think there should be on what they do to take care of people? What tasks are so big that one citizen or one state can't do them alone, so the government must do them or they will not be done?

14. There was a saying by the ancient Roman Juvenal that all the masses needed to be content was "bread and circuses"–food and entertainment. If they had those, they would think the government was doing a fine job. Citizens didn't have to pay when they attended the "bread and circuses," so it felt like they were being given something for nothing by their leaders. What do you think of this? Are many people satisfied that easily?

    Do you think the bread and circuses were truly free? If not, how do you think they were really paid for? Free or not, could the resources used for the bread and circuses have been used for something else?

15. Using bread and circuses to distract citizens as their liberties are being taken away, as happened in Rome, is certainly a poor use of power, but that doesn't make either bread or circuses a bad thing in and of themselves. Circuses are fun! Roman Circuses were large public events such as Gladiator Fights, more like the Olympics than Barnum & Bailey. Making sure the populace content and well-fed is not a bad thing, either. Why do you think references to "bread and circuses" are generally used to indicate perceived bad behavior on the part of the government? What

types of programs does it make you think of? What kind of behavior, promises, and actions from politicians?

What, if anything, do you think modern politicians do that is similar? If you see this type of problem—entertainment and free stuff being used to district citizens from important issues—how can that be changed? Can you think of a better use for any resources going toward "bread and circuses"?

16. Do you think the federal government is doing too much and state sovereignty should be reinforced, or do you think our country needs a powerful central government and states' rights need to be curbed? Should the power of federal government be increased, decreased or stay about the same? What do you think about states nullifying, or ignoring, federal laws that they believe are unconstitutional? Is the federal government responding appropriately, or should it be doing something differently? What, if anything, should it do differently?

17. How do you think changes over the last two hundred years have affected our government? Consider the end of slavery; our increased geographical size and population; population movement from the country to the city to the suburbs; increased diversity; faster transportation and communication; agricultural versus industrial versus service economies; the increase in democracies and republics world-wide compared to monarchies; and new forms of government such as communism. Which changes do you think have been the most important? In what ways is our country more diverse than it was at our founding? How does that impact our government?

18. There are things that need to be regulated and taken care of at the federal and even international level. How would it be to

drive to another state if the roads didn't use the same markings, such as a double yellow line meaning no passing and a dashed yellow line meaning passing zone? Can you imagine if airline pilots *didn't* all speak the same language? What if telephone systems all over the world were not able to work together? Yet, when a government (or company) becomes too large, things become less efficient because they are so big that it is difficult to keep track of anything and everything, among other reasons. A lot of money is wasted when two or more groups are doing the same thing because they don't know (or care) that another group is doing the exact same thing. They could even be doing it in different ways, leading to two different sets of rules citizens are expected to know and follow.

What examples can you think where it makes sense for the federal government to make the rules? Where does it make more sense or improve efficiency for state and local governments to make the rules? What kinds of things are similar or different between these two groups of items? For example, are family, education, or safety related items all grouped together, or are there some at each level?

19. Public health and safety issues are slightly different from individual health and safety issues. Individual health and safety issues, such as high cholesterol or dancing (and falling) in the shower, do not cause problems beyond one family, and certainly not for a whole city or nation. Public health and safety issues, such as an infectious disease or e-coli outbreak, can cause serious health problems for many people throughout a large area. That is the reason we have organizations such as the Centers for Disease Control (CDC) and the Food and Drug Administration

(FDA).

Do you think the government should regulate either or both? How much should they regulate and at what level? Who do you think, federal or state government, has the main responsibility for regulating public health and safety issues? What do you think they should regulate related to individual health and safety? Why? How, and at what point, do individual health and safety issues affect the whole community enough to warrant government involvement?

20. Do you think our government and legal system would be set up and work the same way if we had been part of the Spanish or French empires instead of the British Empire before our Revolution? How might it be different?

21. If the White House and Capitol Building had been built looking across the Potomac at each other, our nation's capital would almost certainly be different because the Virginia parts of D.C. could not have been retroceded easily. The (slave trading) port of Alexandria would almost certainly have been an important part of the Federal City because it was the largest settlement in the area at the time. The Southern states would not have had the extra representatives they received when it was retroceded, tipping the balance ever so slightly toward non-slave states, but slavery would have been harder to end in the District of Columbia.

How could this have affected our history? Here is one example: Arlington National Cemetery, formerly General Robert E. Lee's family plantation (but not his childhood home), is on a piece of retroceded land overlooking the Potomac. Lee did not want to secede from the Union, but he was a Virginian before he was an

American. If he had been a Washingtonian first, he might have led the Union forces instead of the Confederate ones, which would almost certainly have led to an earlier end to the war. What other examples can you think of?

22. How could having the Civil War end after one or two years instead of four have altered our history and our Constitution? The Emancipation Proclamation was not issued until 1863. The 13th, 14th, and 15th Amendments are a direct result of the Civil War but were not passed until after it ended. Like most wars, the Civil War left many men dead and even more permanently unable to work, a large debt, and widespread property damage and economic devastation, particularly in the South. (Gettysburg, Pennsylvania, was the only Northern site of a major Civil War battle.) It was also a spur to get the transcontinental railroad built with all the societal changes that brought with it. Reconstruction left another kind of scars in the South.

23. If the Residence Act establishing D.C. had left all the decisions (funding, final location, etc.) up to Congress, they almost certainly would *not* have gotten it built in the allotted ten years, and Philadelphia (a big city at the time) might have remained the capital permanently. How could having a different capital–a large, important city at that time–have impacted our young country? How do you think having our capital in the middle of nowhere, near nothing, with most of the "residents" and government officials only in residence for part of the year impacted our early years as a nation? How do you think being a federal enclave, not part of any state, impacts the city? Do you think this was a good idea or not? How could it have been/be improved?

24. Slaves are the property of another person, just like a car, piece of

clothing, or farm equipment—that's the definition of a slave. How do you think this made the slaves feel? The slave owner had to pay money to buy them, and they were paid money if they sold them, and some people were worth more than others, just like some cars are worth more than others. How does reading that make you feel? How would it (or does) make you feel if you knew that your ancestors were either the slaves or the slave owners?

When a slave owner freed their slaves, they were giving up a portion of their wealth by simply letting them go free. This is why Jefferson could not free all of his slaves. He died so deeply in debt that most of them were sold to pay off his debts. Despite his intention to free all his slaves, ultimately only his house slaves went free.

Slave owners were still required to care for slaves who were too old or sick to work anymore, although the quality of care varied a lot among owners. How do you think this financial reality influenced the debates on slavery? Do you think it was easy for Franklin, Jefferson, Washington and other slave owners to free their slaves? Do you think they really, truly, in their hearts, wanted to free some or all of them? If so, what stopped them? What do you think their children, who would have inherited the slaves, thought about it? What do you think of John Jay's choice to repeatedly buy and then free slaves?

25. The Founders worked very hard to craft a compromise between the majority who wanted slavery outlawed and the three states that *really* wanted to keep it: North Carolina, South Carolina, and Georgia. Just a few years later, Eli Whitney invented the cotton gin and accidentally started slavery on the path to profitability in

the south.[2] The cotton gin and the developments that accompanied it had a profound impact on our country's development. Do you think the Founders would (or could) have done anything differently if they had known that was going to happen? (Remember that they probably expected the ban on importing slaves after 1808 to signal the beginning of the end of slavery in this nation, per Frederick Douglass.)

What other inventions can you think of that at first glance do not seem related to government but that have impacted how our nation operates? How? What did they do?

26. The Civil Rights Act of 1875 stated, "That all persons ... shall be entitled to full and equal enjoyment of the accommodations, advantages, facilities, and privileges of inns, public conveyances on land or water, theaters, and other places of public amusement." Separate but equal is a very clear violation of this federal law, which the Supreme Court declared unconstitutional in 1883. Shortly after this, Southern states began enacting segregation legislation. How might things have been different if this Act had remained in effect? Do you think we would we have needed the 24th Amendment ending poll taxes?

27. If you could make any change, or amendment, to the Constitution, what would it be? What would that improve? What do you think needs to be done to make that happen? Is there anything you can do to make it happen?

28. If you could go back in time and ask the Founding Fathers what they intended with one part of the Constitution or why they made a certain decision when they were drafting it, what would it be? What else would you ask them?

29. Under what circumstances do you think we should have an Arti-

cle V Convention? What do you think it should consider? What should be off limits? Is it reasonable/possible to truly put something off limits?

If there ever is an Article V Convention, do you think it is more likely that the delegates will not only pass an amendment to completely scrap the current Constitution but also convince at least three fourths of the states to ratify it, or that no amendments the Convention passes will be ratified by enough states to become law? Why? What do you think is the most likely or realistic outcome?

30. The chair George Washington used in Independence Hall during the Constitutional Convention had a sun carved into the back of it. At the time, Franklin said that he had often looked at that sun behind the president without knowing if it was rising or setting, but by the end of the Convention he was certain that it was a rising sun. (The complete quote is on the next page.)

What do you think? Is the sun rising over our nation or setting on us? Why? If you don't like how it is going, what can you do to change things for the better? If you do like how it is going, what can you do to keep it heading that way?

CHAPTER 22

RESOURCES

1. Notes on the State of Virginia
web.archive.org/web/20080914030942/http://etext.lib.virginia.edu/toc/m
odeng/public/JefVirg.html

2. Eli Whitney's Cotton Gin and profitability in the South
www.archives.gov/education/lessons/cotton-gin-patent/

"Whilst the last members were signing [the Constitution], Doctor Franklin, looking towards the Presidents chair, at the back of which a rising sun happened to be painted, observed to a few members near him, that painters had found it difficult to distinguish in their art, a rising, from a setting, sun. I have, said he, often and often, in the course of the session, and the vicissitudes of my hopes and fears as to its issue, looked at that behind the President, without being able to tell whether it was rising or setting; but now at length, I have the happiness to know, that it is a rising, and not a setting sun."

- BENJAMIN FRANKLIN, debates in the Constitutional Convention, Philadelphia, Pennsylvania, September 17, 1787. James Madison, Journal of the Federal Convention, ed. E. H. Scott, p. 763 .

APPENDIX I
CONSTITUTIONAL SUPER-SUMMARY

This is a wild over-simplification of the Constitution and misses many important points, but hopefully it will help you learn and memorize the most basic tenets of the Constitution.

We the People of the United States, in Order to form a more perfect Union, establish Justice, insure domestic Tranquility, provide for the common defense, promote the general Welfare, and secure the Blessings of Liberty to ourselves and our Posterity, do ordain and establish this Constitution for the United States of America.

Article 1 established the Legislative Branch and defined its powers.

Article 2 established the Executive Branch and defined its powers.

Article 3 established the Judicial Branch and defined its powers.

Article 4 discussed the relationship among the states, and between the states and the federal government.

Article 5 established the procedure for amending the Constitution.

Article 6 established that federal laws have precedence over state laws. (In a conflict between the two, federal law wins.) It also stated that government officers must take an oath or affirmation that they will uphold the Constitution, but there cannot be a religious test to be a government officer.

Article 7 established that the Constitution would take effect as soon as nine of the thirteen colonies ratified it.

Amendments.

The 1st Amendment established the freedoms of speech, press, petition, assembly, and religion.

The 2nd Amendment established state militias (now the National Guard) and guaranteed our right to bear arms (own and carry firearms).

The 3rd Amendment forbade the government from forcing citizens to house soldiers.

The 4th Amendment forbade unreasonable searches and seizures by the government.

The 5th Amendment guaranteed the right to a jury trial and to refuse to testify in court if what we say will or could prove we're guilty of a crime. It forbade double jeopardy, which is being tried twice for the same crime once a verdict has been given.

The 6th Amendment guaranteed the right to a speedy jury trial near where the crime was committed, to a lawyer even at government expense, and to be told immediately what crime we are charged with.

The 7th Amendment guaranteed that civil trials are also tried by a jury.

The 8th Amendment forbade excessive bail, excessive fines, and cruel and unusual punishment.

The 9th Amendment established that we have rights that are not listed in the Constitution.

The 10th Amendment established that anything not specifically given to the federal government in the Constitution is the responsibility of the state governments (state sovereignty).

The 11th Amendment limited the ability of citizens to sue states.

THE CONSTITUTION: IT'S THE OS FOR THE US

The 12th Amendment changed the way the President and Vice President are elected.

The 13th Amendment ended slavery.

The 14th Amendment clarified that former slaves were now citizens and should be counted the same as other citizens to determine the numbers of Representatives.

The 15th Amendment guaranteed the right to vote regardless of race or previous condition of servitude (e.g., if you were a freed slave).

The 16th Amendment established the income tax.

The 17th Amendment changed election of senators from state legislatures to citizens.

The 18th Amendment established Prohibition. It was later repealed.

The 19th Amendment gave women the right to vote.

The 20th Amendment clarified how the government should proceed if the President-Elect dies before taking office.

The 21st Amendment repealed the 18th Amendment, Prohibition.

The 22nd Amendment established a two term limit for Presidents.

The 23rd Amendment gave D.C. Electors for Presidential elections.

The 24th Amendment made it illegal to use poll taxes to deny citizens the right to vote.

The 25th Amendment clarified the line of succession for the Presidency.

The 26th Amendment lowered the voting age from 21 to 18.

The 27th Amendment established that that when Congress votes a pay raise for itself, that raise won't take effect until after the next national election.

Appendix II
Constitutional Signatories

William Jackson–Secretary

Delaware

George Read

Gunning Bedford, Jr.

John Dickinson

Richard Bassett

Jacob Broom

Maryland

James McHenry

Daniel of St Thomas Jenifer

Daniel Carroll

Virginia

George Washington–President
and deputy from Virginia

John Blair

James Madison

North Carolina

William Blount

Richard Dobbs Spaight

Hugh Williamson

South Carolina

John Rutledge

Charles Cotesworth Pinckney

Charles Pinckney

Pierce Butler

Georgia

William Few

Abraham Baldwin

New Hampshire

John Langdon

Nicholas Gilman

Massachusetts

Nathanial Gorham

Rufus King

Connecticut

William Samuel Johnson

Roger Sherman

New York

Alexander Hamilton

New Jersey

William Livingston

David Brearley

William Paterson

Jonathan Dayton

Pennsylvania

Benjamin Franklin

Thomas Mifflin

Robert Morris

George Clymer

Thomas FitzSimons

Jared Ingersoll

James Wilson

Gouverneur Morris

APPENDIX III
OATHS OF OFFICE

PRESIDENT:

"I, _____, do solemnly swear (or affirm) that I will support and defend the Constitution of the United States against all enemies, foreign and domestic; that I will bear true faith and allegiance to the same; that I take this obligation freely, without any mental reservation or purpose of evasion; and that I will well and faithfully discharge the duties of the office on which I am about to enter. So help me God."

FEDERAL EMPLOYEES, including Military Personnel, Judges (they take two oaths), and Elected Officials:

"I, _____, do solemnly swear (or affirm) that I will support and defend the Constitution of the United States against all enemies, foreign and domestic; that I will bear true faith and allegiance to the same; that I take this obligation freely, without any mental reservation or purpose of evasion; and that I will well and faithfully discharge the duties of the office on which I am about to enter. So help me God."

JUDICIAL OATH, as revised in 1990:

"I, _____, do solemnly swear (or affirm) that I will administer justice without respect to persons, and do equal right to the poor and to the rich, and that I will faithfully and impartially discharge and perform all the duties incumbent upon me as _____ under the Constitution and laws of the United States. So help me God."

COMBINED OATH (may be taken by Judges instead of the two above):

"I, _____, do solemnly swear (or affirm) that I will administer justice without respect to persons, and do equal right to the poor and to the rich, and that I will faithfully and impartially discharge and perform all the duties incumbent upon me as _____ under the Constitution and laws of the United States; and that I will support and defend the Constitution of the United States against all enemies, foreign and domestic; that I will bear true faith and allegiance to the same; that I take this obligation freely, without any mental reservation or purpose of evasion; and that I will well and faithfully discharge the duties of the office on which I am about to enter. So help me God."

Appendix IV
The Articles of Confederation

The Articles of Confederation.

To all to whom these Presents shall come, we the undersigned Delegates of the States affixed to our Names send greeting.

Articles of Confederation and perpetual Union between the states of New Hampshire, Massachusetts-bay, Rhode Island and Providence Plantations, Connecticut, New York, New Jersey, Pennsylvania, Delaware, Maryland, Virginia, North Carolina, South Carolina and Georgia.

I.

The Stile of this Confederacy shall be **"The United States of America"**.

II.

Each state retains its sovereignty, freedom, and independence, and every power, jurisdiction, and right, which is **not** by this Confederation expressly delegated to the United States, in Congress assembled.

III.

The said States hereby severally enter into a firm league of friendship with each other, for their common defense, the security of their liberties, and their mutual and general welfare, binding themselves to assist each other, against all force offered to, or attacks made upon them, or any of them, on account of religion, sovereignty, trade, or any other pretense whatever.

IV.

The better to secure and perpetuate mutual friendship and intercourse among the people of the different States in this Union, the free inhabitants of each of these States, paupers, vagabonds, and fugitives from justice excepted, shall be entitled to all privileges and immunities of free citizens in the several States; and the people of each State shall have free ingress and regress to and from any other State, and shall enjoy therein all the privileges of trade and commerce, subject to the same duties, impositions, and restrictions as the inhabitants thereof respectively, provided that such restrictions shall not extend so far as to prevent the removal of property imported into any State, to any other State, of which the owner is an inhabitant; provided also that no imposition, duties or restriction shall be laid by any State, on the property of the United States, or either of them.

If any person guilty of, or charged with, treason, felony, or other high misdemeanor in any State, shall flee from justice, and be found in any of the United States, he shall, upon demand of the Governor or executive power of the State from which he fled, be delivered up and removed to the State having jurisdiction of his offense.

Full faith and credit shall be given in each of these States to the records, acts, and judicial proceedings of the courts and magistrates of every other State.

V.

For the most convenient management of the general interests of the United States, delegates shall be annually appointed in such manner as the legislatures of each State shall direct, to meet in Congress on the first Monday in November, in every year, with a power reserved to each State to recall its delegates, or any of them, at any time within the year, and to send others in their stead for the remainder of the year.

No State shall be represented in Congress by less than two, nor more than seven members; and no person shall be capable of being a delegate for more than three years in any term of six years; nor shall any person, being a delegate, be capable of holding any office under the United States, for which he, or another for his benefit, receives any salary, fees or emolument of any kind.

Each State shall maintain its own delegates in a meeting of the States, and while they act as members of the committee of the States.

In determining questions in the United States in Congress assembled, each State shall have one vote.

Freedom of speech and debate in Congress shall not be impeached or questioned in any court or place out of Congress, and the members of Congress shall be protected in their persons from arrests or imprisonments, during the time of their going to and from, and attendance on **Congress, except for treason, felony, or breach of the peace.**

VI.

No State, without the consent of the United States in Congress assembled, shall send any embassy to, or receive any embassy from, or enter into any conference, agreement, alliance or treaty with any King, Prince or State; nor shall any person holding any office of profit or trust under the United States, or any of them, accept any present, emolument, office or title of any kind whatever from any King, Prince or foreign State; nor shall the United States in Congress assembled, or any of them, grant any title of nobility.

No two or more States shall enter into any treaty, confederation or alliance whatever between them, without the consent of the United States in Congress assembled, specifying accurately the purposes for which the same is to be entered into, and how long it shall continue.

No State shall lay any imposts or duties, which may interfere with any stipulations in treaties, entered into by the United States in Congress assembled, with any King, Prince or State, in pursuance of any treaties already proposed by Congress, to the courts of France and Spain.

No vessel of war shall be kept up in time of peace by any State, except such number only, as shall be deemed necessary by the United States in Congress assembled, for the defense of such State, or its trade; nor shall any body of forces be kept up by any State in time of peace, except such number only, as in the judgement of the United States in Congress assembled, shall be deemed requisite to garrison the forts necessary for the defense of such State; but every State shall always keep up a well-regulated and disciplined militia, sufficiently armed and accoutered, and shall provide and constantly have ready for use, in public stores, a due number of field pieces and tents, and a proper quantity of arms, ammunition and camp equipage.

No State shall engage in any war without the consent of the United States in Congress assembled, unless such State be actually invaded by enemies, or shall have received certain advice of a resolution being formed by some nation of Indians to invade such State, and the danger is so imminent as not to admit of a delay till the United States in Congress assembled can be consulted; nor shall any State grant commissions to any ships or vessels of war, nor letters of marque or reprisal, except it be after a declaration of war by the United States in Congress assembled, and then only against the Kingdom or State and the subjects thereof, against which war has been so declared, and under such regulations as shall be established by the United States in Congress assembled, unless such State be infested by pirates, in which case vessels of war may be fitted out for that occasion, and kept so long as the danger shall continue, or until the United States in Congress assembled shall determine otherwise.

VII.

When land forces are raised by any State for the common defense, all officers of or under the rank of colonel, shall be appointed by the legislature of each State respectively, by whom such forces shall be raised, or in such manner as such State shall direct, and all vacancies shall be filled up by the State which first made the appointment.

VIII.

All charges of war, and all other expenses that shall be incurred for the common defense or general welfare, and allowed by the United States in Congress assembled, shall be defrayed out of a common treasury, which shall be supplied by the several States in proportion to the value of all land within each State, granted or surveyed for any person, as such land and the buildings and improvements thereon shall be estimated according to such mode as the United States in Congress assembled, shall from time to time direct and appoint.

The taxes for paying that proportion shall be laid and levied by the authority and direction of the legislatures of the several States within the time agreed upon by the United States in Congress assembled.

IX.

The United States in Congress assembled, shall have the sole and exclusive right and power of determining on peace and war, except in the cases mentioned in the sixth article — of sending and receiving ambassadors — entering into treaties and alliances, provided that no treaty of commerce shall be made whereby the legislative power of the respective States shall be restrained from imposing such imposts and duties on foreigners, as their own people are subjected to, or from prohibiting the exportation or importation of any species of goods or commodities whatsoever — of establishing rules for deciding in all cases, what captures on land or water shall be legal, and in what manner prizes taken by land or naval forces in the service of the United States shall be divided or appropriated — of granting letters of marque and reprisal in times of peace — appointing courts for the trial of piracies and felonies commited on the high seas and establishing courts for receiving and determining finally appeals in all cases of captures, provided that no member of Congress shall be appointed a judge of any of the said courts.

The United States in Congress assembled shall also be the last resort on appeal in all disputes and differences now subsisting or that hereafter may arise between two or more States concerning boundary, jurisdiction or any other causes whatever; which authority shall always be exercised in the manner following. Whenever the legislative or executive authority or lawful agent of any State in controversy with another shall present a petition to Congress stating the matter in question and praying for a hearing, notice thereof shall be given by order of Congress to the legislative or executive authority of the other State in controversy, and a day assigned for the appearance of the parties by their lawful agents, who shall then be directed to appoint by joint consent, commissioners or judges to constitute a court for hearing and determining the matter in question: but if they cannot agree, Congress shall name three persons out of each of the United States, and from the list of such persons each party shall alternately strike out one, the petitioners beginning, until the number shall be reduced to thirteen; and from that number not less than seven, nor more than nine names as Congress shall direct, shall in the presence of Congress be drawn out by lot, and the persons whose names shall be so drawn or any five of them, shall be commissioners or judges, to hear and finally determine the controversy, so always as a major part of the judges who shall hear the cause shall agree in the determination: and if either party shall neglect to attend at the day appointed, without showing reasons, which Congress shall judge sufficient, or being present shall refuse to strike, the Congress shall proceed to nominate three persons out of each State, and the secretary of Congress shall strike in behalf of such party absent or refusing; and the judgement and sentence of the court to be appointed, in the manner before prescribed, shall be final and conclusive; and if any of the parties shall refuse to submit to the authority of such court, or to appear or defend their claim or cause, the court shall nevertheless proceed to pronounce sentence, or judgement, which shall in like manner be final and decisive, the judgement or sentence and other proceedings being in either case transmitted to Congress, and lodged among the acts of Congress for the security of the parties concerned: provided that every commissioner, before he sits in judgement, shall take an oath to be administered by one of the judges of the supreme or superior court of the State, where the cause shall be tried, 'well and truly to hear and determine the matter in question, according to the best of his judgment, without favor, affection or hope of reward': provided also, that no State shall be deprived of territory for the benefit of the United States.

All controversies concerning the private right of soil claimed under different grants of two or more States, whose jurisdictions as they may respect such lands, and the States which passed such grants are adjusted, the said grants or either of them being at the same time claimed to have originated antecedent to such settlement of jurisdiction, shall on the petition of either party to the Congress of the United States, be finally determined as near as may be in the same manner as is before prescribed for deciding disputes respecting territorial jurisdiction between different States.

The United States in Congress assembled shall also have the sole and exclusive right and power of regulating the alloy and value of coin struck by their own authority, or by that of the respective States — fixing the standards of weights and measures throughout the United States — regulating the trade and managing all affairs with the Indians, not members of any of the States, provided that the legislative right of any State within its own limits be not infringed or violated — establishing or regulating post offices from one State to another, throughout all the United States, and exacting such postage on the papers passing through the same as may be requisite to defray the expenses of the said office — appointing all officers of the land forces, in the service of the United States, excepting regimental officers — appointing all the officers of the naval forces, and commissioning all officers whatever in the service of the United States — making rules for the government and regulation of the said land and naval forces, and directing their operations.

The United States in Congress assembled shall have authority to appoint a committee, to sit in the recess of Congress, to be denominated 'A Committee of the States', and to consist of one delegate from each State; and to appoint such other committees and civil officers as may be necessary for managing the general affairs of the United

States under their direction — to appoint one of their members to preside, provided that no person be allowed to serve in the office of president more than one year in any term of three years; to ascertain the necessary sums of money to be raised for the service of the United States, and to appropriate and apply the same for defraying the public expenses — to borrow money, or emit bills on the credit of the United States, transmitting every half-year to the respective States an account of the sums of money so borrowed or emitted — to build and equip a navy — to agree upon the number of land forces, and to make requisitions from each State for its quota, in proportion to the number of white inhabitants in such State; which requisition shall be binding, and thereupon the legislature of each State shall appoint the regimental officers, raise the men and cloath, arm and equip them in a solid-like manner, at the expense of the United States; and the officers and men so cloathed, armed and equipped shall march to the place appointed, and within the time agreed on by the United States in Congress assembled. But if the United States in Congress assembled shall, on consideration of circumstances judge proper that any State should not raise men, or should raise a smaller number of men than the quota thereof, such extra number shall be raised, officered, cloathed, armed and equipped in the same manner as the quota of each State, unless the legislature of such State shall judge that such extra number cannot be safely spread out in the same, in which case they shall raise, officer, cloath, arm and equip as many of such extra number as they judge can be safely spared. And the officers and men so cloathed, armed, and equipped, shall march to the place appointed, and within the time agreed on by the United States in Congress assembled.

The United States in Congress assembled shall never engage in a war, nor grant letters of marque or reprisal in time of peace, nor enter into any treaties or alliances, nor coin money, nor regulate the value thereof, nor ascertain the sums and expenses necessary for the defense and welfare of the United States, or any of them, nor emit bills, nor borrow money on the credit of the United States, nor appropriate money, nor agree upon the number of vessels of war, to be built or purchased, or the number of land or sea forces to be raised, nor appoint a commander in chief of the army or navy, unless nine States assent to the same: nor shall a question on any other point, except for adjourning from day to day be determined, unless by the votes of the majority of the United States in Congress assembled.

The Congress of the United States shall have power to adjourn to any time within the year, and to any place within the United States, so that no period of adjournment be for a longer duration than the space of six months, and shall publish the journal of their proceedings monthly, except such parts thereof relating to treaties, alliances or military operations, as in their judgement require secrecy; and the yeas and nays of the delegates of each State on any question shall be entered on the journal, when it is desired by any delegates of a State, or any of them, at his or their request shall be furnished with a transcript of the said journal, except such parts as are above excepted, to lay before the legislatures of the several States.

X.

The Committee of the States, or any nine of them, shall be authorized to execute, in the recess of Congress, such of the powers of Congress as the United States in Congress assembled, by the consent of the nine States, shall from time to time think expedient to vest them with; provided that no power be delegated to the said Committee, for the exercise of which, by the Articles of Confederation, the voice of nine States in the Congress of the United States assembled be requisite.

XI.

Canada acceding to this confederation, and adjoining in the measures of the United States, shall be admitted into, and entitled to all the advantages of this Union; but no other colony shall be admitted into the same, unless such admission be agreed to by nine States.

XII.

All bills of credit emitted, monies borrowed, and debts contracted by, or under the authority of Congress, before the assembling of the

United States, in pursuance of the present confederation, shall be deemed and considered as a charge against the United States, for payment and satisfaction whereof the said United States, and the public faith are hereby solemnly pleged.

XIII.

Every State shall abide by the determination of the United States in Congress assembled, on all questions which by this confederation are submitted to them. And the Articles of this Confederation shall be inviolably observed by every State, and the Union shall be perpetual; nor shall any alteration at any time hereafter be made in any of them; unless such alteration be agreed to in a Congress of the United States, and be afterwards confirmed by the legislatures of every State.

And Whereas it hath pleased the Great Governor of the World to incline the hearts of the legislatures we respectively represent in Congress, to approve of, and to authorize us to ratify the said Articles of Confederation and perpetual Union. Know Ye that we the undersigned delegates, by virtue of the power and authority to us given for that purpose, do by these presents, in the name and in behalf of our respective constituents, fully and entirely ratify and confirm each and every of the said Articles of Confederation and perpetual Union, and all and singular the matters and things therein contained: And we do further solemnly plight and engage the faith of our respective constituents, that they shall abide by the determinations of the United States in Congress assembled, on all questions, which by the said Confederation are submitted to them. And that the Articles thereof shall be inviolably observed by the States we respectively represent, and that the Union shall be perpetual.

In Witness whereof we have hereunto set our hands in Congress. Done at Philadelphia in the State of Pennsylvania the ninth day of July in the Year of our Lord One Thousand Seven Hundred and Seventy-Eight, and in the Third Year of the independence of America.

Agreed to by Congress November 15, 1777. In force after ratification

APPENDIXES

by Maryland, March 1, 1781

APPENDIX V
VIRGINIA DECLARATION OF RIGHTS

Virginia's Declaration of Rights was drawn upon by Thomas Jefferson for the opening paragraphs of the Declaration of Independence. It was widely copied by the other colonies and became the basis of the Bill of Rights. Written by George Mason, it was adopted by the Virginia Constitutional Convention on June 12, 1776.

VIRGINIA DECLARATION OF RIGHTS

A DECLARATION OF RIGHTS made by the representatives of the good people of Virginia, assembled in full and free convention which rights do pertain to them and their posterity, as the basis and foundation of government.

Section 1. That all men are by nature equally free and independent and have certain inherent rights, of which, when they enter into a state of society, they cannot, by any compact, deprive or divest their posterity; namely, the enjoyment of life and liberty, with the means of acquiring and possessing property, and pursuing and obtaining happiness and safety.

Section 2. That all power is vested in, and consequently derived from, the people; that magistrates are their trustees and servants and at all times amenable to them.

Section 3. That government is, or ought to be, instituted for the common benefit, protection, and security of the people, nation, or community; of all the various modes and forms of government, that is best which is capable of producing the greatest degree of happiness and safety and is most effectually secured against the danger of maladministration. And that, when any government shall be found inadequate or contrary to these purposes, a majority of the community has an indubitable, inalienable, and indefeasible right to reform, alter, or abolish it, in such manner as shall be judged most conducive to the public weal.

Section 4. That no man, or set of men, is entitled to exclusive or separate emoluments or privileges from the community, but in consideration of public services; which, nor being descendible, neither ought the offices of magistrate, legislator, or judge to be hereditary.

Section 5. That the legislative and executive powers of the state should be separate and distinct from the judiciary; and that the members of the two first may be restrained from oppression, by feeling and participating the burdens of the people, they should, at fixed periods, be reduced to a private station, return into that body from which they were originally taken, and the vacancies be supplied by frequent, certain, and regular elections, in which all, or any part, of the former members, to be again eligible, or ineligible, as the laws shall direct.

Section 6. That elections of members to serve as representatives of the people, in assembly ought to be free; and that all men, having sufficient evidence of permanent common interest with, and attachment to, the community, have the right of suffrage and cannot be taxed or deprived of their property for public uses without their own consent or that of their representatives so elected, nor bound by any law to which they have not, in like manner, assembled for the public good.

Section 7. That all power of suspending laws, or the execution of laws, by any authority, without consent of the representatives of the people, is injurious to their rights and ought not to be exercised.

Section 8. That in all capital or criminal prosecutions a man has a right to demand the cause and nature of his accusation, to be confronted with the accusers and witnesses, to call for evidence in his favor, and to a speedy trial by an impartial jury of twelve men of his vicinage, without whose unanimous consent he cannot be found guilty; nor can he be compelled to give evidence against himself; that no man be deprived of his liberty except by the law of the land or the judgment of his peers.

Section 9. That excessive bail ought not to be required, nor excessive fines imposed, nor cruel and unusual punishments inflicted.

Section 10. That general warrants, whereby an officer or messenger may be commanded to search suspected places without evidence of a fact committed, or to seize any person or persons not named, or whose offense is not particularly described and supported by evidence, are grievous and oppressive and ought not to be granted.

Section 11. That in controversies respecting property, and in suits between man and man, the ancient trial by jury is preferable to any other and ought to be held sacred.

Section 12. That the freedom of the press is one of the great bulwarks of liberty, and can never be restrained but by despotic governments.

Section 13. That a well-regulated militia, composed of the body of the people, trained to arms, is the proper, natural, and safe defense of a free state; that standing armies, in time of peace, should be avoided as dangerous to liberty; and that in all cases the military should be under strict subordination to, and governed by, the civil power.

Section 14. That the people have a right to uniform government; and, therefore, that no government separate from or independent of the government of Virginia ought to be erected or established within the limits thereof.

Section 15. That no free government, or the blessings of liberty, can be preserved to any people but by a firm adherence to justice, moderation, temperance, frugality, and virtue and by frequent recurrence to fundamental principles.

Section 16. That religion, or the duty which we owe to our Creator, and the manner of discharging it, can be directed only by reason and conviction, not by force or violence; and therefore all men are equally entitled to the free exercise of religion, according to the dictates of conscience; and that it is the mutual duty of all to practise Christian forbearance, love, and charity toward each other.

Appendix VI
Virginia Statute for Religious Freedom

Well aware that the opinions and belief of men depend not on their own will, but follow involuntarily the evidence proposed to their minds; that Almighty God hath created the mind free, and manifested his supreme will that free it shall remain by making it altogether insusceptible of restraint; that all attempts to influence it by temporal punishments, or burthens, or by civil incapacitations, tend only to beget habits of hypocrisy and meanness, and are a departure from the plan of the holy author of our religion, who being lord both of body and mind, yet chose not to propagate it by coercions on either, as was in his Almighty power to do, but to extend it by its influence on reason alone; that the impious presumption of legislators and rulers, civil as well as ecclesiastical, who, being themselves but fallible and uninspired men, have assumed dominion over the faith of others, setting up their own opinions and modes of thinking as the only true and infallible, and as such endeavoring to impose them on others, hath established and maintained false religions over the greatest part of the world and through all time: That to compel a man to furnish contributions of money for the propagation of opinions which he disbelieves and abhors, is sinful and tyrannical; that even the forcing him to support this or that teacher of his own religious persuasion, is depriving him of the comfortable liberty of giving his contributions to the particular pastor whose morals he would make his pattern, and whose powers he feels most persuasive to righteousness; and is withdrawing from the ministry those temporary rewards, which proceeding from an approbation of their personal conduct, are an additional incitement to earnest and unremitting labours for the instruction of mankind; that our civil rights have no dependance on our religious opinions, any more than our opinions in physics or geometry; that therefore the proscribing any citizen as unworthy the public confidence by laying upon him an incapacity of being called to offices of trust and emolument, unless he profess or renounce this or that religious opinion, is depriving him injuriously of those privileges and advantages to which, in common with his fellow citizens, he has a natural right; that it tends also to corrupt the principles of that very religion it is meant to encourage, by bribing, with a monopoly of worldly honours and emoluments, those who will externally profess and conform to it; that though indeed these are criminal who do not withstand such temptation, yet neither are those innocent who lay the bait in their way; that the opinions of men are not the object of civil government, nor under its jurisdiction; that to suffer the civil magistrate to intrude his powers into the field of opinion and to restrain the profession or propagation of principles on supposition of their ill tendency is a dangerous falacy, which at once destroys all religious liberty, because he being of course judge of that tendency will make his opinions the rule of judgment, and approve or condemn the sentiments of others only as they shall square with or differ from his own; that it is time enough for the rightful purposes of civil government for its officers to interfere when principles break out into overt acts against peace and good order; and finally, that truth is great and will prevail if left to herself; that she is the proper and sufficient antagonist to error, and has nothing to fear from the conflict unless by human interposition disarmed of her natural weapons, free argument and debate; errors ceasing to be dangerous when it is permitted freely to contradict them.

We the General Assembly of Virginia do enact that no man shall be compelled to frequent or support any religious worship, place, or ministry whatsoever, nor shall be enforced, restrained, molested, or burthened in his body or goods, nor shall otherwise suffer, on account of his religious opinions or belief; but that all men shall be free to profess, and by argument to maintain, their opinions in matters of religion, and that the same shall in no wise diminish, enlarge, or affect their civil capacities.

And though we well know that this Assembly, elected by the people for the ordinary purposes of legislation only, have no power to restrain the acts of succeeding Assemblies, constituted with powers equal to our own, and that therefore to declare this act irrevocable would be of no effect in law; yet we are free to declare, and do declare, that the rights hereby asserted are of the natural rights of mankind, and that if any act shall be hereafter passed to repeal the present or to narrow its operation, such act will be an infringement of natural right

APPENDIX VII
THOMAS JEFFERSON'S DANBURY LETTER

B oth versions of this letter are copied from the June 1998 Library of Congress (LOC) Information Bulletin on the LOC website. It is included here because of its frequent use in interpreting and discussing the 1st Amendment. It is also included so you can read two different versions of one very important letter. Think about how they differ and what those differences might mean. The Bulletin these came from (link below) contains an excellent article on this point. http://www.loc.gov/loc/lcib/9806/danpost.html

THE DRAFT AND RECENTLY DISCOVERED TEXT

To messers Nehemiah Dodge, Ephraim Robbins, & Stephen S. Nelson, a committee of the Danbury Baptist association in the state of Connecticut.

Gentlemen

The affectionate sentiments of esteem & approbation which you are so good as to express towards me, on behalf of the Danbury Baptist association, give me the highest satisfaction. my duties dictate a faithful & zealous pursuit of the interests of my constituents, and, in proportion as they are persuaded of my fidelity to those duties, the discharge of them becomes more & more pleasing.

Believing with you that religion is a matter which lies solely between man & his god, that he owes account to none other for his faith or his worship, that the legitimate powers of government reach actions only and not opinions, I contemplate with sovereign reverence that act of the whole American people which declared that their legislature should "make no law respecting an establishment of religion, or prohibiting the free exercise thereof;" thus building a wall of eternal separation between Church & State. Congress thus inhibited from acts respecting religion, and the Executive authorised only to execute their acts, I have refrained from prescribing even those occasional performances of devotion, practiced indeed by the Executive of another nation as the legal head of its church, but subject here, as religious exercises only to the voluntary regulations and discipline of each respective sect,

[Jefferson first wrote: *"confining myself therefore to the duties of my station, which are merely temporal, be assured that your religious rights shall never be infringed by any act of mine and that."* These lines he crossed out and then wrote: *"concurring with"*; having crossed out these two words, he wrote: *"Adhering to this great act of national legislation in behalf of the rights of conscience"*; next he crossed out these words and wrote: *"Adhering to this expression of the supreme will of the nation in behalf of the rights of conscience I shall see with friendly dispositions the progress of those sentiments which tend to restore to man all his natural rights, convinced that he has no natural rights in opposition to his social duties."*]

I reciprocate your kind prayers for the protection & blessing of the common father and creator of man, and tender you for yourselves & the Danbury Baptist [your religious] association assurances of my high respect & esteem.

Th Jefferson
Jan. 1. 1802.

APPENDIXES

The Final Letter, As Sent

To messers. Nehemiah Dodge, Ephraim Robbins, & Stephen S. Nelson, a committee of the Danbury Baptist association in the state of Connecticut.

Gentlemen

The affectionate sentiments of esteem and approbation which you are so good as to express towards me, on behalf of the Danbury Baptist association, give me the highest satisfaction. my duties dictate a faithful and zealous pursuit of the interests of my constituents, & in proportion as they are persuaded of my fidelity to those duties, the discharge of them becomes more and more pleasing.

Believing with you that religion is a matter which lies solely between Man & his God, that he owes account to none other for his faith or his worship, that the legitimate powers of government reach actions only, & not opinions, I contemplate with sovereign reverence that act of the whole American people which declared that their legislature should "make no law respecting an establishment of religion, or prohibiting the free exercise thereof," thus building a wall of separation between Church & State. Adhering to this expression of the supreme will of the nation in behalf of the rights of conscience, I shall see with sincere satisfaction the progress of those sentiments which tend to restore to man all his natural rights, convinced he has no natural right in opposition to his social duties.

I reciprocate your kind prayers for the protection & blessing of the common father and creator of man, and tender you for yourselves & your religious association, assurances of my high respect & esteem.

Th Jefferson
Jan. 1. 1802.

Appendix VIII
Methodology,
or How I Researched This

I did most of the research for this book online. I even used Wikipedia, sort of. Wikipedia is not a source you can trust to be completely accurate, but it's not bad if you think of it as a conversation. You might talk to a friend about something, a sports team perhaps. They tell you that a certain team won a championship by a certain score. Maybe they are remembering correctly, maybe not. You can go home search out the correct information. The same is true of Wikipedia. A book I was reading mentioned the Edict of Nantes, which sounded like the law that was revoked and caused John Jay's grandfather to lose everything but I knew nothing about it. When I read the Wikipedia article, it mentioned the Revocation of the Edict of Nantes, so I Googled that. The Google™ results included the Hanover Historical Texts project, which includes the actual text of the Revocation of the Edict of Nantes. I could read it myself! Did I rely on Wikipedia? Yes, to point me in a general direction to do more research. Did I rely on it as a source? No, and the difference is important.

What kind of websites did I rely on as sources? Most of them are government and university sites. I trust that Cornell University's Law School has accurate basic information on the Equal Protection Clause. I trust that the US Senate has an accurate list of all our Vice Presidents and their terms of office, and I trust that the White House information on Presidents is accurate. There really is an amazing amount of information on these websites, including on topics you might not expect. For example, the Senate website has a section on the art in the Senate. Sites I used include:

- Official Armed Services websites, including the Army (www.army.mil), Navy (www.navy.mil), and Coast Guard (www.uscg.mil).
- Government information sources, including the Library of Congress (www.loc.gov), the National Archives (www.archives.gov), and Patent Office (www.uspto.gov).
- The official House (www.house.gov), Senate (www.senate.gov), Supreme Court (www.supremecourt.gov), and White House (www.whitehouse.gov) websites, and the section of the Library of Congress devoted to Congressional activities (thomas.loc.gov).

My research included many other sites, of course, but my intent here is to explain how this book was researched, not to list every detail. Even if you already know how to do research, hopefully this will show that the primary sources used are as neutral as possible. The few times websites were selected knowing that they might have a particular political bias, it was because most coverage of the topic is biased at this point in time and two or more sites were selected with opposite views to balance each other out. It would be like reading the coverage of an event like John Brown's 1859 Harpers Ferry Raid from one Southern pro-slavery paper and one Northern abolitionist paper. Neither one would give a fair and impartial view because they felt strongly, but by reading both you get a better idea of the truth.

Some historical figures, such as Benedict Arnold, Frederick Douglass, and Thomas Jefferson, have entire websites devoted to their life and history. For example, Jefferson's home is an estate, research center, and tourist attraction named Monticello (www.monticello.org). Other sources are websites from well-known and trusted organizations or companies, such as the Smithsonian (www.Smithsonian.org) and PBS (www.pbs.org). In other cases where there isn't a single clear authority, I researched multiple websites and if they all have the same basic information (but not cut and pasted from the same source), then I accepted that as generally accurate information.

ABOUT THE AUTHOR

Bethanne Kim is from a family of historians. All those family visits to historical sites and national parks helped her learn to love and appreciate American history from a very young age. This was not apparent to her parents when she was complaining about going to see the Liberty Bell (again) or when she started reciting the docent's monologue at Liberty Hall with them.

Kim received her BA in International Relations from The Johns Hopkins University. It is a multi-disciplinary degree that requires studying political science, economics, history, and foreign language, but not zombies. All students of The Johns Hopkins University learn two things their first day: both the "The" and the "s" in Johns are part of the name. Do not skip them. Ever. Seriously. It really bugs the administrators.

More than twenty years after her high school civics class, she became interested in better understanding the Constitution and went in search of a non-partisan book that wasn't full of legalese and case law. After failing in her mission, Kim set out to write the book she wanted to read. This book is the result of that.

It is extremely hard to keep all personal opinions out of a book like this. You may be curious what she really thinks on these issues. Since you have read this far, here are a few of her opinions. .

THE CONSTITUTION: IT'S THE OS FOR THE US

- DC should not have their own Congressional or Electoral representation. They should be part of the Maryland delegation since the land DC occupies was all formerly part of Maryland. They should, however, keep their non-voting member to handle DC-specific issues as long as Congress retains control of the District.
- Electoral College votes should be distributed based on Congressional Districts, not winner-take-all. The state winner receives both Senate votes unless the difference between the top two candidates is less than five percent, in which case each candidate receives one Elector. Ditto for primary elections.
- The Congress should be able to over-ride Supreme Court decisions without having to pass a Constitutional Amendment, but that should require a high bar. Requiring two thirds or even three quarters of Congress to vote in favor of any law over-riding the Supreme Court could be the answer.

The Constitution isn't her only interest. Despite the complete lack of any academic need, Liz learned so much about zombies over the last few years that she wrote the young adult/middle grade series *Not the Zombies!* She is currently finishing the third book in the series. It is a source of significant irritation to her teenage son who assures her she has "ruined zombies" for him.

OTHER BOOKS

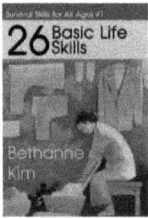

Survival Skills for All Ages Book 1: Basic Life Skills covers skills so simple most emergency preparedness books skip right over them. In true emergencies, knowing how to sharpen kitchen knives and basic sanitation can be literal life savers. Skills were chosen for their value in everyday life as well as emergencies.

Survival Skills for All Ages Book 2: 52⁺ Recipes for Everyday & Emergencies is full of simple recipes that can be cooked on or off-grid, so you can serve normal meals even without power, and recipes for staples such as mayonnaise, baking powder, and crackers.

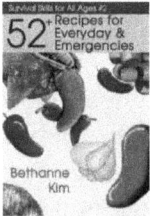

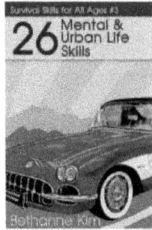

Survival Skills for All Ages Book 3: 26 Mental & Urban Life Skills covers financial skills, staying safe while traveling, self-defense, cyber security, hiding from danger, handling your emotions (including stress and anger), and more. These skills can help kids and adults throughout life, not just in emergencies.

Cubmastering: Getting Started as Cubmaster is an introduction for new Cubmasters. Topics covered include organizational structure, training, recruiting, and recharter. This is about more than just the nuts and bolts of Scouting, though. It also covers dealing with difficult parents and planning special pack events.

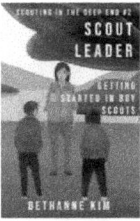

Scout Leader: An Introduction to Boy Scouts focuses on the nuts and bolts of the Boy Scouts of America with particular emphasis on how units in Cub Scouts and Scouts BSA are supposed to work. Recharter, training, common BSA meetings (such as Roundtable), and much more are described. Each chapter starts with a quote from Lord Baden Powell.

Citizenship in the World: Teaching the Merit Badge is, quite simply, a guide to assist merit badge counselors in teaching the BSA Eagle-required merit badge "Citizenship in the World." It includes the merit badge requirements, and information and tips for teaching it.

The Organized Wedding: Planning Everything from Your Engagement to Your Marriage is chock full of checklists. No detail is too small! What truly sets it apart is including the actual wedding ceremony and a chapter on your marriage with questions on financial priorities, family health history, and all your doctors.

OMG! Not the Zombies! Book 1 A group of teens goes for a hike and accidentally starts the zombie apocalypse. Being good at being prepared, they start setting up a safe community in the old Indian cliff houses and stocking it with supplies to save themselves and their families while the adults are still pretending life is normal.

BRB! Not the Zombies! Book 2 As their group grows, they discover a new mission: Get crucial information and items to the CDC to help with efforts to create a cure for the Infection. They fight their way through zombie-infested towns and to find the "impregnable" CDC research station their hopes are pinned on.

YOLO! Not the Zombies! Book 3 Have you ever wondered how a hurricane might affect the zombie apocalypse? Or how undead would fare in a sandstorm? (Hint: Hope they aren't wearing a helmet.) These and other natural disasters are explored in these zombie short stories.

APPENDIXES

FORTHCOMING:

Survival Skills for All Ages: 26 Outdoor Life Skills covers basic camping skills such as knot tying, fire building, outdoor cooking, and choosing a tent. It also covers hunting, fishing, and foraging for food; finding your way using maps, compasses, and GPSs; and truly basic skills such as managing time and water safety (tides, currents, etc.).

Survival Skills for All Ages: Special Needs Prepping may sound like something only "other people" need but the truth is that most families have special needs. Babies, elderly parents, diabetes, asthma, allergies—most of us have at least one of these and even if we don't, a simple sprained ankle or back injury can make us (temporarily) special needs.

Contact the Author

Bethanne Kim would love to hear from you! She maintains two blogs. The Moderate Mom focuses on politics. Wise Fathers avoids politics.

You can connect with her through:

Email–theWiseMom@WiseFathers.com

Blogs–TheModerateMom.com; WiseFathers.com

Facebook–The Moderate Mom; Wise Fathers

Pinterest–TheModerateMom; WiseFathers

Twitter–@TheModerateMom; @Wisefatherss

Because Amazon reviews really do matter, especially for indie authors, please take a few minutes and post a review of this book on Amazon.com.

www.ingramcontent.com/pod-product-compliance
Lightning Source LLC
Chambersburg PA
CBHW062147080426
42734CB00010B/1596